BLACK AMERICA SERIES

MORGAN COUNTY
GEORGIA

BLACK AMERICA SERIES

MORGAN COUNTY
GEORGIA

Lynn Robinson Camp

ARCADIA
PUBLISHING

ISBN 978-0-7385-1747-6

Published by Arcadia Publishing
Charleston, South Carolina

Printed in the United States of America

Library of Congress Catalog Card Number: 2004111795

For all general information contact Arcadia Publishing at:
Telephone 843-853-2070
Fax 843-853-0044
E-mail sales@arcadiapublishing.com
For customer service and orders:
Toll-Free 1-888-313-2665

Visit us on the Internet at www.arcadiapublishing.com

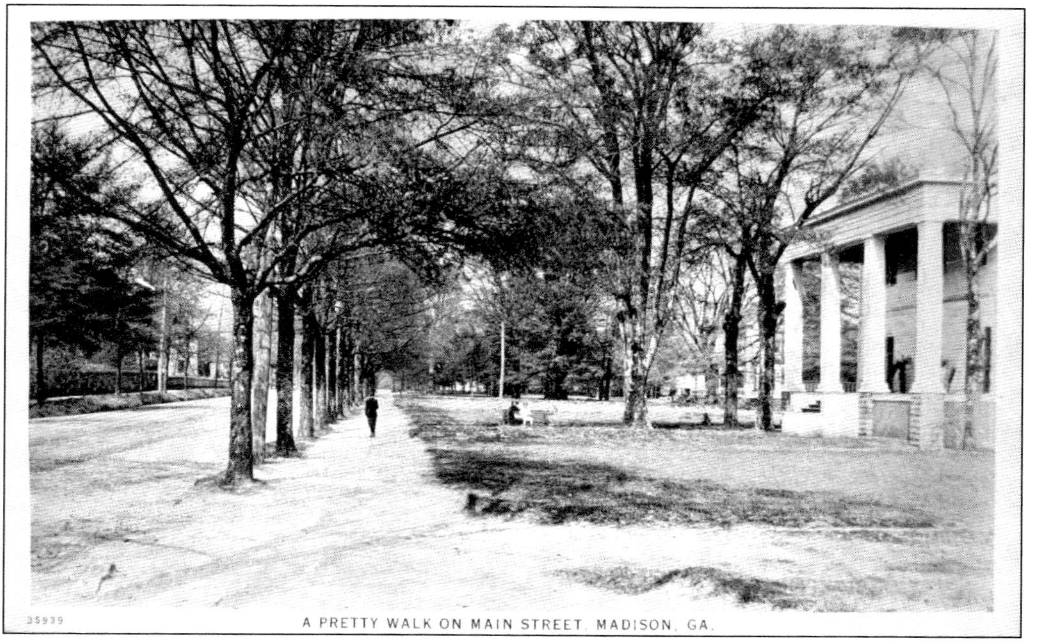

This is Main Street in Madison, Georgia, the county seat of Morgan County, as it appeared during the early 1900s. (Courtesy Georgia Division of Archives and History, Office of Secretary of State.)

Contents

ACKNOWLEDGMENTS

Praises, honor, and glory to God—the almighty power that flowed through me so that this project could come to fruition.

First, I must thank Katie White and Arcadia Publishing for giving me an opportunity for creative expression and celebration of my heritage. I will be eternally grateful to the Morgan County community for welcoming me, sharing your history and treasured photographs, and embracing this project with such gusto. My intent was simple: to honor you with my work and creativity. I trust the contents of this book represent you all in an honorable light.

I was first inspired to write when I was three years old sitting in Gresham Grove Church, watching my mother, Tessie Robinson, take notes for the Georgia Colored Men's Benevolent Society. Thanks to my soul mate, John Chambers, for keeping me grounded and being loving and patient with me when I'm engrossed in my projects. Having the love of Tarik, Paige, and Tate gives me courage to keep on moving.

Rev. Fred Perriman and the staff of the Morgan County African-American Museum, your support was invaluable. Thanks to Adelaide Ponder, an elegant lady and journalist, for writing the foreword, and Minnie Peek, who got as excited as I did, for her introduction. I felt honored when I got the enthusiastic support of Benny Andrews. Thanks to Dr. Rosalyn Mitchell Patterson and Jennifer E. Cheeks-Collins for the support and encouragement. Thanks to all contributors whose names appear throughout this book, along with Bessie White, Rita Harris, Herman Robertson, and Pastor John Hyman; all of you were important to the success of this project. Special thanks for Steven W. Engerrand, Gail Deloach, and the staff of Georgia Division of Archives and History, Office of Secretary of State, for all of your assistance. Also, thanks to Molly Gilbert, Georgia Department of Industry, Trade, and Tourism, and the staff of the Morgan County Archives.

The following websites, books, and publications were referenced: *Morgan County Heritage 1807–1997*; *The Madisonian* 1978 and 1992; *History of the Town of Buckhead, Georgia 1786–1975*, compiled by Martha McWhorter Nunnally; *The Atlanta Journal and Constitution*; *The Atlanta Tribune*; *The Atlanta Daily World*; *The Morgan County Citizen*; *Unbank the Fire-Visions for the Education of African-American Children* by Janice E. Hale; *Before the Mayflower* by Lerone Bennett Jr.; *Once Upon a Time in Atlanta* by Raymond Andrews; *The Dot Man: George Andrews of Madison, Georgia*, by J. Richard Gruber; *Southern Living;* www.dca.state.ga.us; www.gasou.edu; www.horseshoes.com; www.rootsweb.com; www.blackmidwives.org; *Jackson Grove Baptist Church 100th Anniversary* souvenir book with history by Maxie Jones; *USA Today*; *Art Papers* September/October 1991, volume 15 number 6; *American Visions*, June/July 1992; *Macon Telegraph and News*, February 16, 1990; *Imprint*; *Go Down, Moses: A Study of 21 Successful Negro Rural Pastors* by Ralph A Felton; and *A History of the Wesley Moore Home* by Marshall W. Williams.

Finally, I acknowledge my father, Huel Robinson (in memory), a Morgan County farmer who kept me connected to Morgan County after we moved because of his love and devotion to Mt. Perry Missionary Baptist Church. I also acknowledge my sister girl, Sharon Chambers (in memory), who shared many fond memories of growing up in Morgan County and fantasized with me about us writing a book together. The book has been written.

Love, Peace, and Joy!
Lynn

Foreword

In the years prior to the American Revolution, the Creek Indians inhabited what is now Morgan County. Soon after the Revolutionary War, white settlers bearing land grants for service or enticed by the land lotteries for territory ceded by the Indians came to the area. Some acquired large holdings and built fine houses and service buildings.

But the settlers found that they could not operate their estates without help, which proved hard to find. Thus, they joined in a practice that was becoming prevalent in the South—they purchased African slaves brought to this county by slave traders. These slaves, many highly intelligent, tended the land and worked in the houses.

As time went on, many were able to purchase their freedom or were freed by sympathetic property owners. Some were able to buy their own land, whereas other worked for wages or as sharecroppers, whereby they earned a part of the crop they produced.

All were freed by the Emancipation Proclamation, although some stayed on, as they had no other place to go. By the early 20th century, many had become successful businessmen, operating restaurants, barbershops, beauty parlors, shoe shops, undertaking parlors, dry-cleaning establishments, contracting businesses, filling stations, machine shops, or other forms of free enterprise.

A host of African Americans in Morgan County were among these hard-working farmers and businessmen and women. They also entered professions, especially excelling in medicine and education. These highly regarded African-American citizens were greatly admired and respected. Early entrepreneurs, they won a special place in the heart of the community.

But things were not easy for them. The schools were still segregated, and the opportunities for young whites were much greater than those for young blacks. The desegregation of schools changed this, and today, many of Morgan County's most successful citizens are African American. They excel in all walks of life.

Morgan County owes much to those early pioneers who prevailed against great hardships and disadvantage. They are an inspiration and their lives deserve recognition.

Now comes Lynn Camp, who has put together a remarkable book depicting the story of many of these early African Americans in Morgan County. Theirs is a story that needs to be told, and she has done it beautifully.

Adelaide Ponder

INTRODUCTION

According to the Georgia Society of Historical Research, Morgan County was named for Revolutionary War general Daniel Morgan. The land, inhabited by the Creek Indians before the arrival of the white man, was obtained by treaty entered into at Fort Wilkerson on June 18, 1803. The territory acquired by this treaty was divided into three counties: Baldwin, Wayne and Wilkerson. Morgan County was cut off from Baldwin County and created on December 10, 1807.

The state conducted a lottery to open the lands in an act of legislature approved by Gov. John Milledge on May 11, 1803. Each free white male between age 31 and 50 had one chance. The cost of lots varied because of the quality of land.

By the Act of 1808, Madison was made the county seat and place for public buildings. Madison, which received its charter in December 1809, was named after James Madison, father of the U.S. Constitution. Madison grew slowly in size and importance. The 1860 census gave the population of Morgan County as 9,997 and included 2,984 whites, 7,006 slaves, and 7 free blacks. Today, the town's population reflects more than black and white. The county is multicultural with people from other counties. This has caused the school system to recruit teachers of foreign languages to accommodate the language barriers and meet the need of all students.

Madison is known as the town where Gen. William Tecumseh Sherman trod softly. Sen. Joshua Hill, a friend of a family member of General Sherman, pleaded on behalf of the town. A compromise was made; down went the depot, a cotton gin, and a cloth factory. Other things were destroyed, but the tree-lined avenues with their charming houses were untouched.

Land was given to some blacks after slavery was abolished. They built small houses and churches that served as schools for the community. These churches are no longer serving as schools, and much history has been eradicated.

Madison's Burney Street School, which housed both elementary and high school pupils. had a library because of philanthropist members of the white race. The presiding Elder Simmons, Rev. E.P. Johnson, Albert Hollis, and Mollie Jones were contributors. Pupils from different parts of the county and different towns would board in the city to attend this school. The three African-American schools in the county were Bostwick Elementary, Springfield Elementary, and Pearl Elementary and High School. Most students could be transported by school buses, with the exception of students who lived in the city limits or near the schools. When the Morgan County School System integrated in 1970, Springfield and Bostwick Elementary Schools were closed, and Pearl Elementary and High became Morgan County Middle School. The Morgan County Middle School has been renovated, and more classrooms were added. Rededication took place on August 9, 2004. Many efforts have been made to improve race relationships and educational opportunities, and all students are given equal opportunity to learn and excel.

This publication of *Black America: Morgan County, Georgia* emphasizes African Americans, past and present, who have lived or still live in Morgan County. It features landowners, sharecroppers, educators, churches, black businesses, and families, their ways of life, accomplishments, and careers. Read, learn, and enjoy!

Minnie Shepherd Peek

One

Pioneers of Progress
From Slavery through the Jim Crow Era

If you see [the Negro] plowing the open field, leveling the forest, at work with a spade, a rake, a hoe, a pick-ax, or a bill—let him alone; he has a right to work.
Frederick Douglass

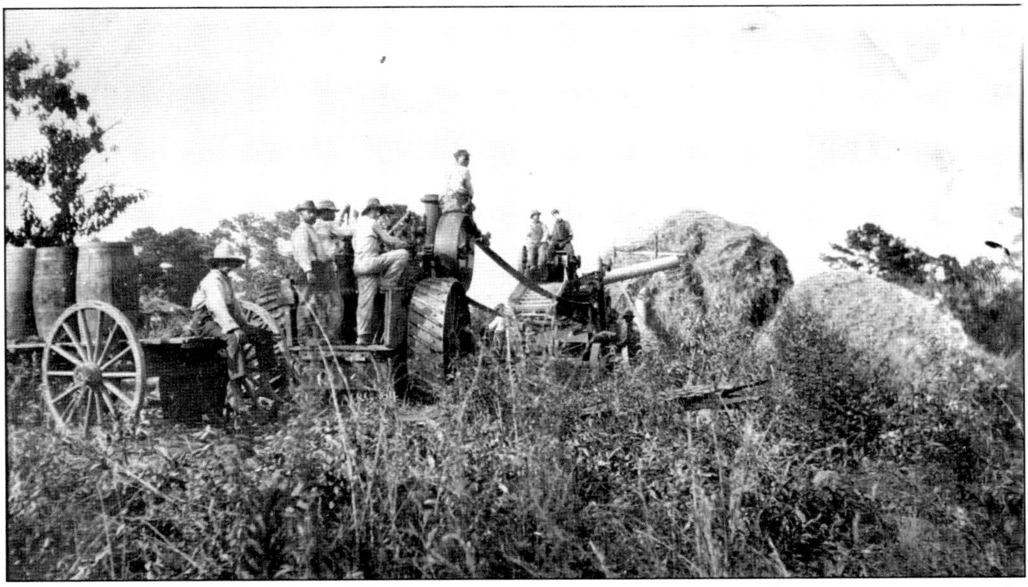

These African-American men are harvesting a crop. For many years, hay, cotton, and cattle were a major source of incomes for Morgan County residents. The rich Piedmont soil and mild temperatures made conditions favorable for agriculture. During the early years, African Americans provided slave labor to build the economy in Morgan County. There were a few African-American freemen, however. (Courtesy Georgia Division of Archives and History, Office of Secretary of State.)

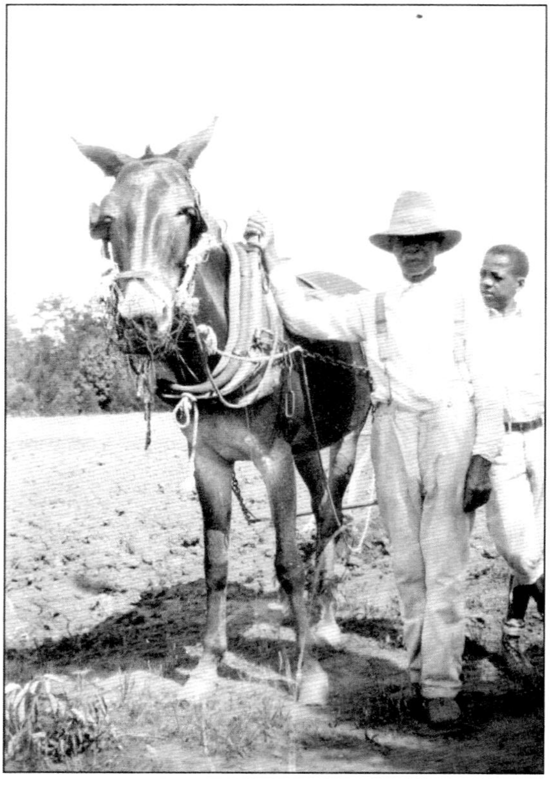

Rev. Alex Stanfield and one of his nine grandsons, Montague Harris, are pictured with Old Red, the mule. Mules were used for plowing and pulling buggies and wagons. (Courtesy Georgia Division of Archives and History, Office of Secretary of State.)

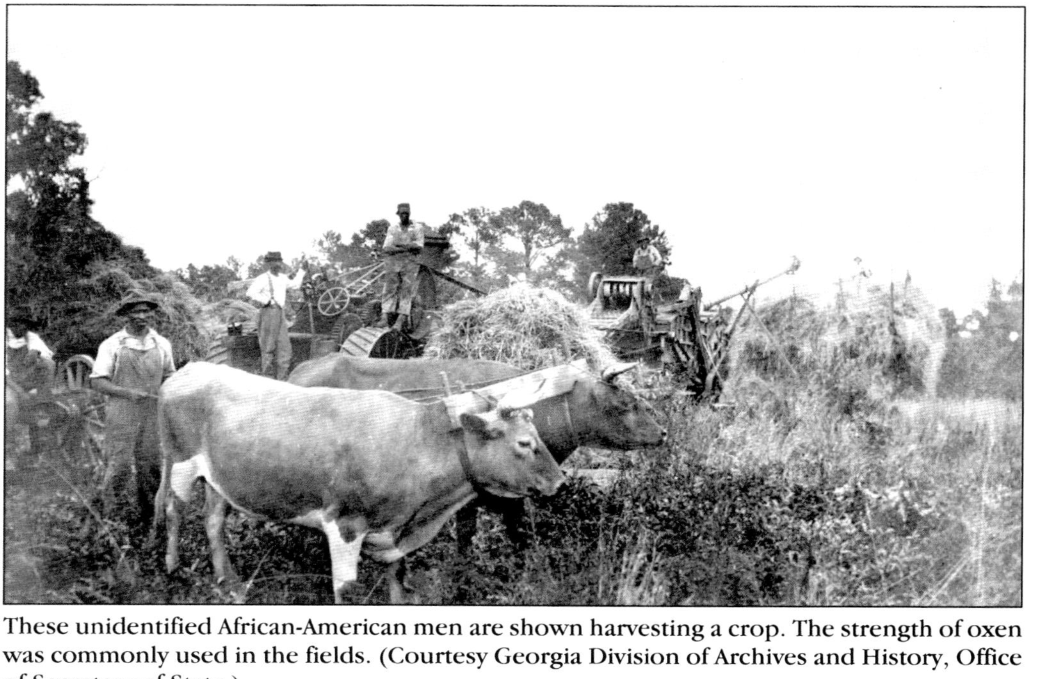

These unidentified African-American men are shown harvesting a crop. The strength of oxen was commonly used in the fields. (Courtesy Georgia Division of Archives and History, Office of Secretary of State.)

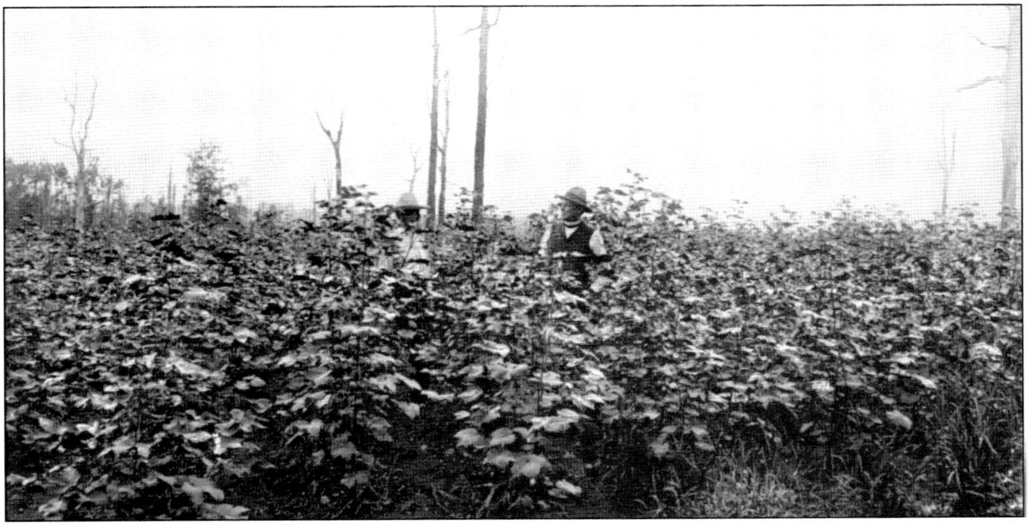

These men are shown in a field of cotton. It was common for families to work in fields like this in the largely agricultural Morgan County. (Courtesy Georgia Division of Archives and History, Office of Secretary of State.)

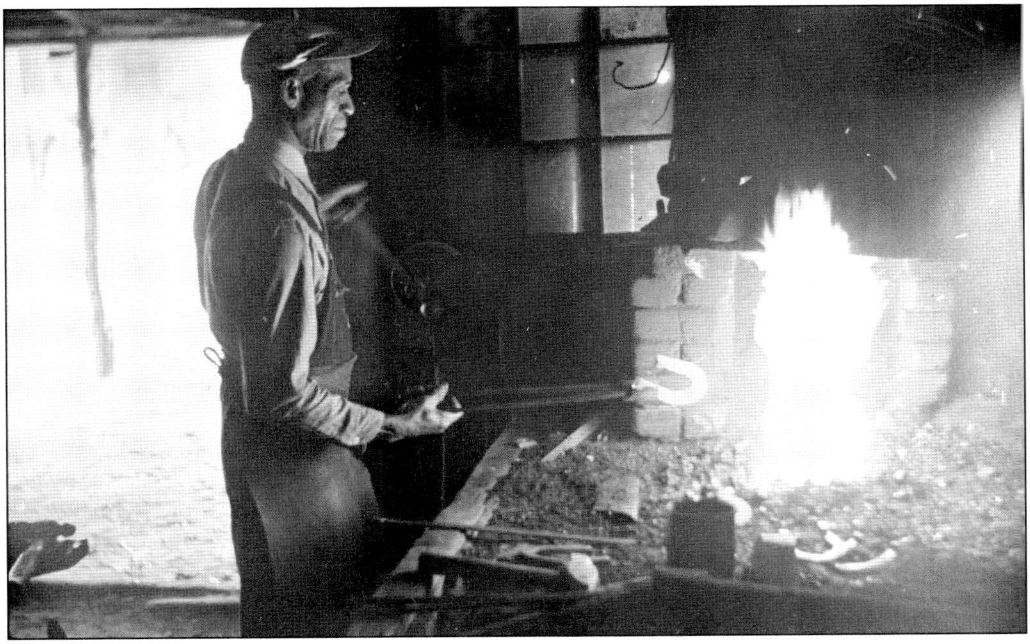

This blacksmith works on horseshoes near Madison *c.* 1940–1943. Blacksmithing was once an essential skill in a community. The Great Depression and World War II ended a renaissance in decorative ironwork. By the time of this photograph, the blacksmith's main work was shifting from shoeing workhorses to pleasure horses. Machines had also begun to do many jobs. The Senoufo people of Africa still hold the blacksmith in high esteem today. They believe he is endowed with special powers because of his relationship with the earth and his work with iron and fire. (Courtesy Georgia Division of Archives and History, Office of Secretary of State.)

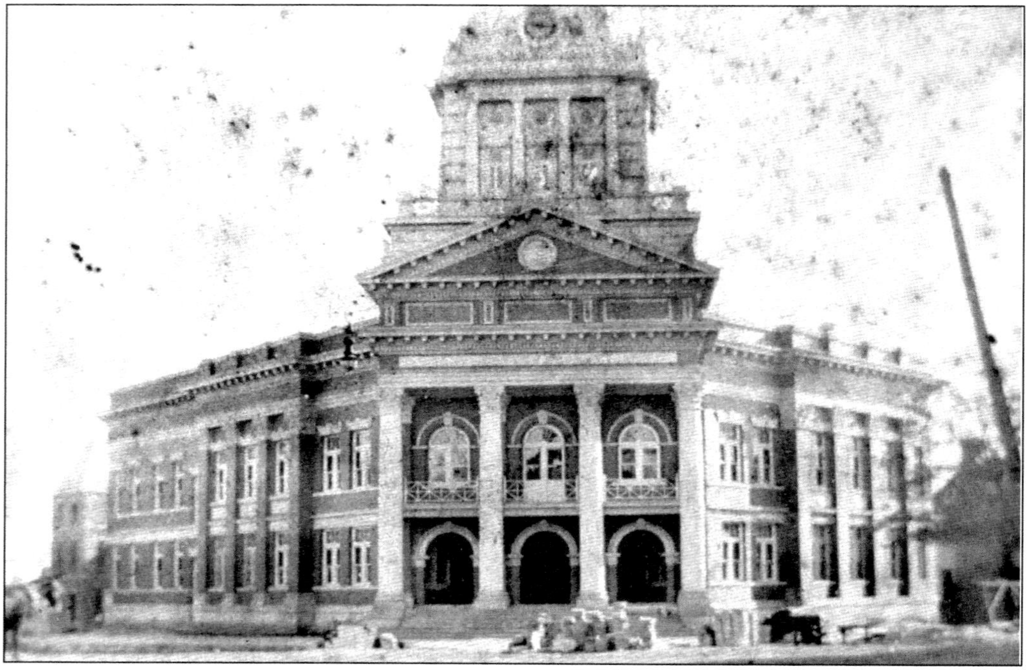

The Morgan County Courthouse, pictured in 1906, is now listed on the National Register of Historic Places. Located on the square in downtown Madison, its architectural design is considered neoclassical. (Courtesy Georgia Division of Archives and History, Office of Secretary of State.)

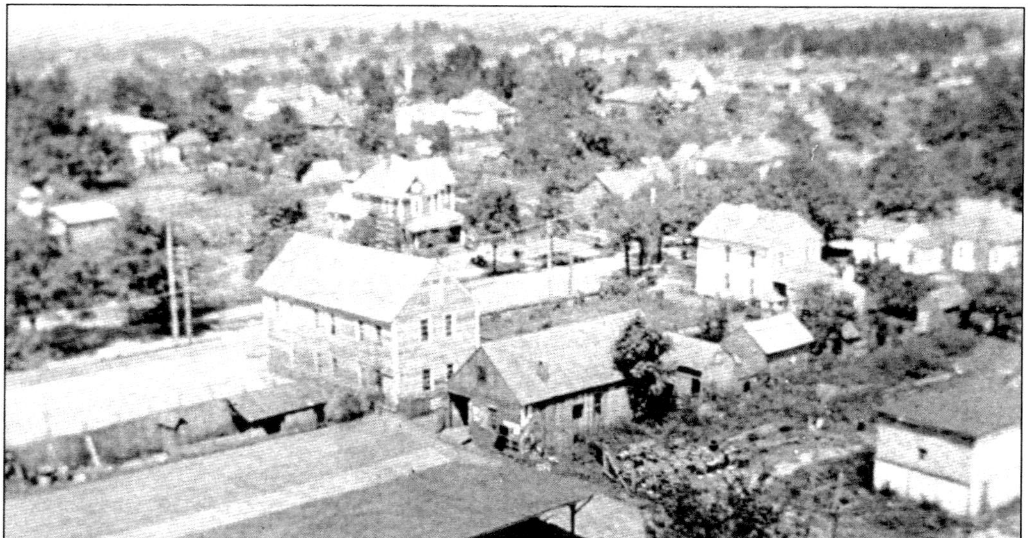

This is an aerial view of Main Street in Madison sometime between 1900 and 1908. To the far right is Old Rock Jail, which was built in 1892 and used as the county and sometimes city jail until the late 1970s. Old Rock Jail was the scene of the early 1920s lynching of Epoliam (E-port) Langston. (Courtesy Georgia Division of Archives and History, Office of Secretary of State.)

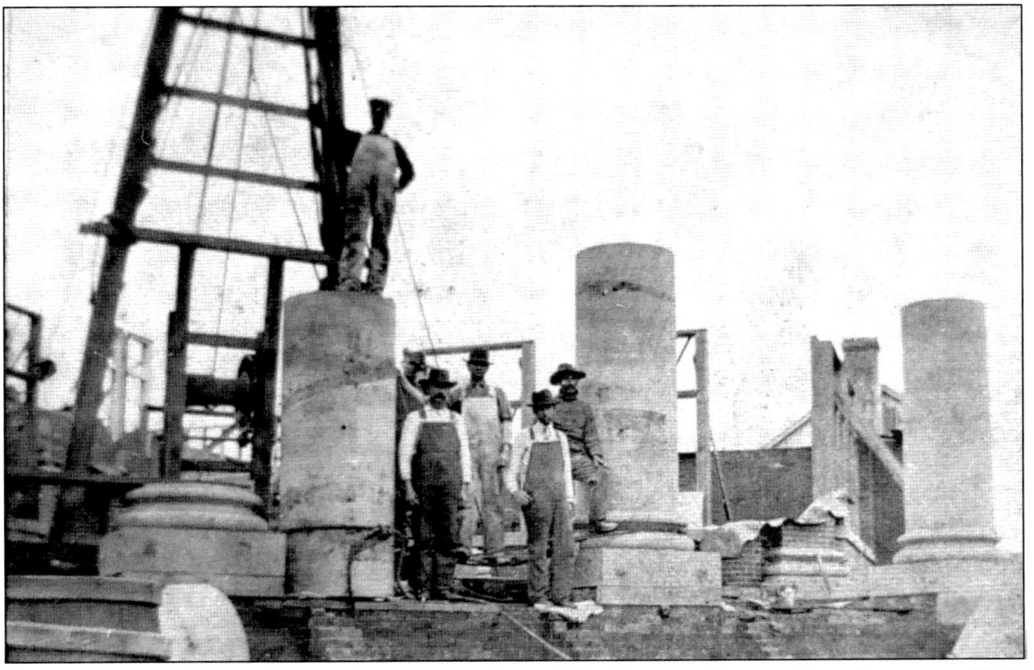

These men are shown during the construction of the Morgan County Courthouse, *c.* 1905 (Courtesy Georgia Division of Archives and History, Office of Secretary of State.)

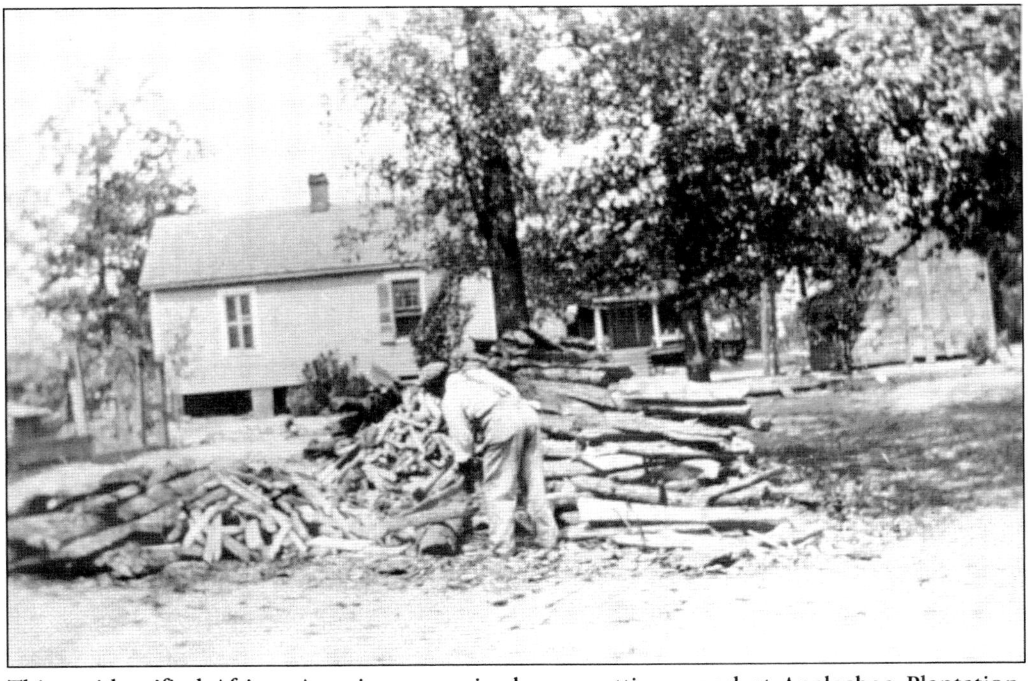

This unidentified African-American man is shown cutting wood at Apalachee Plantation, home of Joseph C. Few, *c.* 1880. (Courtesy Georgia Division of Archives and History, Office of Secretary of State.)

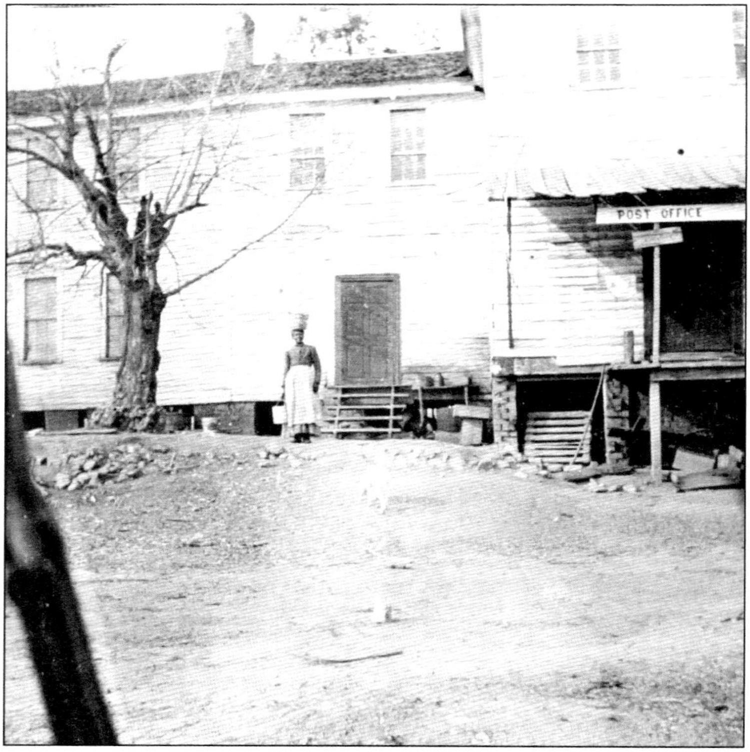

This unidentified woman stands at the Parks Mill House in 1906. The parcel of land on which the house was built was given to James Park during the 1805 land lottery. Richard Park purchased the land from his father and built the L-shaped home sometime between 1809 and 1811. The home served as a traveler's inn, blacksmith shop, and a livery stable. (Courtesy Georgia Division of Archives and History, Office of Secretary of State.)

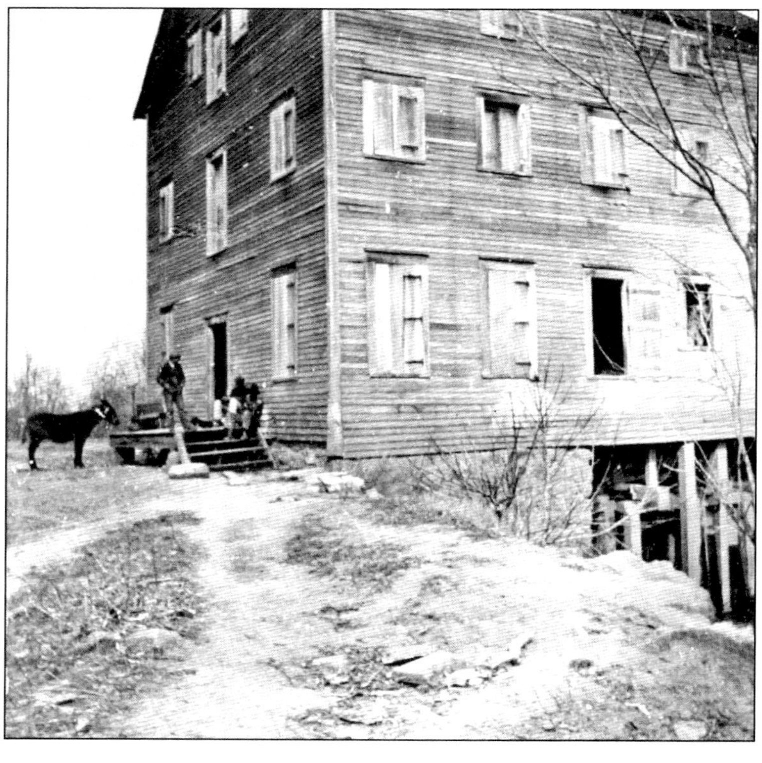

Park's Mill featured a ferry, a gristmill, and a "mud mill," a place where bricks were made. The mill was burned by Union troops in 1864. Cyrus Park, a slave, climbed to the roof of the home and put out the fire with wet blankets. Edgar Brown (1883–1981), whose father had been a slave in the community, said there was a lot of work in the mill during wheat season. (Courtesy Georgia Division of Archives and History, Office of Secretary of State.)

Moses Bass (1847–1918) purchased 100 acres of land, making him the first freedman to purchase land in the county. Mr. Bass signed the deed with an X because he was unable to read or write. Because he did not have the opportunity to have an education, he encouraged his children to become educated and independent. He was the great-grandfather of Marie Bass Martin and Martin Bass Jr. (Courtesy Marie Bass Martin.)

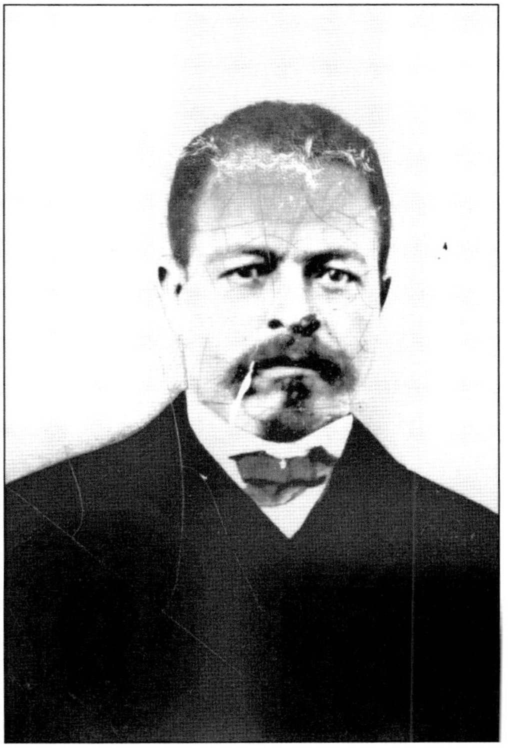

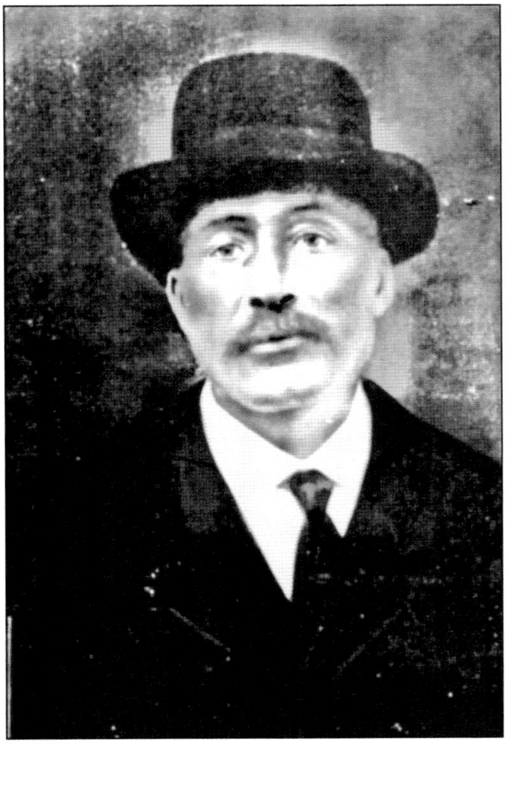

Floyd Jordan Sr. was a farmer and deacon at Mt. Perry Missionary Baptist Church. He enjoyed hosting large family dinners featuring his special pit-cooked pork barbecue. (Courtesy Elzata Brown.)

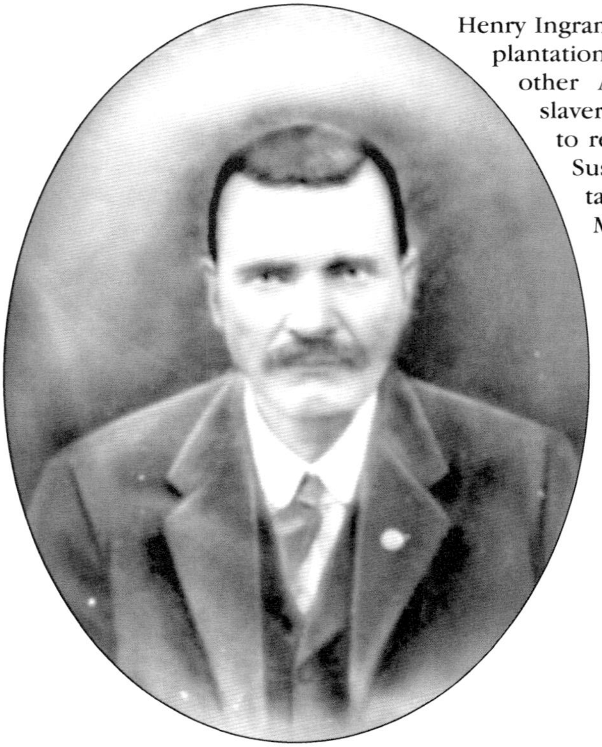

Henry Ingram was born in 1854 and worked on a plantation, but he was never a slave. Like many other African-American men born before slavery was abolished, he did not learn to read and write as a child. He married Susie Williams, a schoolteacher who taught him to read and write. (Courtesy Minnie Peek.)

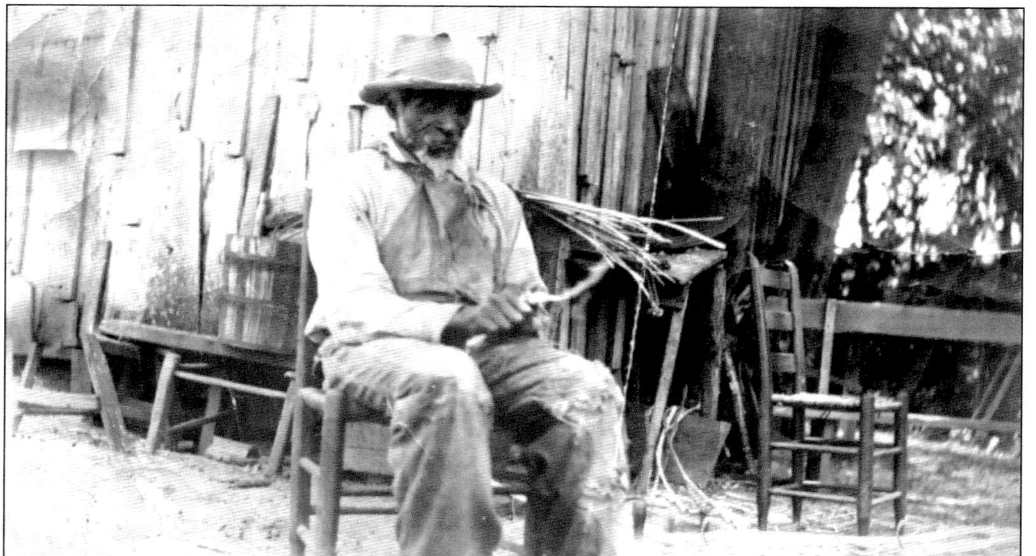

This unidentified Morgan County man is shown making straw bottoms for chairs, *c.* 1900. (Courtesy Minnie Peek.)

Harold L. Murray was born in Wilkes County, left Georgia at 17, and became a self-educated man. He graduated from Chicago Institute of Technology where he studied brick masonry. He worked across the United States and Canada. Often, work on buildings in Madison would stop, awaiting Mr. Murray's return so he could "do that fancy work finish." Buildings he worked on include Madison First United Methodist Church, McGeary Hospital, Pearl High School, and the first motel on Eatonton Road. (Courtesy Wauline Baptiste.)

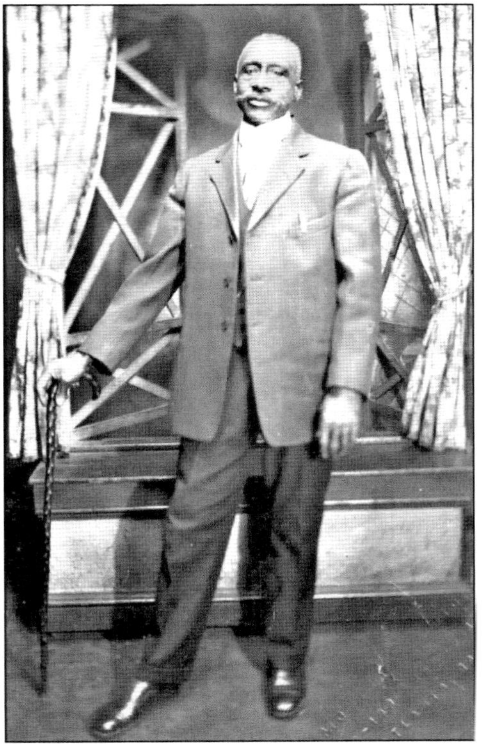

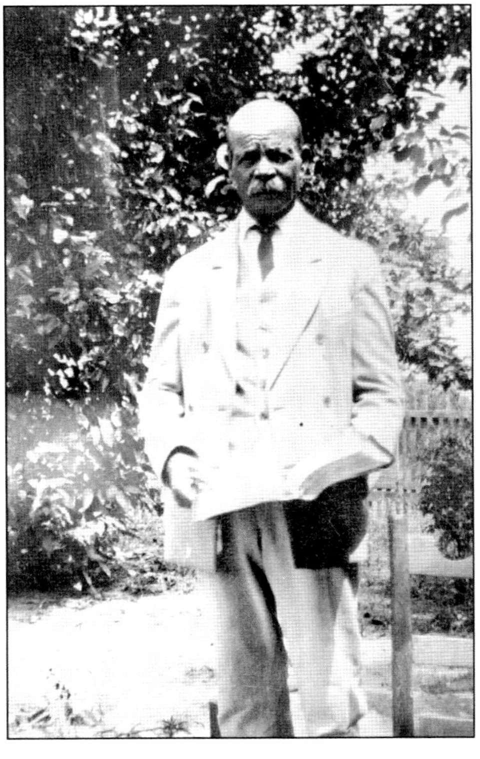

Rev. Alex Stanfield was born in 1855. He lived in Buckhead, one of the oldest settlements in Morgan County, all his life. During Stanfield's time, Buckhead was a thriving town. Trains traveling from Atlanta and Augusta turned around in Buckhead. The town had four general stores, restaurants, a hotel, a couple of drugstores, a barbershop, a cotton buyer's office, and a meat market. (Courtesy Georgia Division of Archives and History, Office of Secretary of State.)

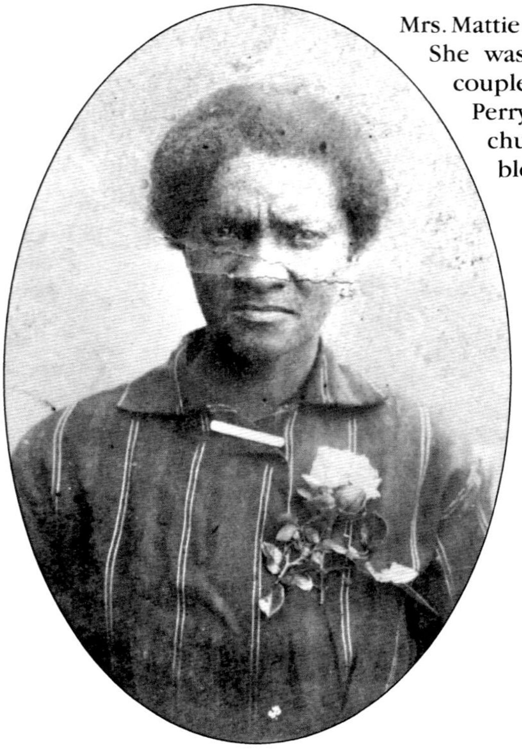

Mrs. Mattie Evans is shown in this early 1900s photograph. She was the wife of Deacon Fleming Evans. The couple lived in the Rehoboot Community near Mt. Perry Church, where she was a missionary of the church. She displays a live rose corsage on her blouse. (Courtesy Elzata Brown.)

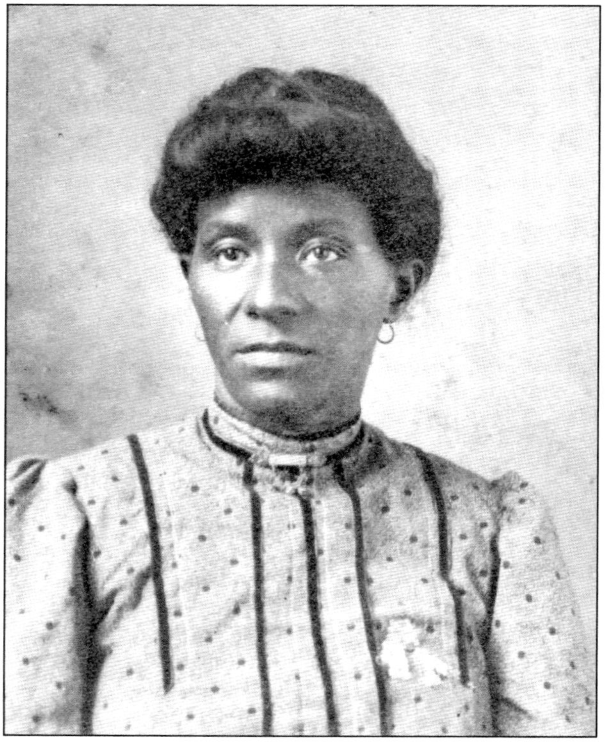

Salina Love Jordan was the wife of Floyd Jordan Sr. She cared for the home and the family's six children, and she also worked on the farm. (Courtesy Elzata Brown.)

The second wife of Henry Ingram, Susie Williams Ingram was a schoolteacher in the rural schools of Morgan County. The family lived on a farm in the Park's Mill community. Their children were William, Corine, John, Julia, and Annie. Susie's parents were George and Harriet Williams. The family attended Jefferson Baptist Church, and one of Susie's brothers, Albert, was a prominent community leader. (Courtesy Minnie Peek.)

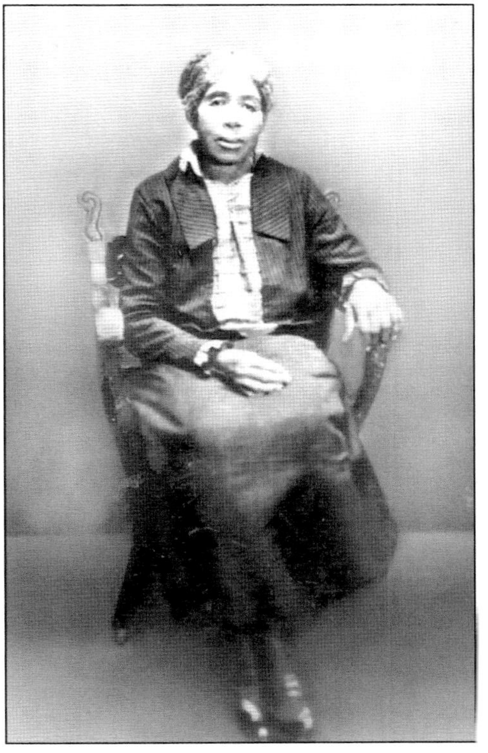

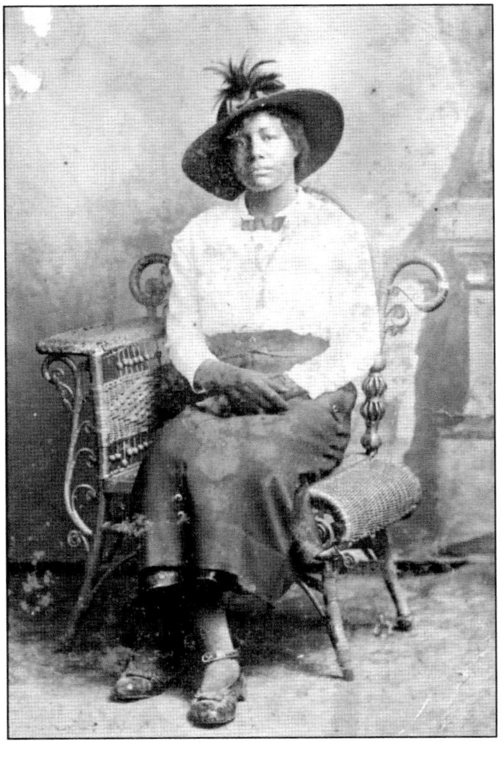

Lila Jordan Lee of Morgan County is the subject of this photograph. Notice the dust on her shoes, which are obviously well worn. This indicates that she, like many others during the early days, walked most places she went. Lila was one of the six children of Floyd Jordan Sr. and Salina Love Jordan. (Courtesy Elzata Brown.)

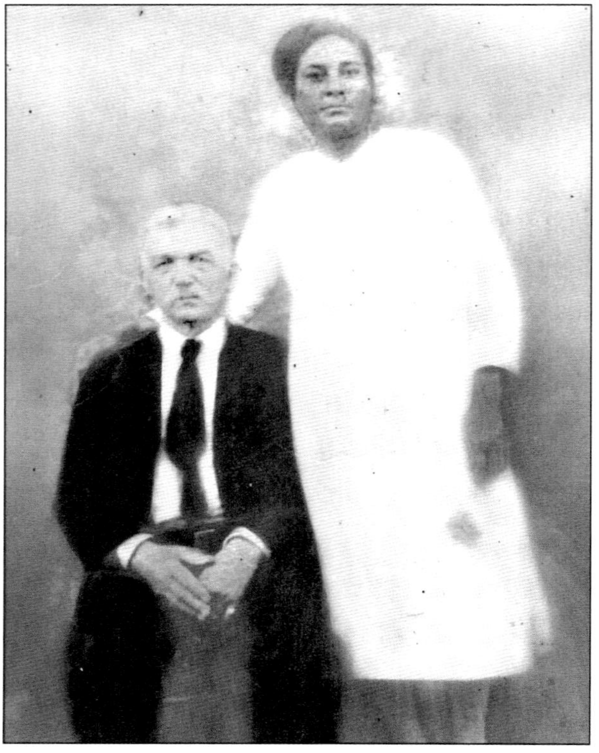

Banks Rollin (1865–1945) and Fannie Boswell Rollin (1869–1959) were both born in Putnam County and moved to Morgan County with their family around 1920. The couple had 15 children—12 girls and 3 boys. Many couples had large families during the early days. (Courtesy Carrie Chambers.)

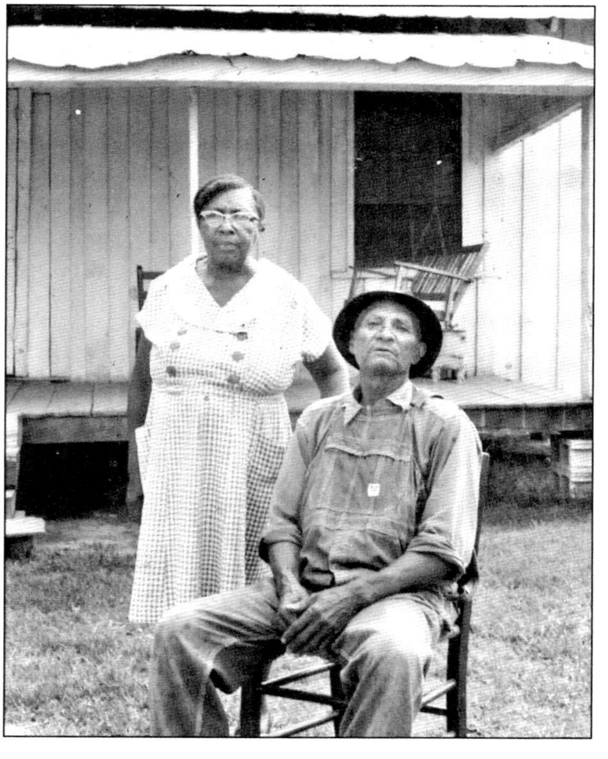

Julia Jackson Rollin (1893–1990) and Albert Rollin (1873–1979) lived on a farm on the Eatonton Highway in Morgan County. They raised "cotton, corn, delicious watermelon, cantaloupe and all kinds of vegetables as well as cows, hog, and chickens." The couple had 12 children: Annie Mae, Alice, Albert, Mildred, Arthur, Miller, Fannie Mae, Charlie, Shepherd, Ella Belle, and Carrie Belle. (Courtesy Carrie Chambers.)

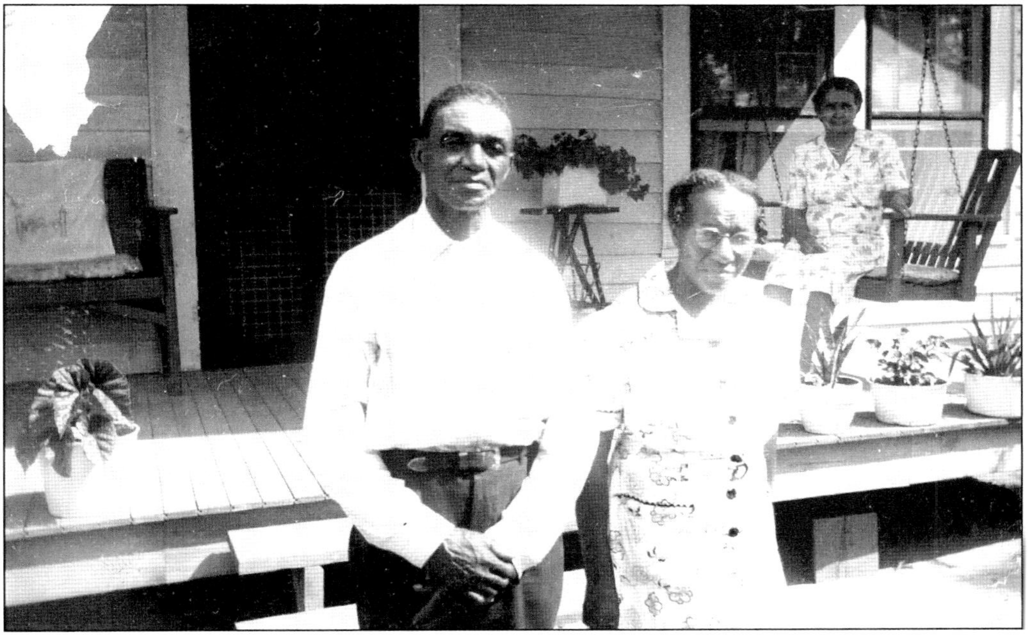

Leegree and Willie Ann Booker sharecropped for 20 years before purchasing their 100-acre farm. In the early 1950s, the Bookers raised over $6,000 worth of cotton. Mrs. Booker helped her husband on the farm while caring for their nine children. She enjoyed cooking and growing flowers. They were among the families advised by Rev. W.M. Mitchell to become self-sufficient by securing an FHA loan and purchasing a farm, as opposed to continuing to sharecrop. (Courtesy Elzata Brown.)

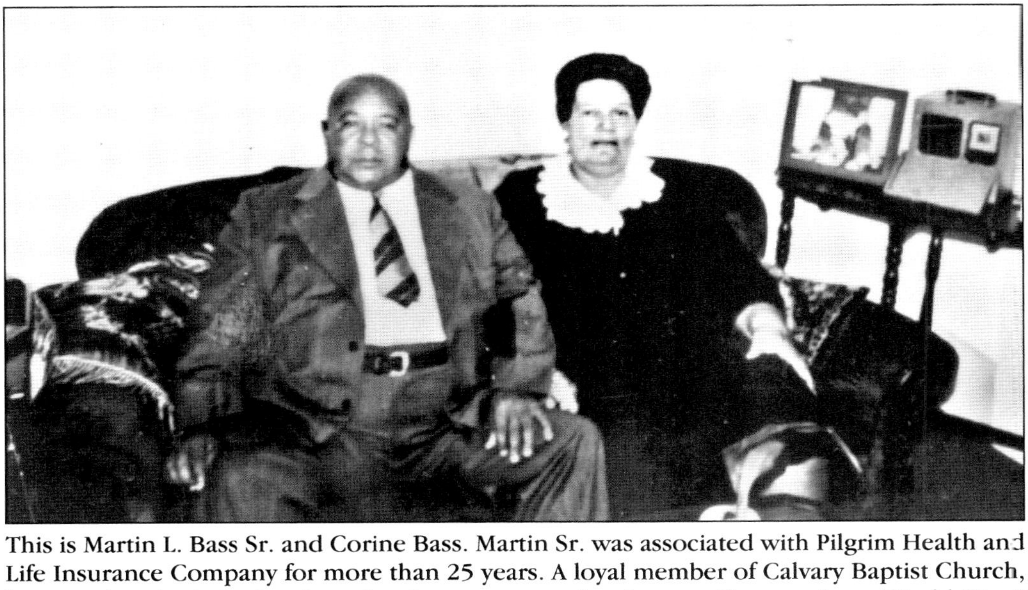

This is Martin L. Bass Sr. and Corine Bass. Martin Sr. was associated with Pilgrim Health and Life Insurance Company for more than 25 years. A loyal member of Calvary Baptist Church, he was church clerk, Sunday school treasurer, and a deacon. He was also a World War I veteran. Corine was a devoted mother and housewife. They were the parents of Martin L. Bass Jr. and Marie Bass Martin (Courtesy Marie Bass Martin.)

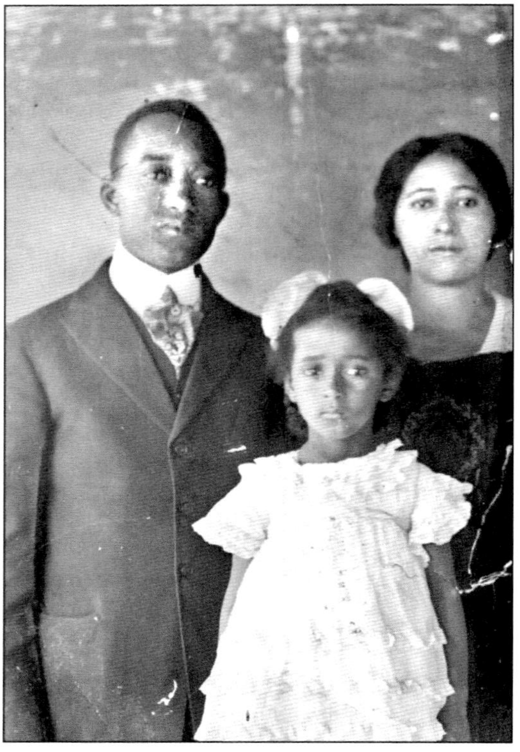

Joe L. Love and his wife, Fannie, are shown with their daughter, Margaret, in this early 1900s family portrait. Love was a tailor by trade and operated the "Pressing Club," a drycleaners, in Madison from 1912 to 1914. Fannie Love taught first grade until the late 1950s. She also taught piano lessons in Morgan County. A large portrait of this family now hangs in the Moore Parlor of the Morgan County African-American Museum. (Courtesy Elzata Brown.)

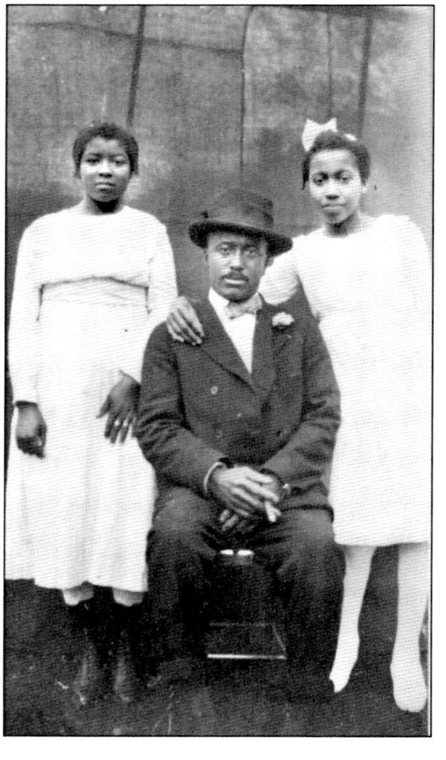

Joe Jordan and family of Morgan County are shown in this family photograph. (Courtesy Elzata Brown.)

The Howard family of Morgan County is shown in this 1940s photograph. Notice the accessories worn in this photograph, which include a broach, tie clip, and purse. These signify that this is a well-dressed family of the times. (Courtesy Elzata Brown.)

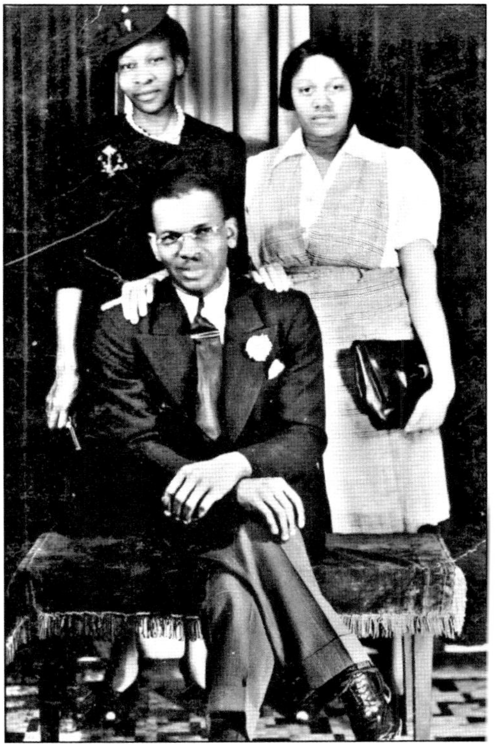

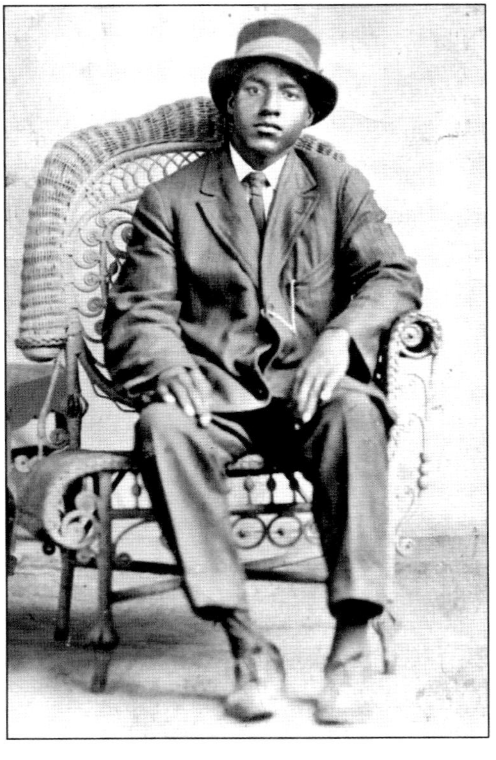

Floyd Jordan Jr. was born in Morgan County, where he lived until his death in 1994. He was around 98 years old at the time of his death. He was a farmer and deacon at Mt. Perry Missionary Baptist Church. (Courtesy Elzata Brown.)

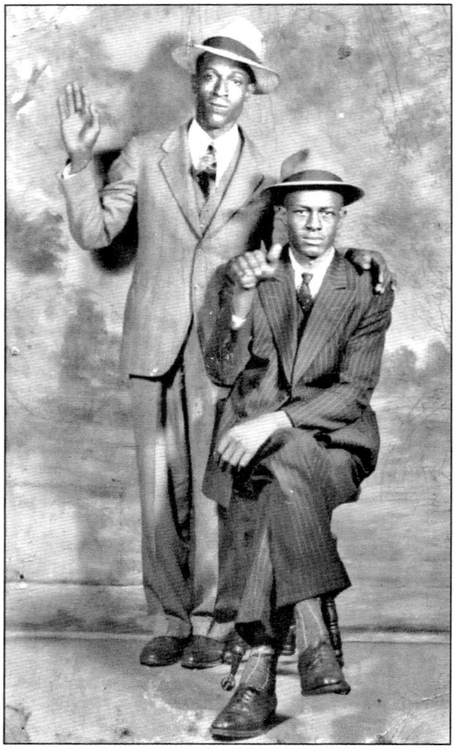

These two unidentified Morgan County men are shown waving at the camera. (Courtesy Elzata Brown.)

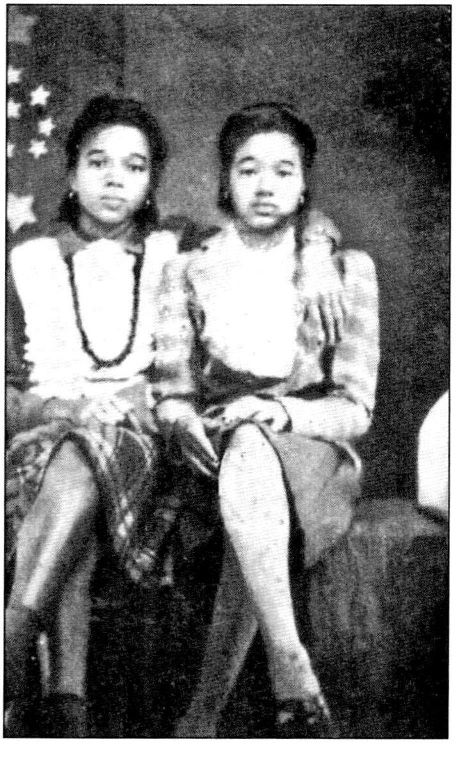

Ida Rebecca and Hattie Booker, *c*. 1940, are two of nine children of Leegree and Willie Ann Booker. This photo was taken during the girls' late teenage years. Considered to be among Morgan County's stunning beauties of their times, Ida Rebecca (named for her grandmother Becky and her aunt Ida) was even given the nickname "Cute." (Courtesy Elzata Brown.)

Rev. Walter Melvin (W.M.) Mitchell, *c.* 1936, the "farmer-preacher-carpenter," implemented the "Lord's Acre Plan." He encouraged congregations to dedicate two rows of a crop to the Lord. Reverend Mitchell built houses and did repairs on houses and churches. He assisted farmers in securing FHA loans in the community. During the 1940s, Reverend Mitchell became a pioneer civil-rights activist and community organizer who worked to consolidate schools and end disparity. (Courtesy Dr. Rosalyn Mitchell Patterson.)

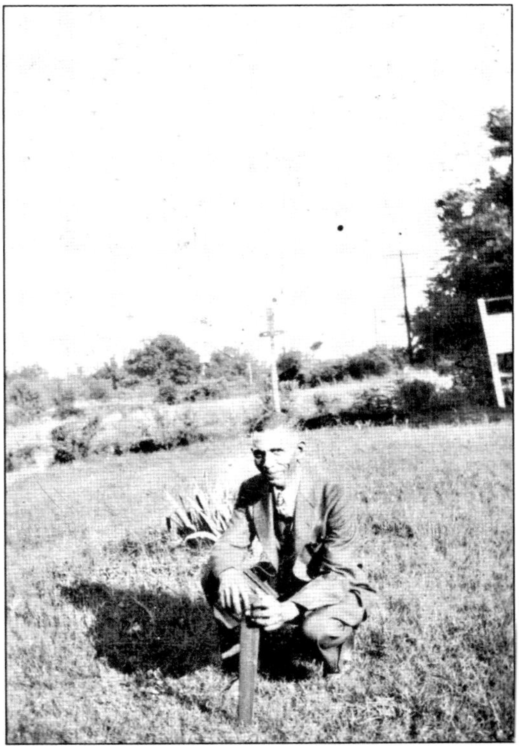

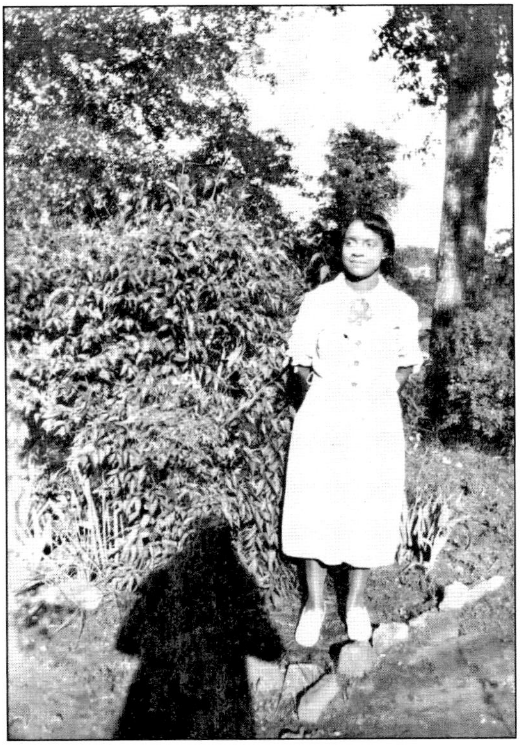

Mrs. Hazeltine Jones Mitchell, seen *c.* 1936, was born in Madison. She taught in the rural Siloam School, which her husband built from scrap lumber after remodeling Smyrna Baptist Church. Mrs. Mitchell gradated from the Nurses Training Program at Spelman College in 1927 and became the first registered nurse to work at McGeary Hospital in Morgan County. She also established the first nursery school for black children in Madison, under the Works Progress Administration (WPA). (Courtesy Dr. Rosalyn Mitchell Patterson.)

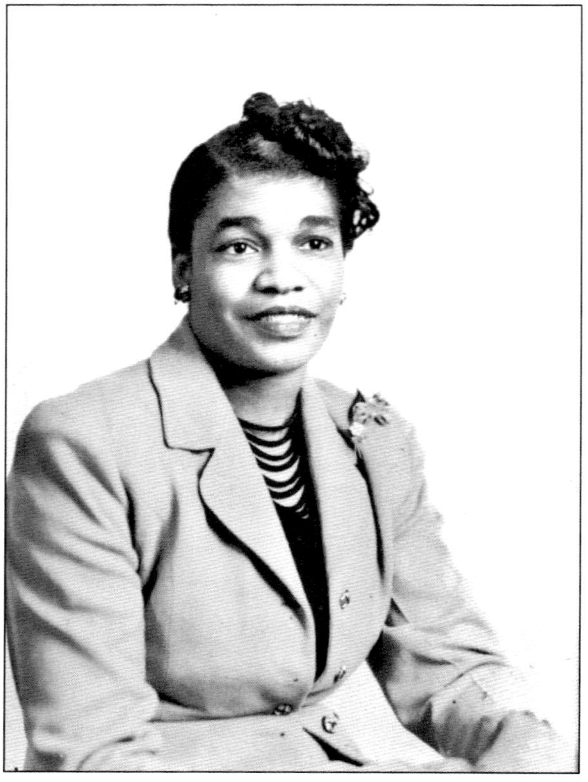

Ruby L. Robertson Booker, daughter of Troy Robertson of Morgan County and wife of Albert Booker, moved to Philadelphia during the 1940s, like many other Southern African Americans during this era. Approximately 6.5 million African Americans moved from the South between 1910 and 1970. After moving, she enjoyed traveling to different states with her new church family at Welling Temple Church of Philadelphia. (Courtesy Elzata Brown.)

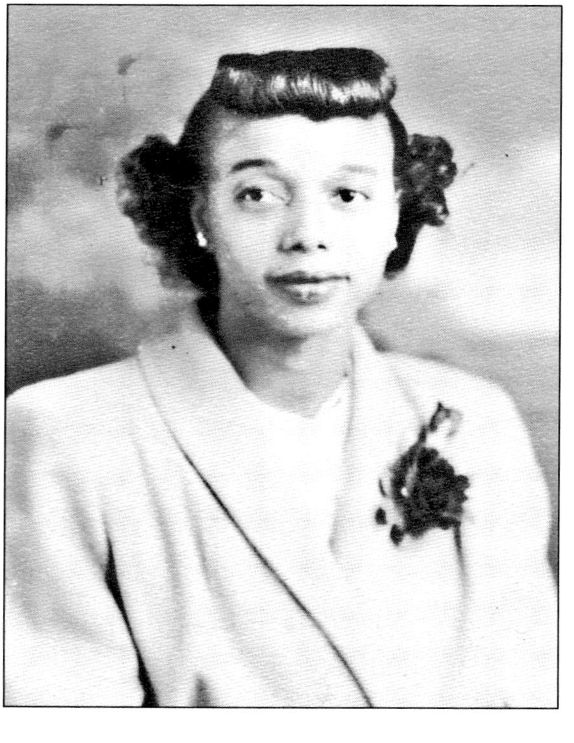

Rebecca Booker is shown here in the early 1950s. She graduated from Burney Street High School and then attended Georgia Normal School, which later became Savannah State College. She taught at rural Morgan County schools such as St. Paul School in Apalachee, Buckhead, and Wallace Grove. She collected famous quotes and loved poetry. She believed in setting goals and encouraged young people to further their education. (Courtesy Elzata Brown.)

Emma Booker, seen *c.* 1930, is the oldest daughter of Morgan County farmers Leegree and Willie Ann Booker. Emma is the mother of Elzata Brown, who became a community leader, educator, and community activist. She is 91 years old and still lives in Morgan County. (Courtesy Elzata Brown.)

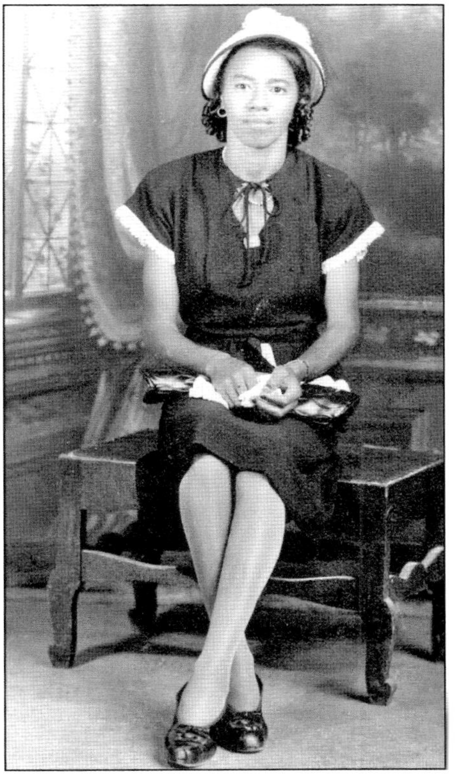

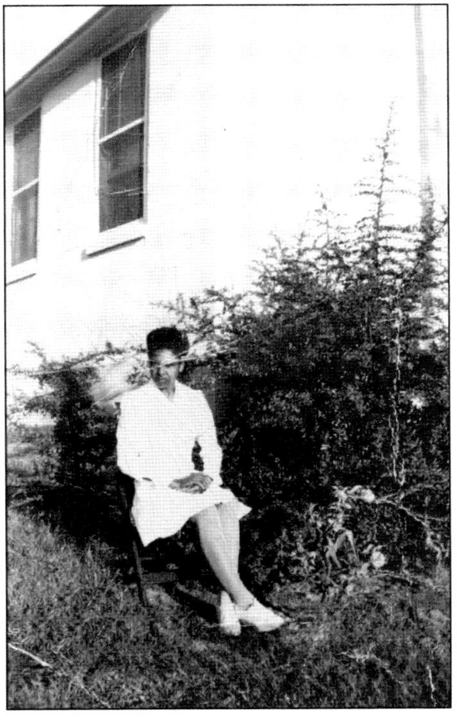

Louise Ingram became a licensed practical nurse after attend school in Morgan County and completing her G.E.D. She moved from Morgan County in order to have more job opportunities and left her two daughters in the care of her parents. This was fairly common during the early days, since more career opportunities existed in the cities. (Courtesy Minnie Peek.)

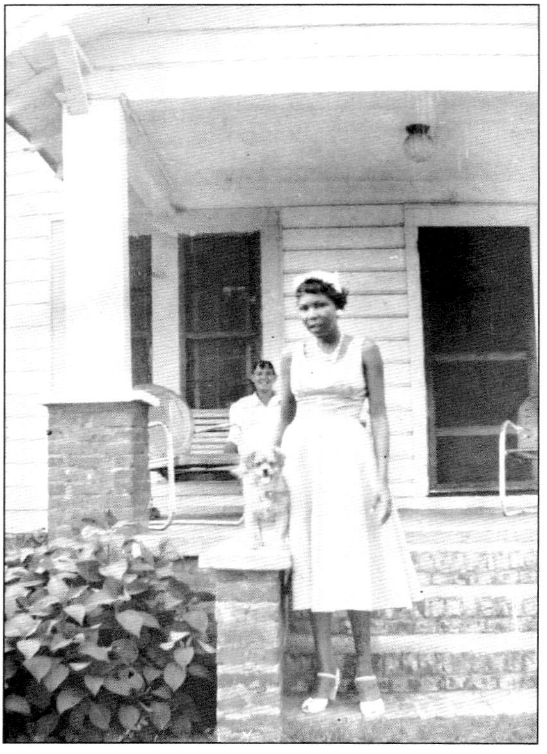

Minnie Shepherd and her grandmother, Mary Lucy Ingram, are on the porch of the Ingram home on Greensboro Road. This is where Minnie Shepherd and her sister grew up. (Courtesy Minnie Peek.)

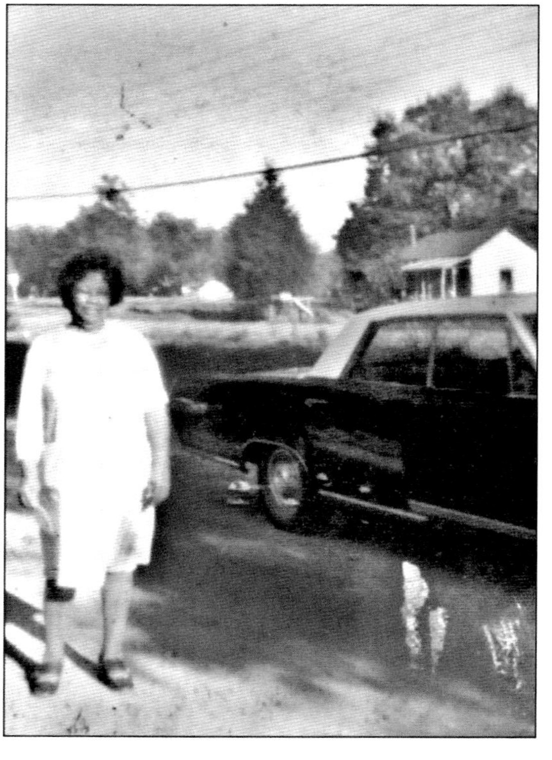

Opra Ingram Dallas is shown *c.* 1960 with her home in the background. Ed Ingram had the two-room house built for his daughter Louise Ingram. (Courtesy Minnie Peek.)

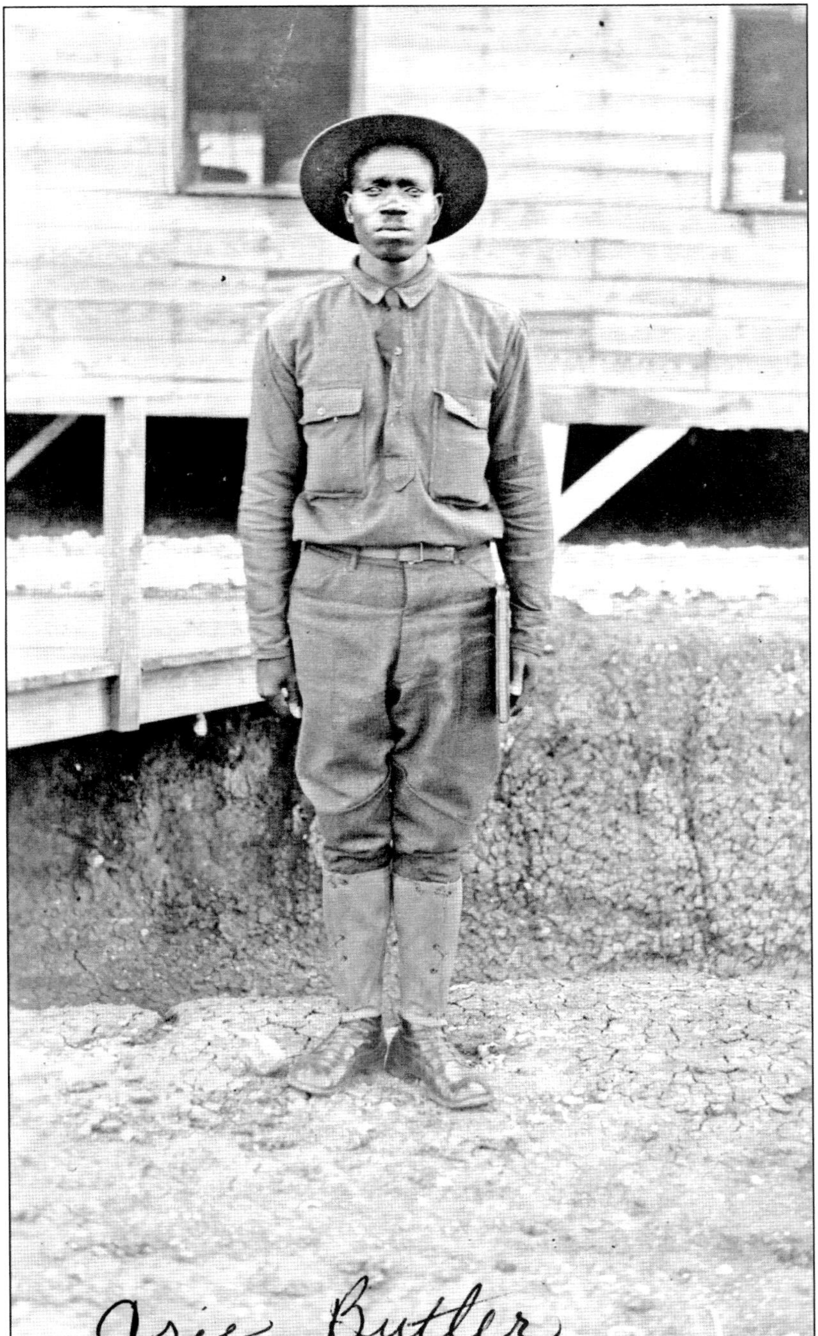

Asie Butler is shown here in full military attire *c*. 1940s. During the Civil War, eager volunteers desiring to become soldiers thronged recruiting stations only to be sent home with an understanding that the war was a "white man's war." Therefore, many African Americans wore their uniforms with pride when their roles as soldiers were finally recognized. (Courtesy Elzata Brown.)

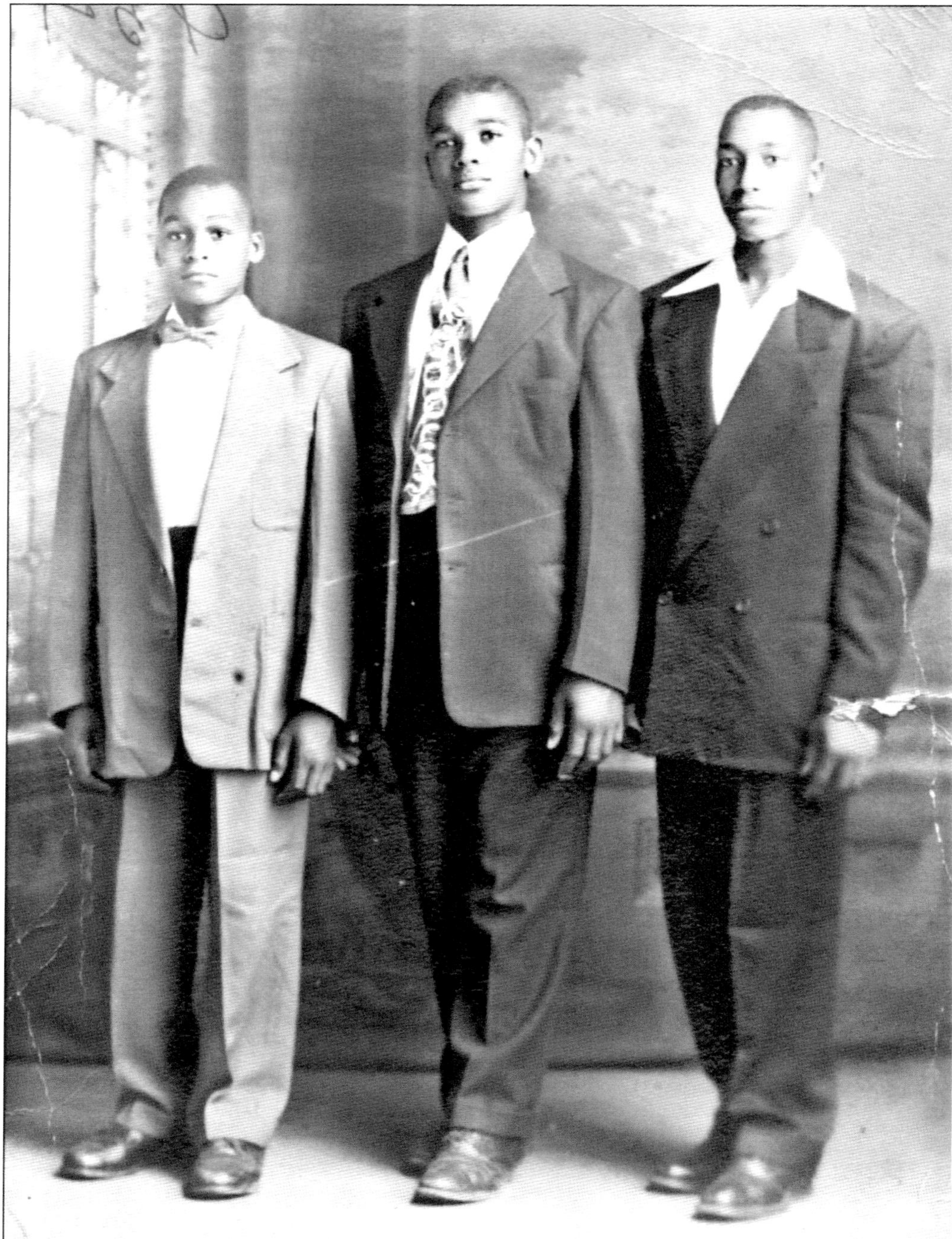

Leegree, Detroy, and Leroy Booker, sons of Albert and Ruby Booker, are shown in this 1950s photograph. They lived with their grandparents on the Booker farm where they helped by chopping and picking cotton. A story that has been passed down says the boys would complain that their backs were hurting. Their uncle George would tell them "You ain't got no back—all you got is a gristle—now get back to work!" (Courtesy Elzata Brown.)

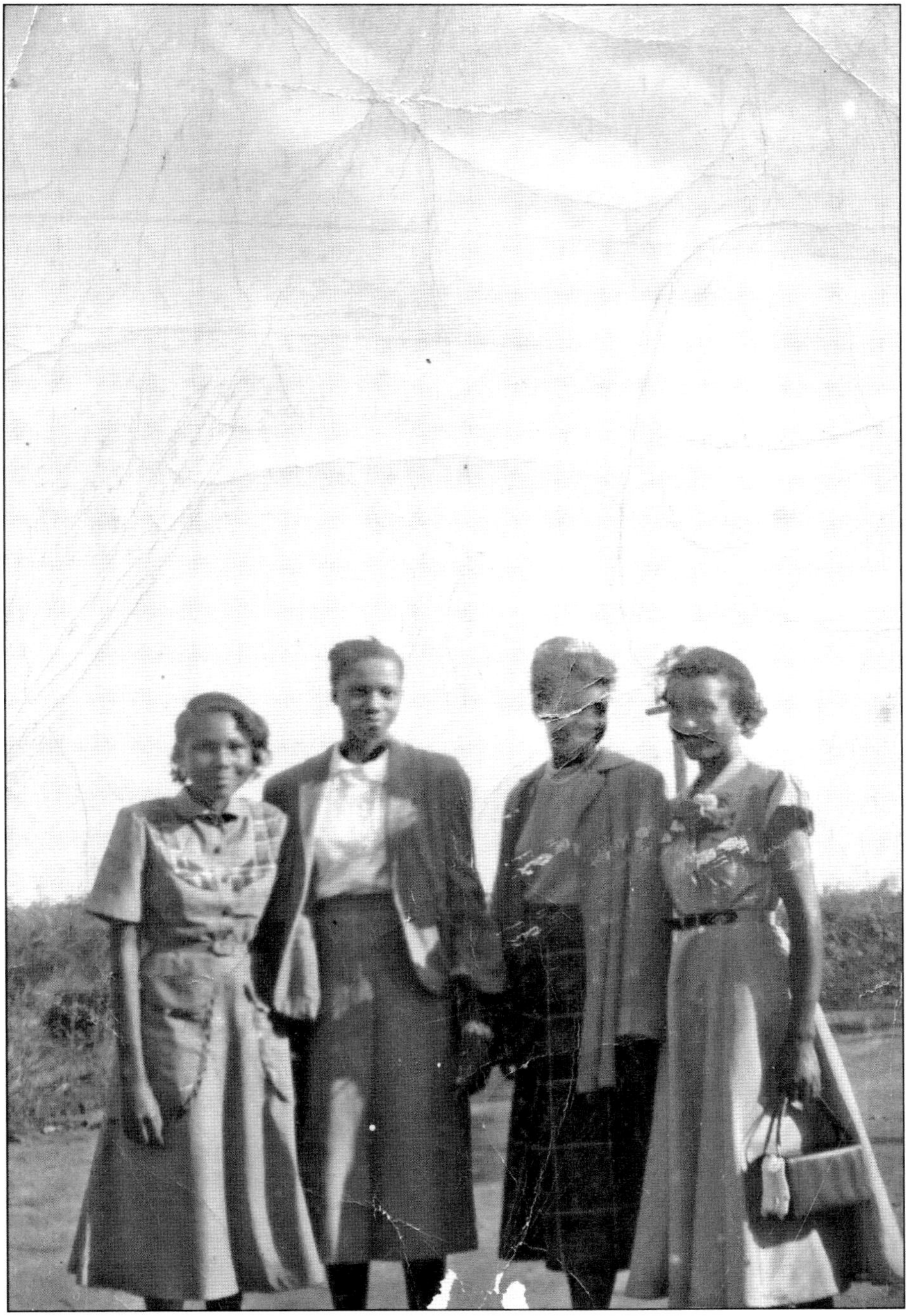

Minnie Shepherd, Elzata Brown, Barbara Henry, and Franzetta Hawkins are shown in this early 1950s photo taken after a union meeting. Union meetings were held every fifth Sunday, when four churches—Jackson Grove, Smyrna, Plainview, and Holland Springs Baptist Church—would convene for young people to present songs and speeches to the congregation. These meetings served to develop leadership skills and build self-confidence in the youth of these times. (Courtesy Minnie Peek.)

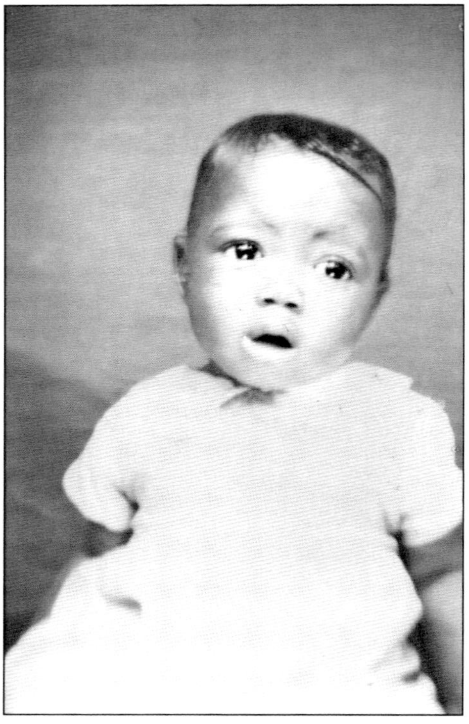

Elzata Brown is shown here as an infant *c.* 1935. There were many large families during the early days, but some children, like Elzata, had no siblings. (Courtesy Elzata Brown.)

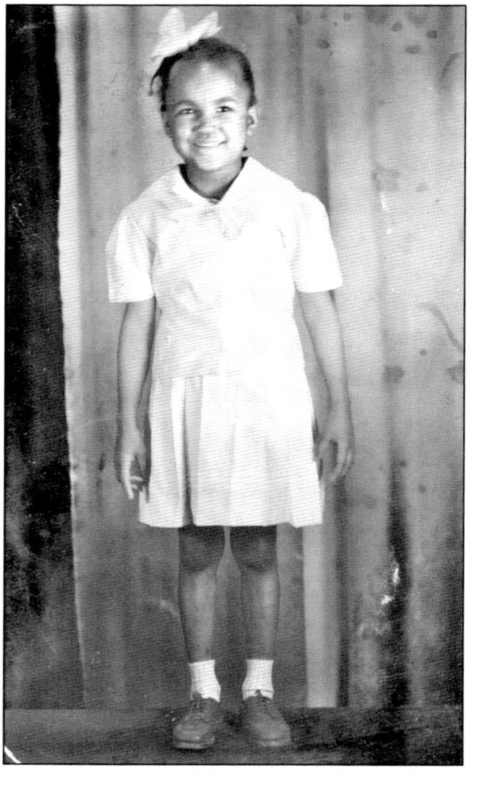

Margaret Ree Holloman is shown around five years old in this photograph. She is the daughter of Taylor and Jimmie Lee Holloman of Bostwick. Her father, a farmer and landowner, served on the Morgan County Board of Education during the late 1970s and early 1980s. Margaret married Amos Jones of Morgan County and had two children, Zonna and Bernard. She is now a retired teacher. (Courtesy Elzata Brown.)

Salina Jordan's grandchildren, Mae Frances Butler and Leola Jordan, pictured *c.* 1940, enjoyed spending summer vacations in Morgan County with their grandmother. (Courtesy Elzata Brown.)

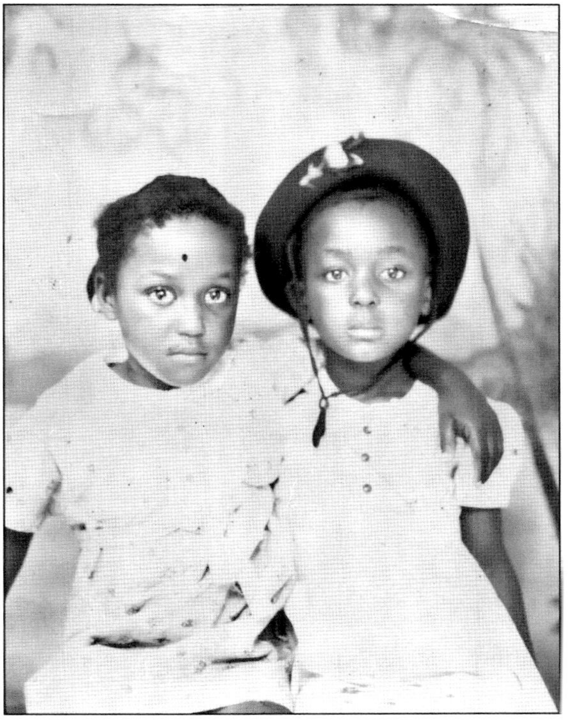

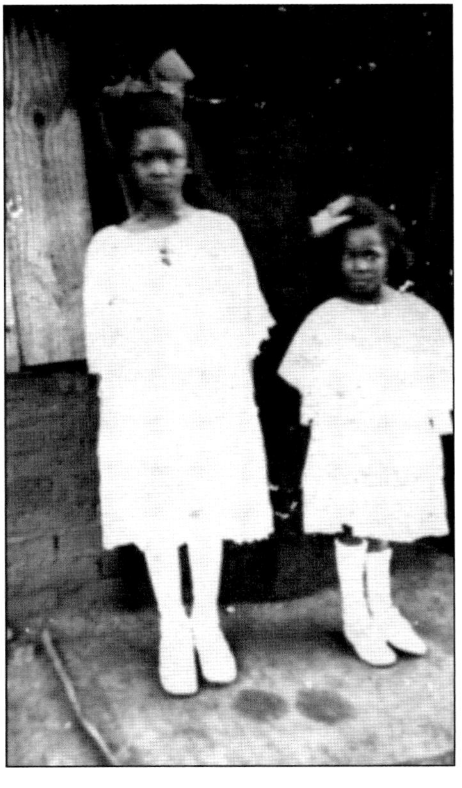

Louise and Lillie Pearl Ingram attended Mt. Zion School, a rural church school, in Morgan County. The girls are the daughters of Ed Ingram and Mattie Mae Johnson. Ed later married Mary Lucy Moseley, who reared the girls, after the death of their mother. (Courtesy Minnie Peek.)

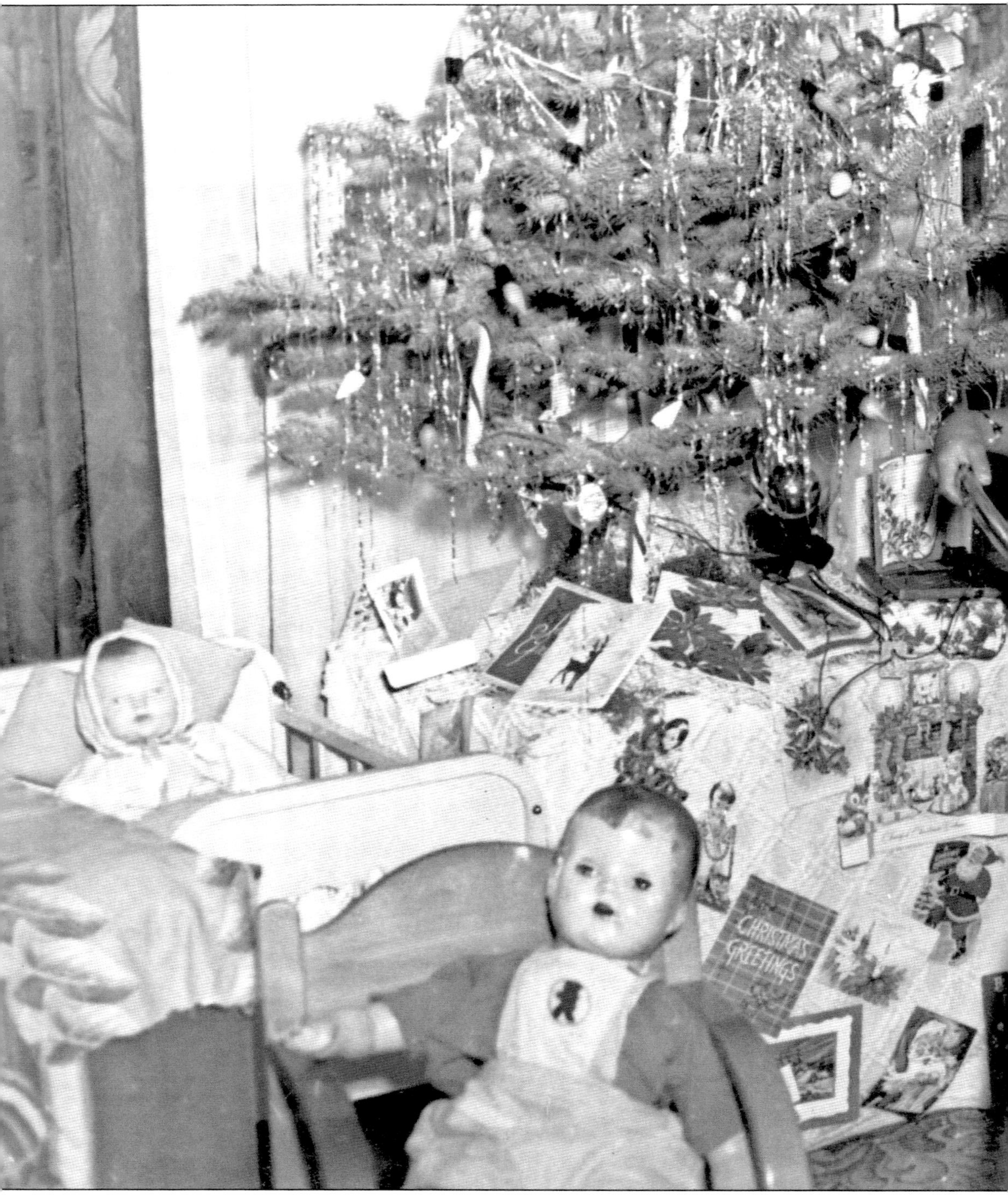

Geraldine Booker is shown at five years old on December 22, 1951. Like many other children during this time, she found white dolls under the Christmas tree, since black ones were not easily accessible. African-American children were sometimes discouraged

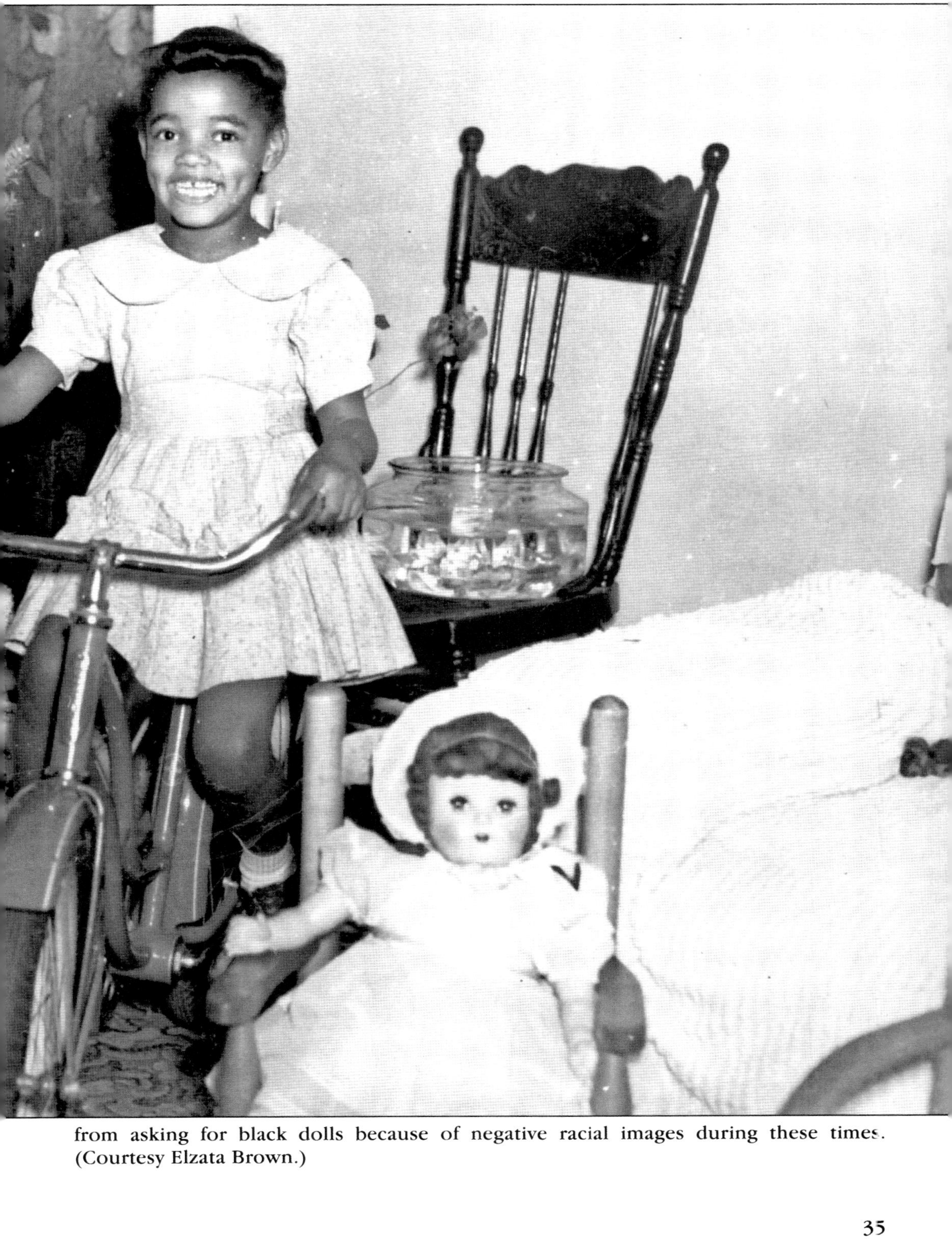

from asking for black dolls because of negative racial images during these times. (Courtesy Elzata Brown.)

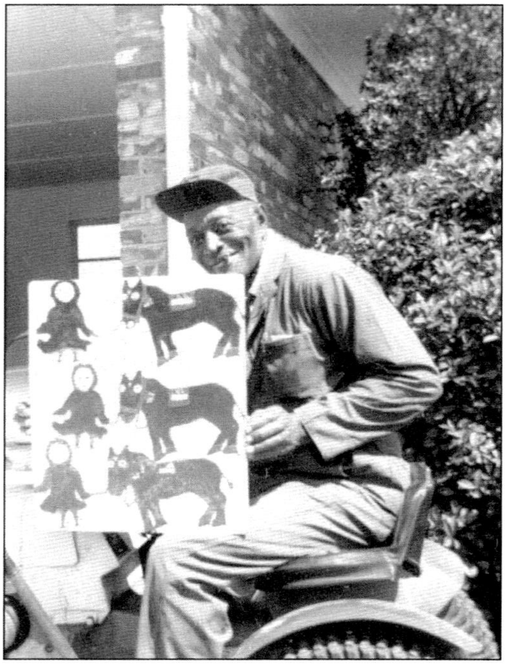

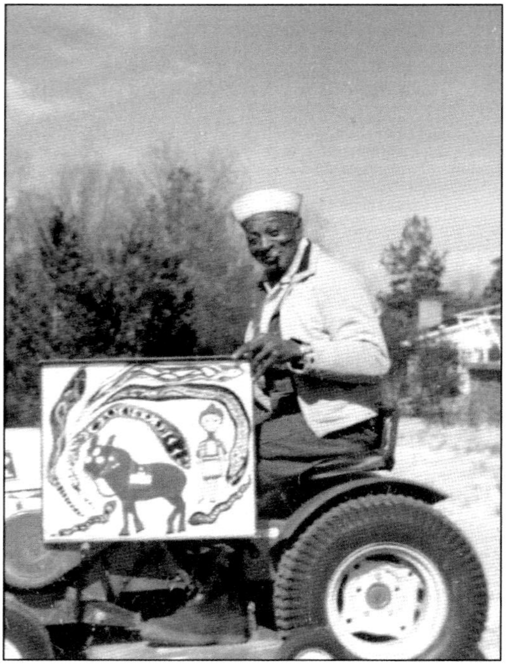

(Left) Will Jones was a local folk artist in Morgan County. (Courtesy Georgia Division of Archives and History, Office of Secretary of State.)
(Right) Will Jones shows off one of his paintings. Snakes, birds, and other animals appear in a lot of African-American folk art (Courtesy Georgia Division of Archives and History, Office of Secretary of State.)

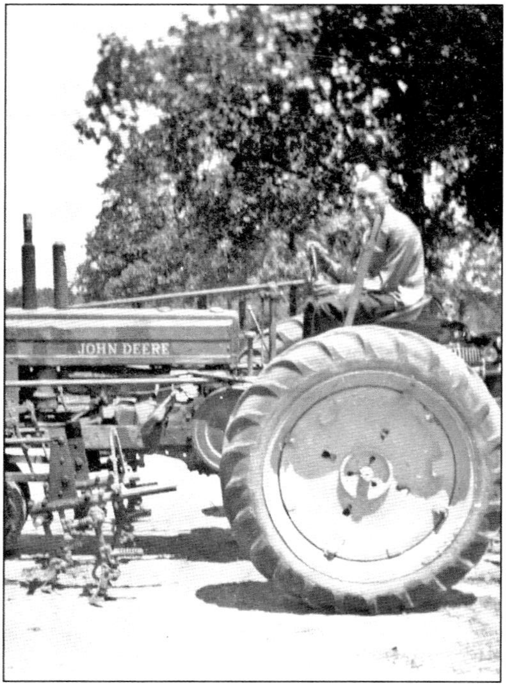

Joe Booker had a home built for his family close to the Booker homestead in order to help his father on the farm. He is pictured *c.* 1955 on a John Deere tractor. During this time, family-operated farms accounted for a significant portion of crop production in the county. (Courtesy Elzata Brown.)

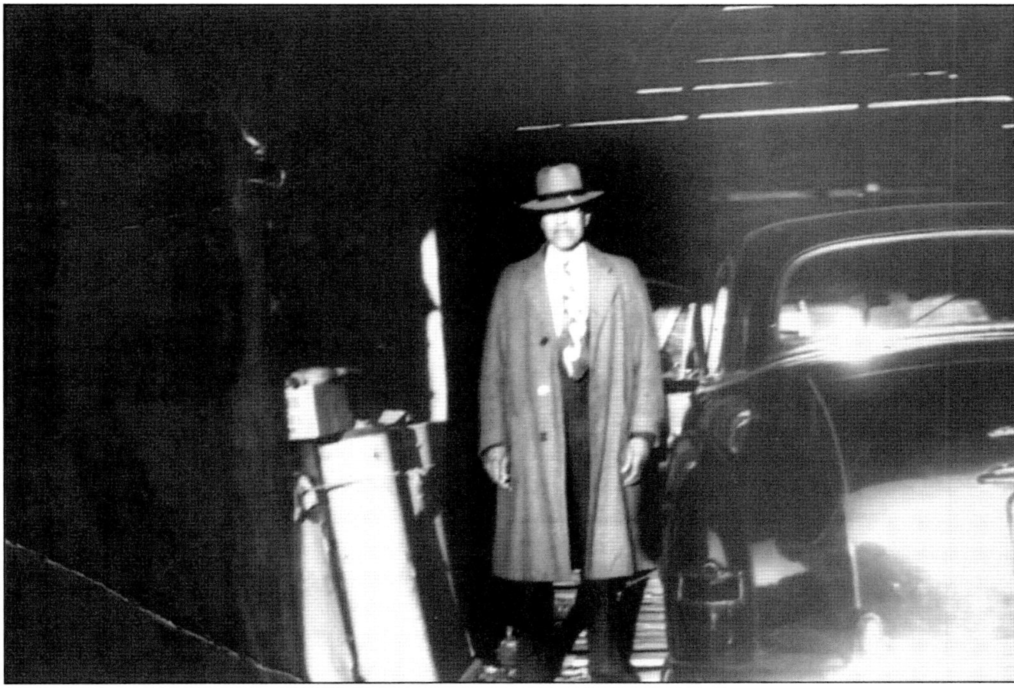

Ed Ingram enjoyed dressing up and riding to church in his car. He purchased a different car or truck every few years. (Courtesy Minnie Peek.)

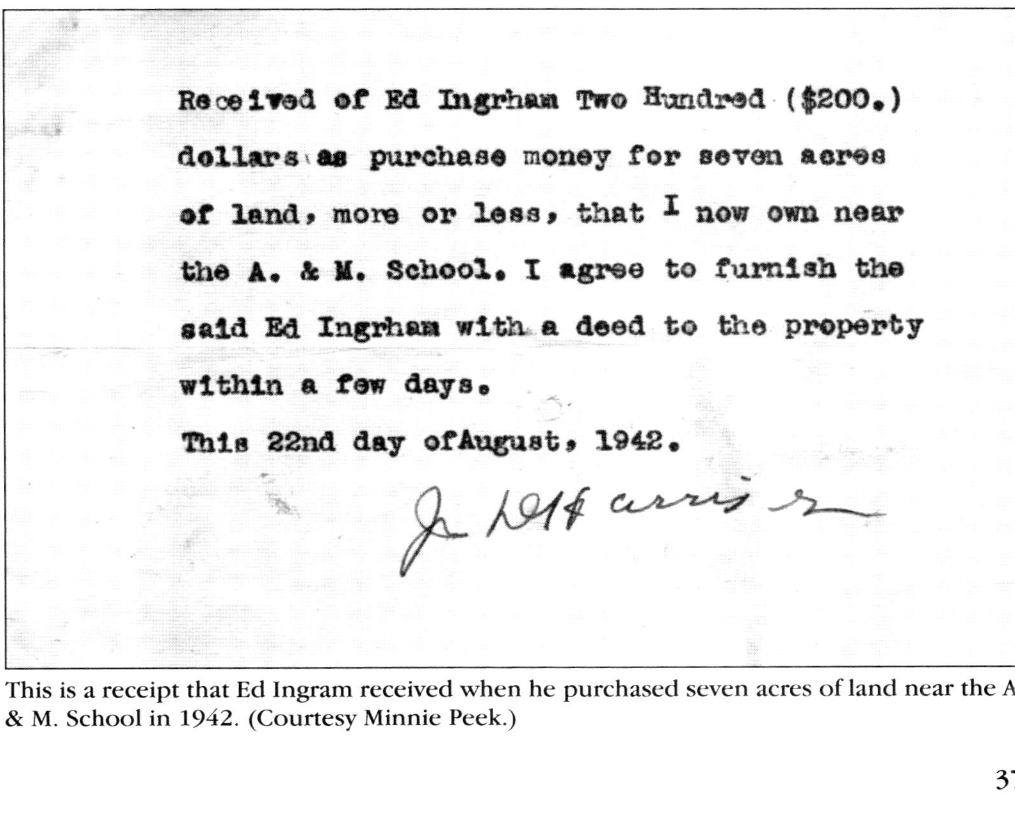

Received of Ed Ingrham Two Hundred ($200.) dollars as purchase money for seven acres of land, more or less, that I now own near the A. & M. School. I agree to furnish the said Ed Ingrham with a deed to the property within a few days.

This 22nd day ofAugust, 1942.

This is a receipt that Ed Ingram received when he purchased seven acres of land near the A. & M. School in 1942. (Courtesy Minnie Peek.)

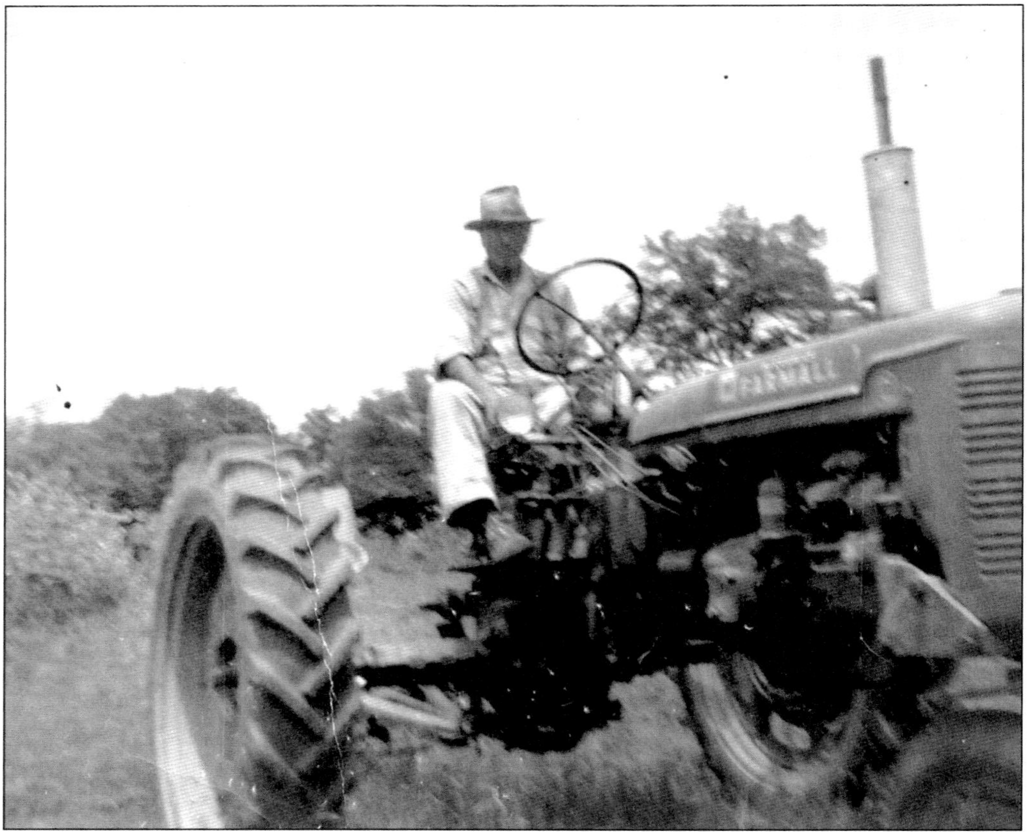

Ed "Eddie" Gooden Ingram (1888–1987) is shown on his tractor. Ed quit school in the third grade to help his parents on the farm. This was common during the early days, as the family's labor was the source of its income. He became well known in Morgan County as a hard-working landowner who provided a home for his children, his wife's two younger sisters, and later two granddaughters. Beloved by many in the community, he and his wife were called "Mama" and "Papa." (Courtesy Minnie Peek.)

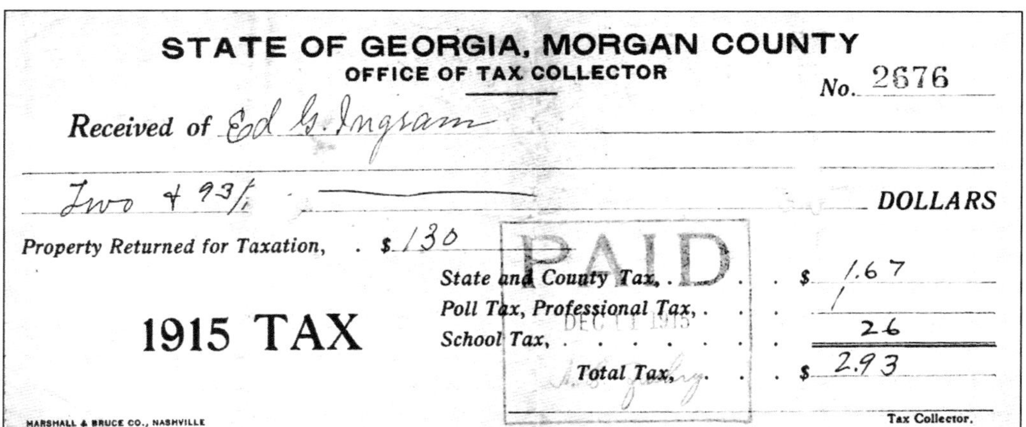

STATE OF GEORGIA, MORGAN COUNTY
OFFICE OF TAX COLLECTOR

No. 2676

Received of Ed G. Ingram

Two + 93/100 **DOLLARS**

Property Returned for Taxation, $130

1915 TAX

State and County Tax,	$ 1.67
Poll Tax, Professional Tax,	1
School Tax,	26
Total Tax,	$ 2.93

PAID
DEC 11 1915

Tax Collector.

MARSHALL & BRUCE CO., NASHVILLE

This is a tax receipt for the payment of property tax in 1915. (Courtesy Minnie Peek.)

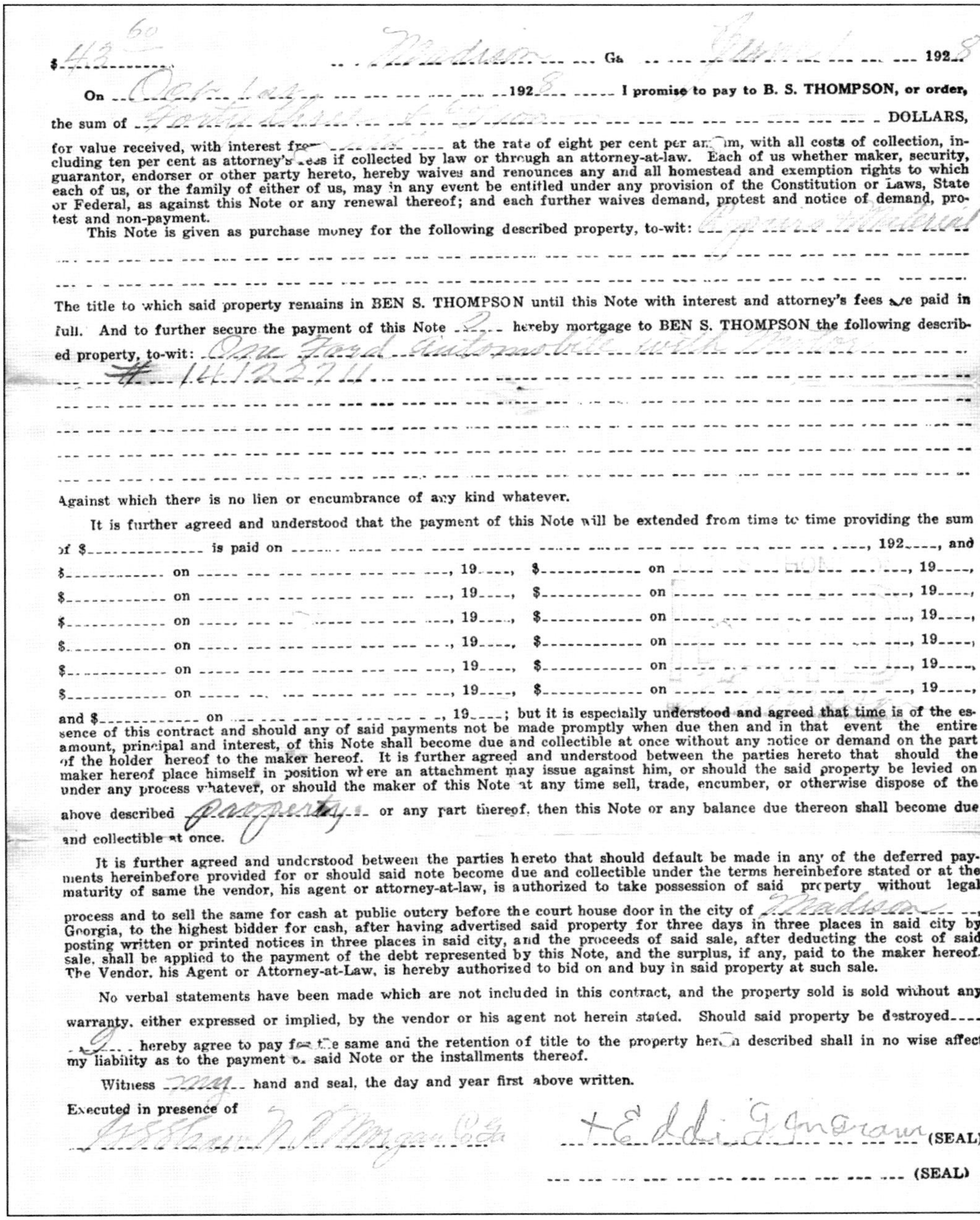

$ 42 60/100 ..... Madison ..... Ga 192 8

On Oct. 1st ..... 192 8 ..... I promise to pay to B. S. THOMPSON, or order, the sum of Forty three & 60/100 ..... DOLLARS,

for value received, with interest from ..... at the rate of eight per cent per annum, with all costs of collection, including ten per cent as attorney's fees if collected by law or through an attorney-at-law. Each of us whether maker, security, guarantor, endorser or other party hereto, hereby waives and renounces any and all homestead and exemption rights to which each of us, or the family of either of us, may in any event be entitled under any provision of the Constitution or Laws, State or Federal, as against this Note or any renewal thereof; and each further waives demand, protest and notice of demand, protest and non-payment.

This Note is given as purchase money for the following described property, to-wit: Repairs & Material

The title to which said property remains in BEN S. THOMPSON until this Note with interest and attorney's fees are paid in full. And to further secure the payment of this Note I hereby mortgage to BEN S. THOMPSON the following described property, to-wit: One Ford Automobile with Motor # 14122711

Against which there is no lien or encumbrance of any kind whatever.

It is further agreed and understood that the payment of this Note will be extended from time to time providing the sum of $..... is paid on ....., 192...., and

$..... on ....., 19...., $..... on ....., 19....,
$..... on ....., 19...., $..... on ....., 19....,
$..... on ....., 19...., $..... on ....., 19....,
$..... on ....., 19...., $..... on ....., 19....,
$..... on ....., 19...., $..... on ....., 19....,
$..... on ....., 19...., $..... on ....., 19....,

and $..... on ....., 19....; but it is especially understood and agreed that time is of the essence of this contract and should any of said payments not be made promptly when due then and in that event the entire amount, principal and interest, of this Note shall become due and collectible at once without any notice or demand on the part of the holder hereof to the maker hereof. It is further agreed and understood between the parties hereto that should the maker hereof place himself in position where an attachment may issue against him, or should the said property be levied on under any process whatever, or should the maker of this Note at any time sell, trade, encumber, or otherwise dispose of the above described property or any part thereof, then this Note or any balance due thereon shall become due and collectible at once.

It is further agreed and understood between the parties hereto that should default be made in any of the deferred payments hereinbefore provided for or should said note become due and collectible under the terms hereinbefore stated or at the maturity of same the vendor, his agent or attorney-at-law, is authorized to take possession of said property without legal process and to sell the same for cash at public outcry before the court house door in the city of Madison, Georgia, to the highest bidder for cash, after having advertised said property for three days in three places in said city by posting written or printed notices in three places in said city, and the proceeds of said sale, after deducting the cost of said sale, shall be applied to the payment of the debt represented by this Note, and the surplus, if any, paid to the maker hereof. The Vendor, his Agent or Attorney-at-Law, is hereby authorized to bid on and buy in said property at such sale.

No verbal statements have been made which are not included in this contract, and the property sold is sold without any warranty, either expressed or implied, by the vendor or his agent not herein stated. Should said property be destroyed I hereby agree to pay for the same and the retention of title to the property herein described shall in no wise affect my liability as to the payment of said Note or the installments thereof.

Witness my hand and seal, the day and year first above written.

Executed in presence of

W. S. Thompson N. P. Morgan Co. Ga. + Eddie G. Ingram (SEAL)

..... (SEAL)

This 1928 note was issued to Ed Ingram for the purchase of repairs and material. Ed, a good provider for his family, raised wheat, corn, and sugarcane. Ed and his neighbor Edgar Brown sawed wood for stoves, fireplaces, and heaters. Their wives, Mary Lucy Ingram and Minnie Brown, canned fruits and vegetables. The neighbors also washed clothes outside in wash pots, made lye soap, and killed hogs together. (Courtesy Minnie Peek.)

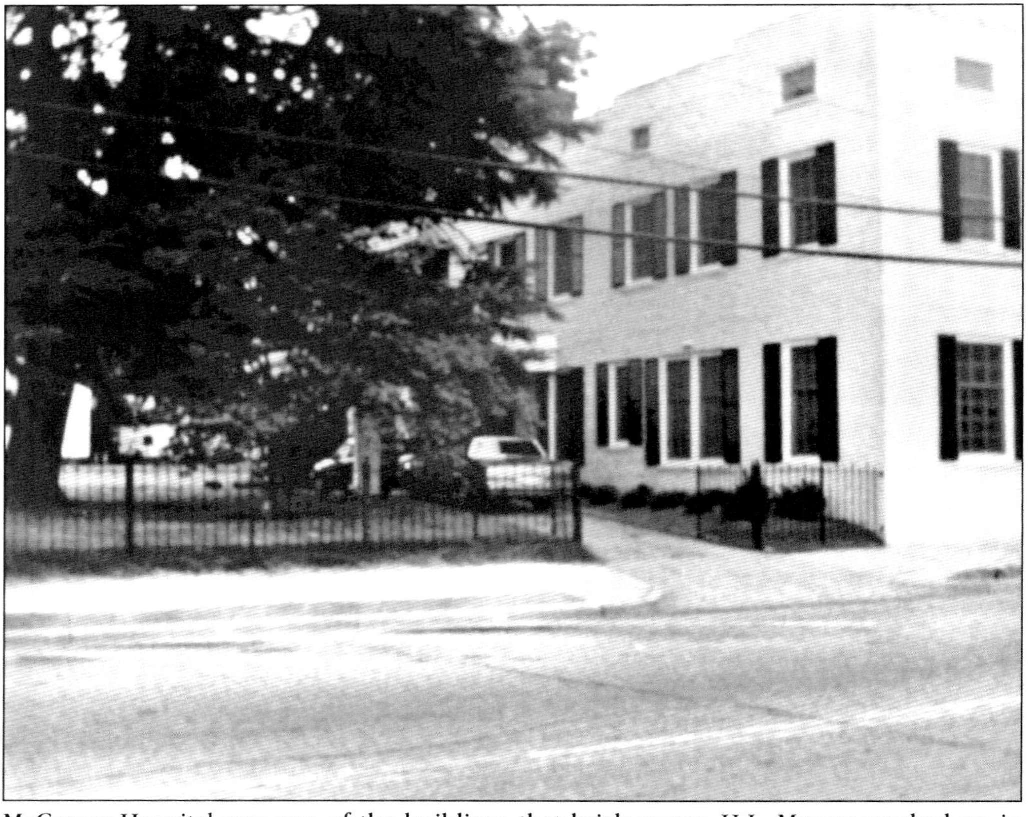

McGreary Hospital was one of the buildings that brick mason H.L. Murray worked on in Morgan County. It is also the hospital where Hazeltine Mitchell practiced as a registered nurse in the 1930s. This was Madison's first hospital, and it served Madison and surrounding counties from 1931 to 1954. (Courtesy Dr. Rosalyn Mitchell Patterson.)

Two

DAILY LIFE
School, Work, and Community Activities

A community is a place where hope lives next door to expectation, where infinite goals and a myriad of possibilities reside under the same roof, and where the pieces of our dreams can be woven together with new ideas.

Author unknown

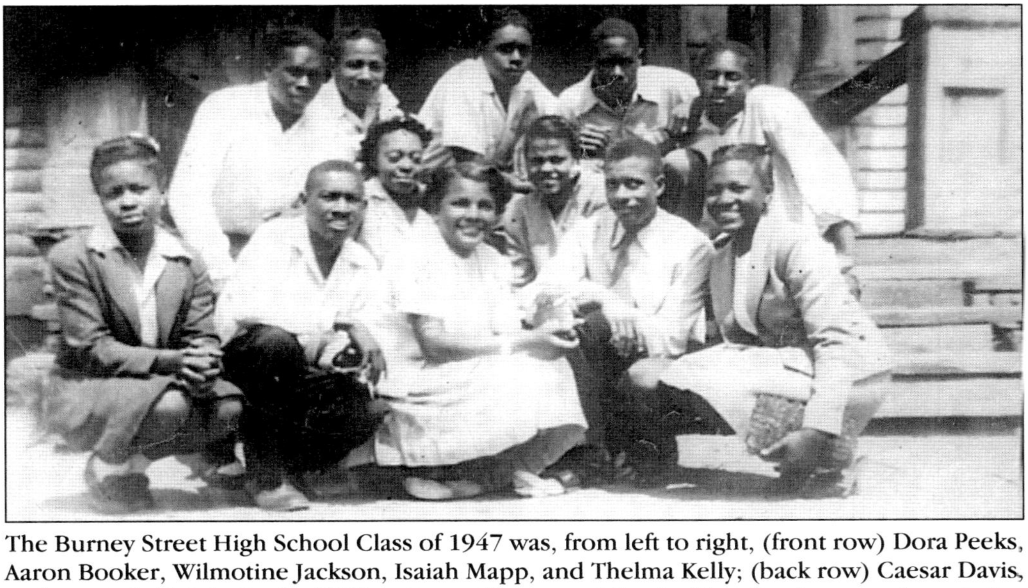

The Burney Street High School Class of 1947 was, from left to right, (front row) Dora Peeks, Aaron Booker, Wilmotine Jackson, Isaiah Mapp, and Thelma Kelly; (back row) Caesar Davis, Walter Mitchell, Jake Drake, William James Henry, and Travis Allen. Students graduated after the 11th grade. Reconstruction governments in the South created the public school systems, and these early primary schools were attended by men and women as well as children. The community was involved in improving the school environment and purchasing equipment with philanthropic assistance. The school's opening enrollment was 206 pupils, and students from different cities and towns boarded in Madison to attend here. The principal in 1918 was H.L. Flemister. (Courtesy Dora Peeks Boswell.)

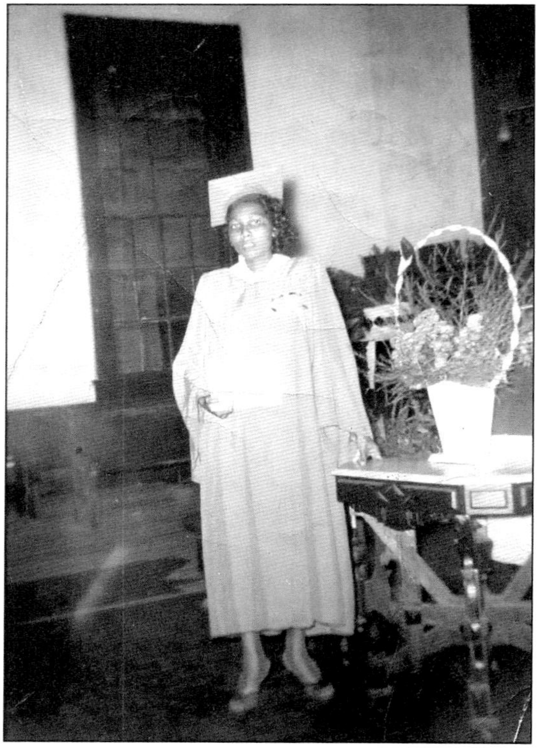

Minnie Bell Shepherd graduated from Pearl High School in 1954. She walked a couple of miles to attend Jackson Grove School, then later Burney Street School, riding a bus to school for the first time in ninth grade. She attended school during the summer months but picked cotton in the fall. After the construction of Pearl High School, African-American students in Morgan County had the opportunity to complete 12th grade. (Courtesy Minnie Peek.)

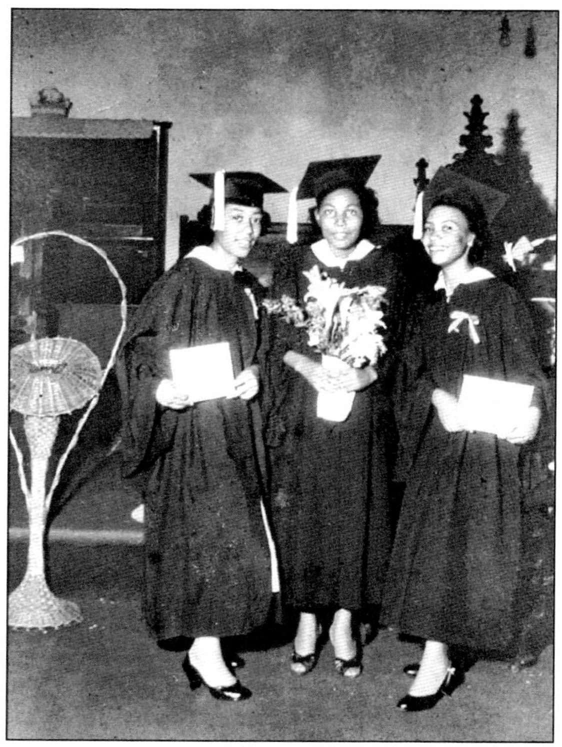

Three top-ranking students of the Pearl High School 1954 graduating class—Gladys White, Minnie Shepherd, and Rosalyn Mitchell—are pictured here. The commencement ceremony was held in the sanctuary of Calvary Baptist Church on Academy Street in Madison. The class motto was "Today we climb the stairs of yesterday's mistakes." The class flower was the red rose, and the class colors were red and white. (Courtesy Dr. Rosalyn Mitchell Patterson.)

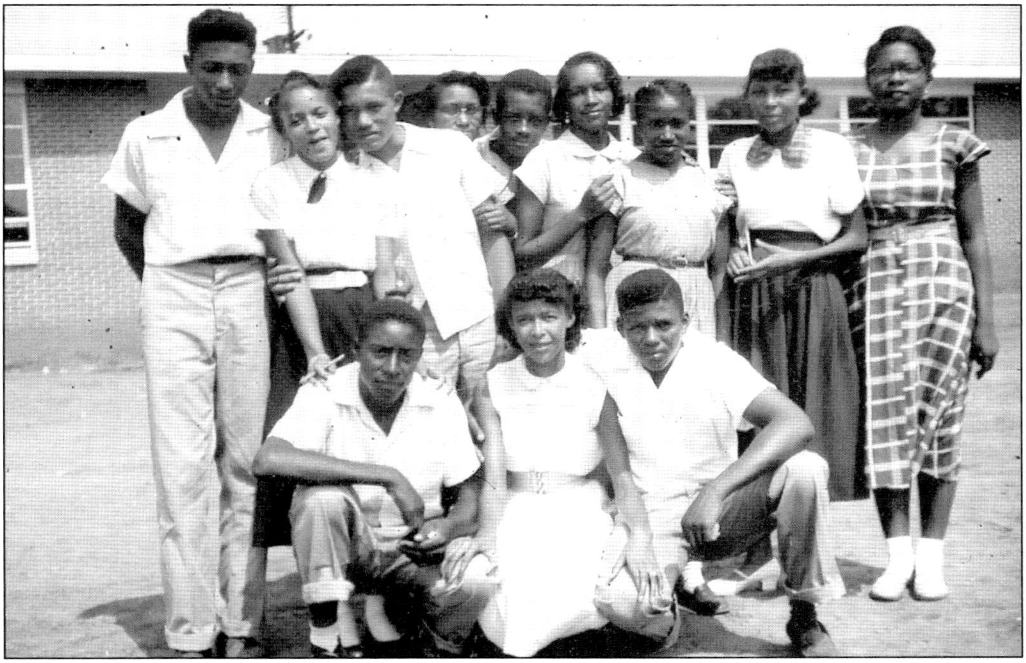

Members of the 1954 graduating class of Pearl High School pose in front of the school, a landmark in Morgan County. The building now houses Morgan County Middle School. The Pearl-Burney High School alumni, recognizing its significance in the community, have erected a monument. (Courtesy Dr. Rosalyn Mitchell Patterson.)

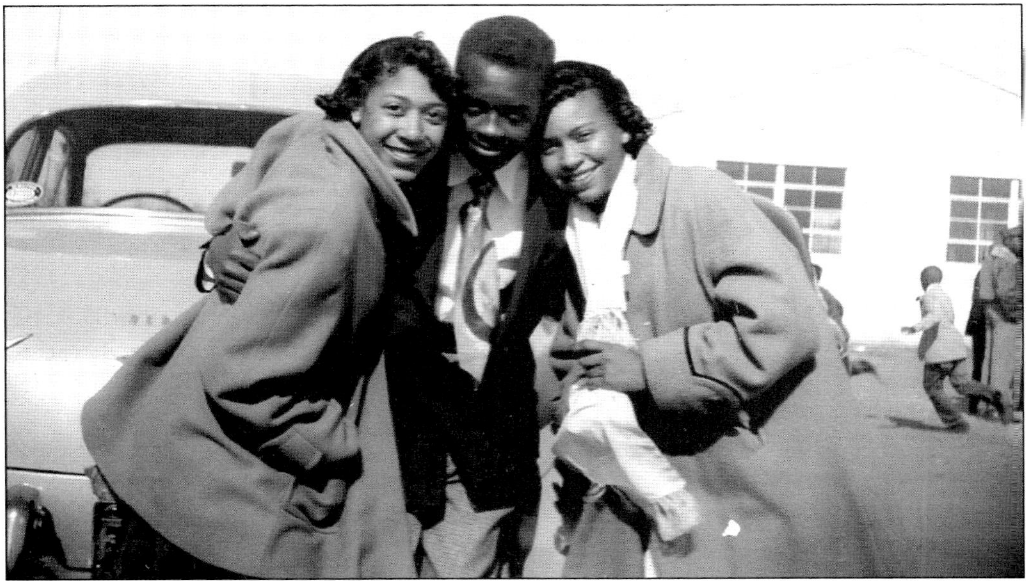

Gladys White, Franklin Jones, and Rosalyn Mitchell smile for the camera during recess their senior year of high school. Younger children are playing in the background. Pearl High School housed elementary and high school students before schools were integrated in Madison. (Courtesy Dr. Rosalyn Mitchell Patterson.)

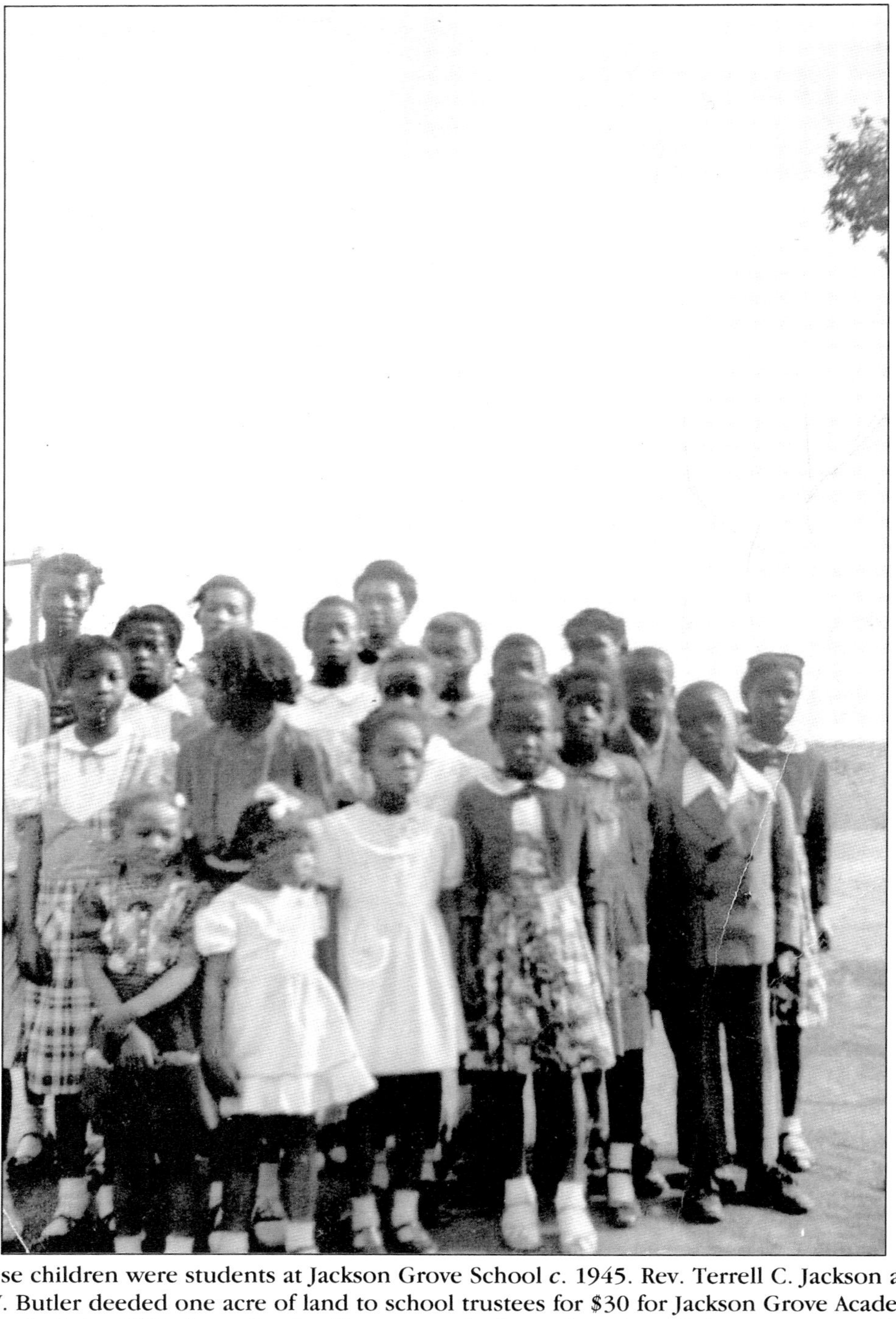

These children were students at Jackson Grove School *c.* 1945. Rev. Terrell C. Jackson and E.W. Butler deeded one acre of land to school trustees for $30 for Jackson Grove Academy to be built in 1897. A small schoolhouse was built on the edge of the property in 1900. Older children would bring in wood that their parents cut at home for the pot-bellied stove used for heating. The school had one cabinet of hand-me-down books for the students' use. (Courtesy Minnie Peek.)

Minnie Bell Shepherd Peek began to dream of going to college instead of the cotton field when she was in high school. After graduating from Pearl High School at the age of 16, she attended Savannah State College in Savannah, Georgia, and returned to Morgan County as a science teacher. (Courtesy Minnie Peek.)

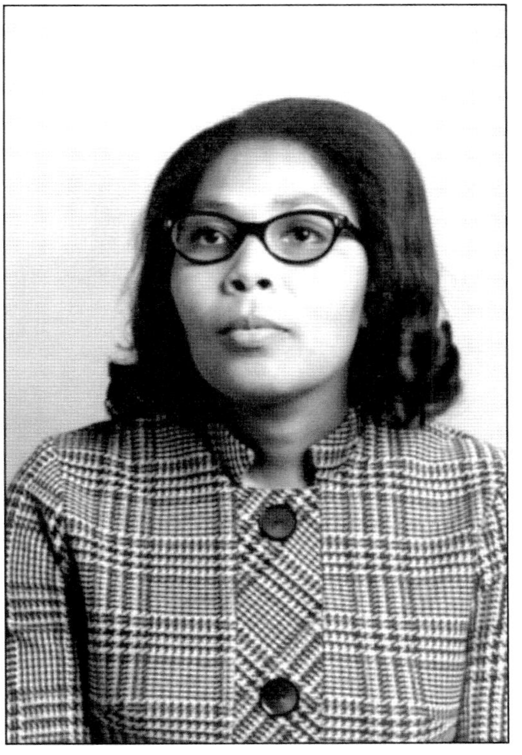

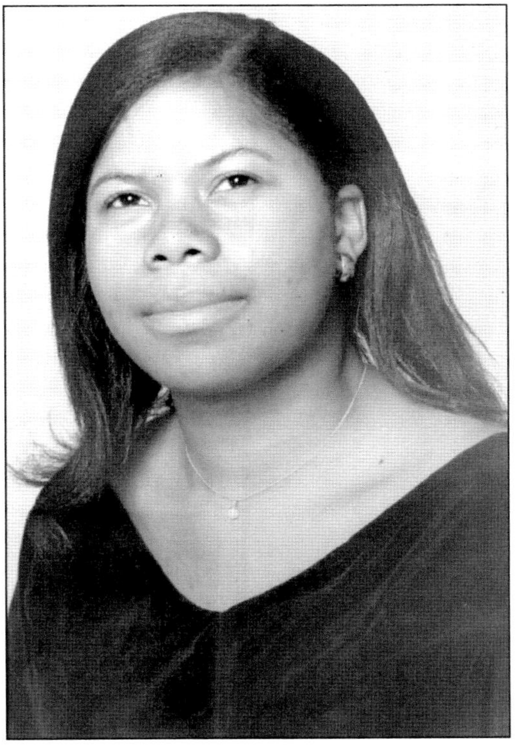

Sharon Vonetta Chambers (1954–2002) graduated from Morgan County High School in 1972 and was on the Homecoming Court. She played clarinet and oboe in the band as a student at Pearl High School. After graduation, Sharon attended Talladega College and Atlanta Medical College. She worked as a medical assistant in Atlanta and had one daughter, Alreca. (Courtesy Carrie Chambers.)

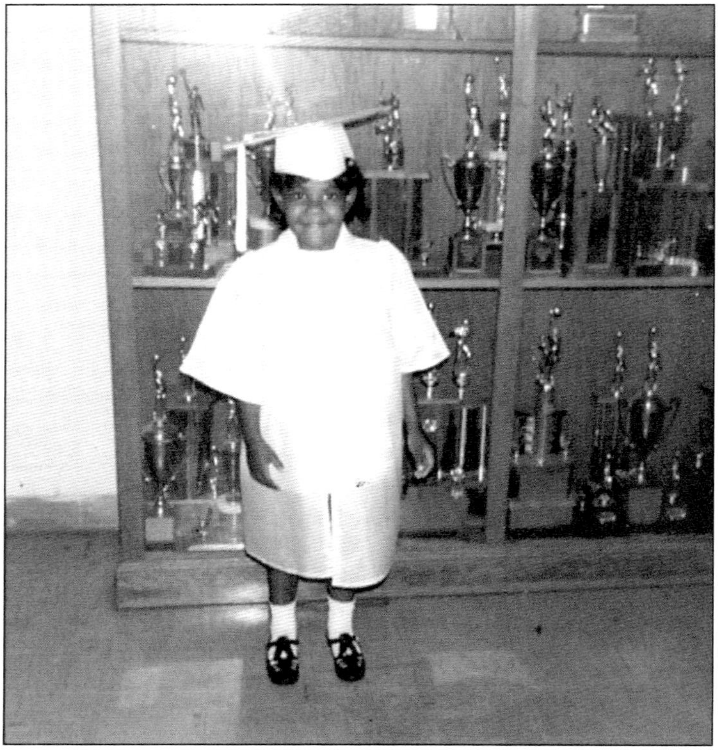

LaWuane Peek is five years old in this 1971 photograph. She attended kindergarten in nearby Oconee County, Georgia, as there was not a state-funded kindergarten program in Morgan County at the time. (Courtesy Minnie Peek.)

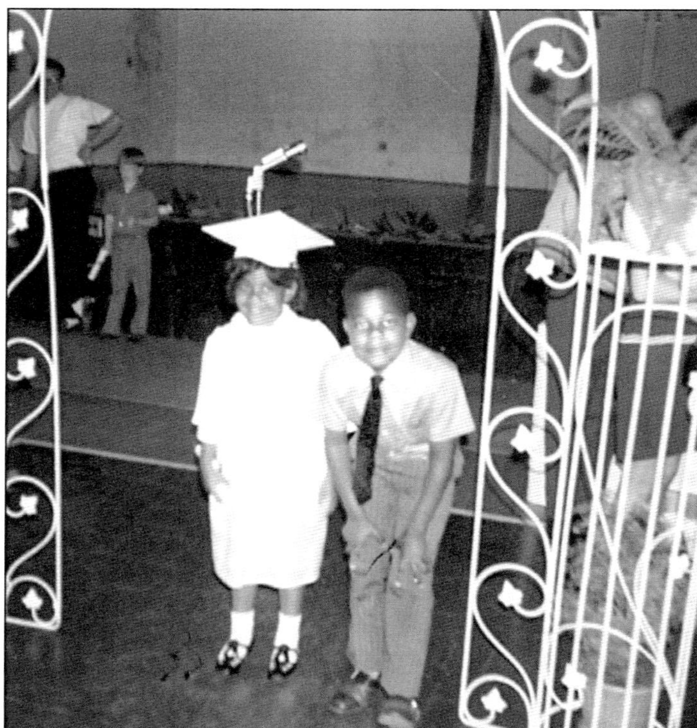

LaWuane Peek is shown after the kindergarten commencement program with her brother, Reginald. (Courtesy Minnie Peek.)

Mary Nell Brown, *c.* 1960, held her brother, Mike, after service at Mt. Vernon Baptist Church, where their father was the pastor. Older children would help their parents by caring for younger children during service. Mary Nell and Mike are two of the offsprings of George and Stella "Sis" Brown. The family lived in the Sowhatchet community. (Courtesy Tessie Robinson.)

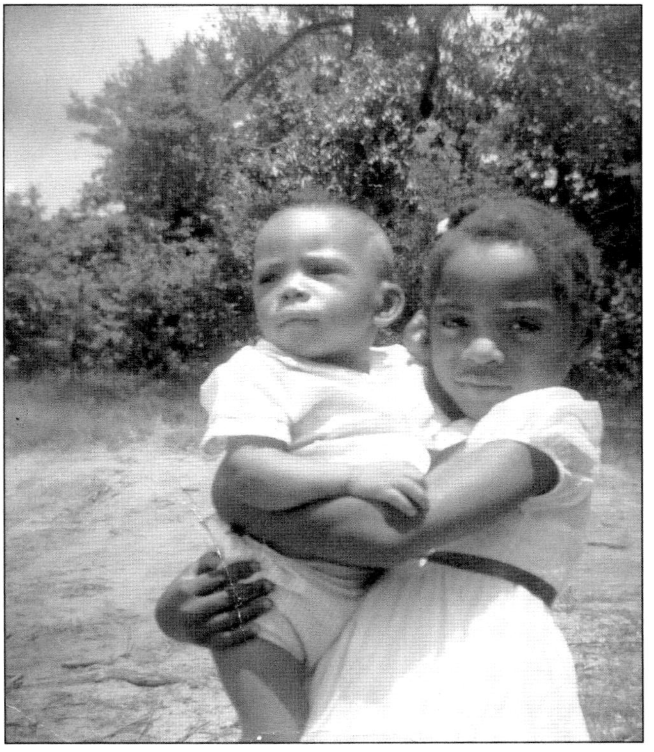

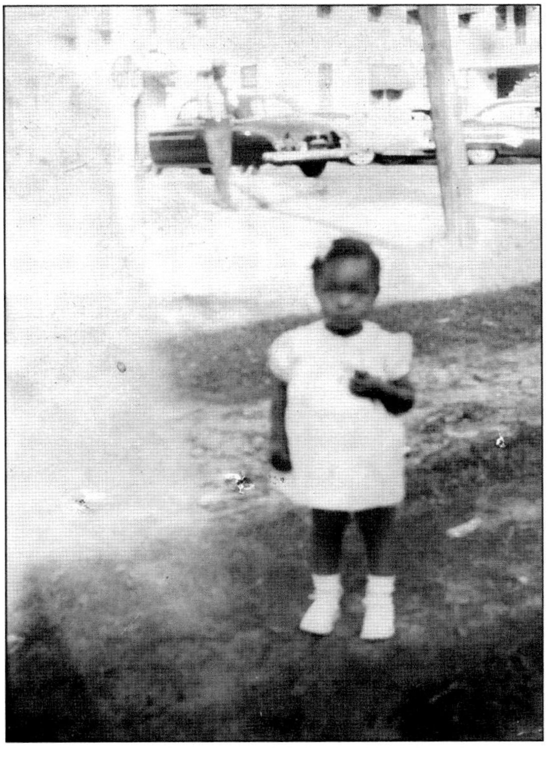

Ruby Lynn Robinson, *c.* 1954, stands on a street in downtown Madison. The Robinson family lived on a farm in Hardeman Mill Road in Bostwick until 1956. The child enjoyed the Saturday visits to town with her parents, which included shopping at Mack's Department Store, eating ice cream from the drugstore, and dining on barbecue pork, Brunswick stew, and pork rinds. Shown here at age two, she is the author of this book. (Courtesy the author.)

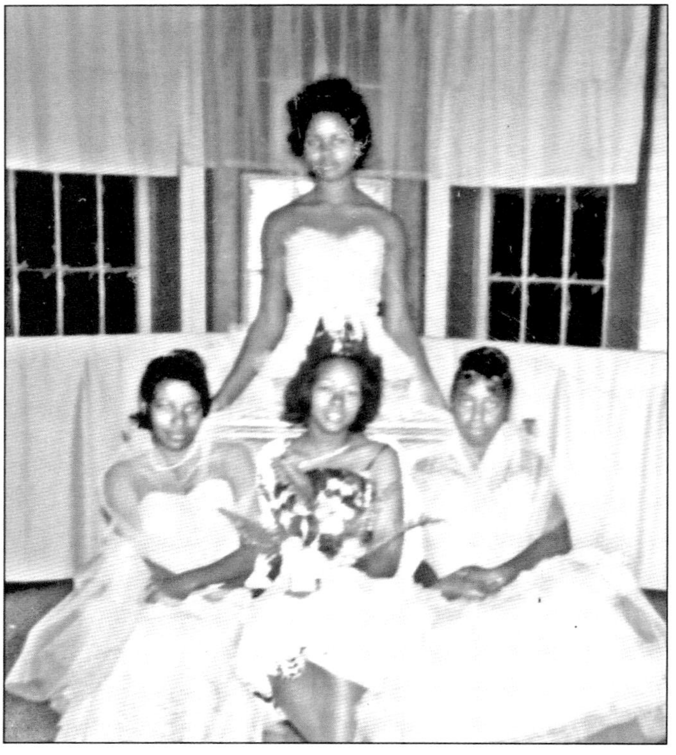

Clara Jones was crowned Community Queen in this 1960s photograph. This pageant was held as a fund-raiser at Mt. Perry Missionary Baptist Church. (Courtesy Elzata Brown.)

Seated from left to right on the second row are newly crowned community queens Ruby Lynn Robinson, Agnes Mae Payne, and Collie Butler. Other contestants and program participants are also pictured. Churches in the community sent youth representatives to participate in this event in 1962. (Courtesy the author.)

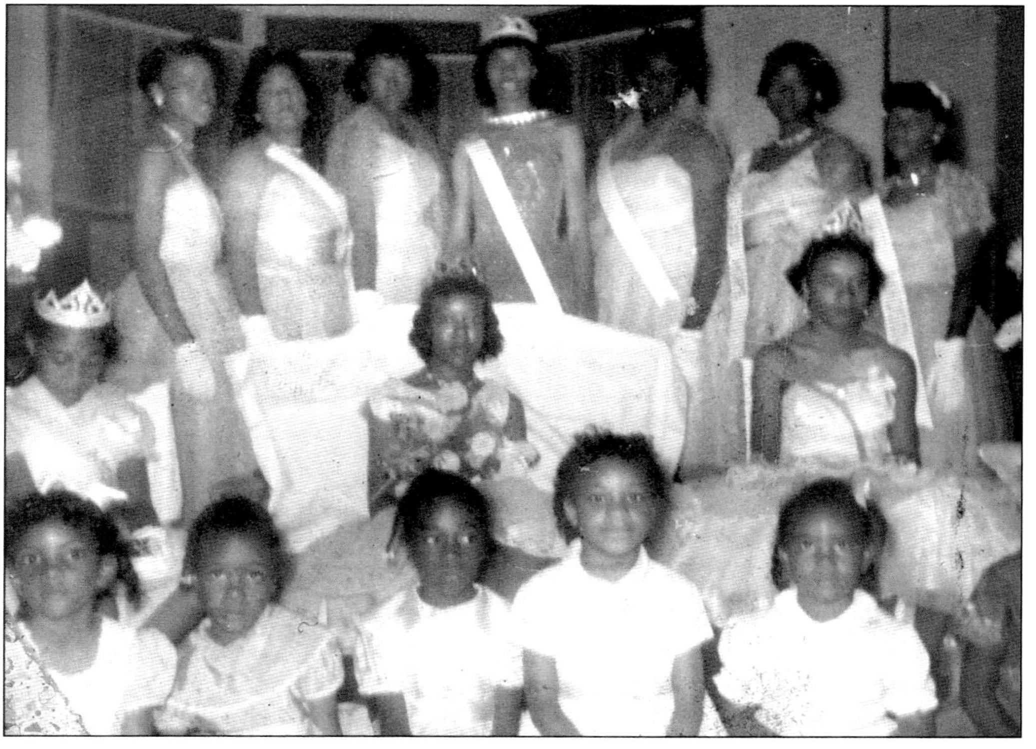

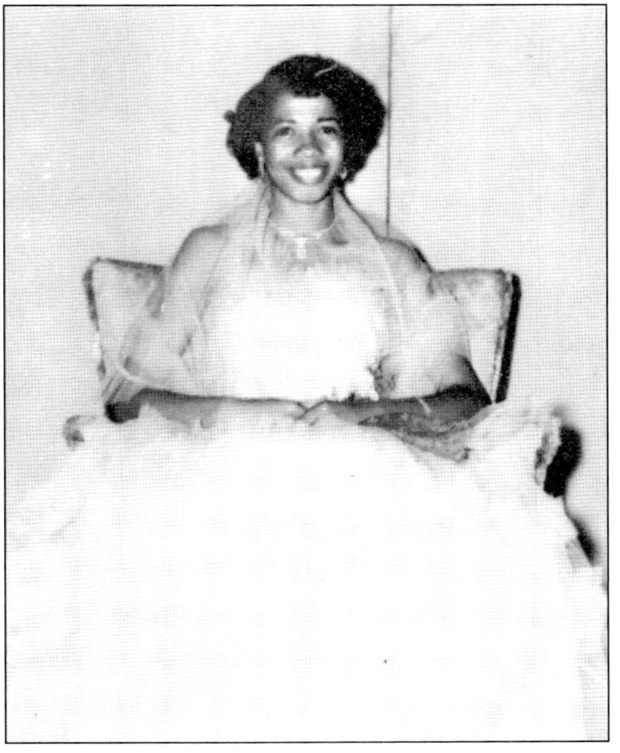

Elzata Brown is dressed for the high school prom, *c.* early 1950s. She signed this photo "Velverlyn," the middle name she gave herself in high school, since her birth name did not include one like some of her classmates. (Courtesy Elzata Brown.)

Emma Booker was crowned Millennium Queen of the Madison Missionary Baptist Association in 2000. She is shown here with the moderator of the association, Rev. William Smith. (Courtesy Elzata Brown.)

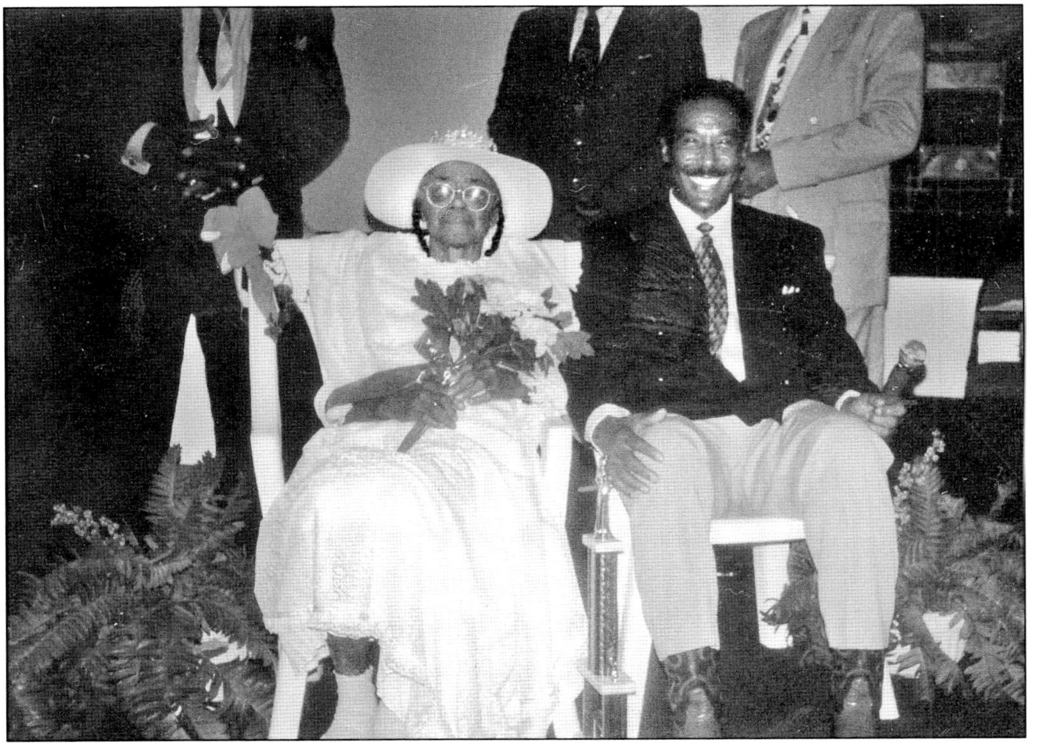

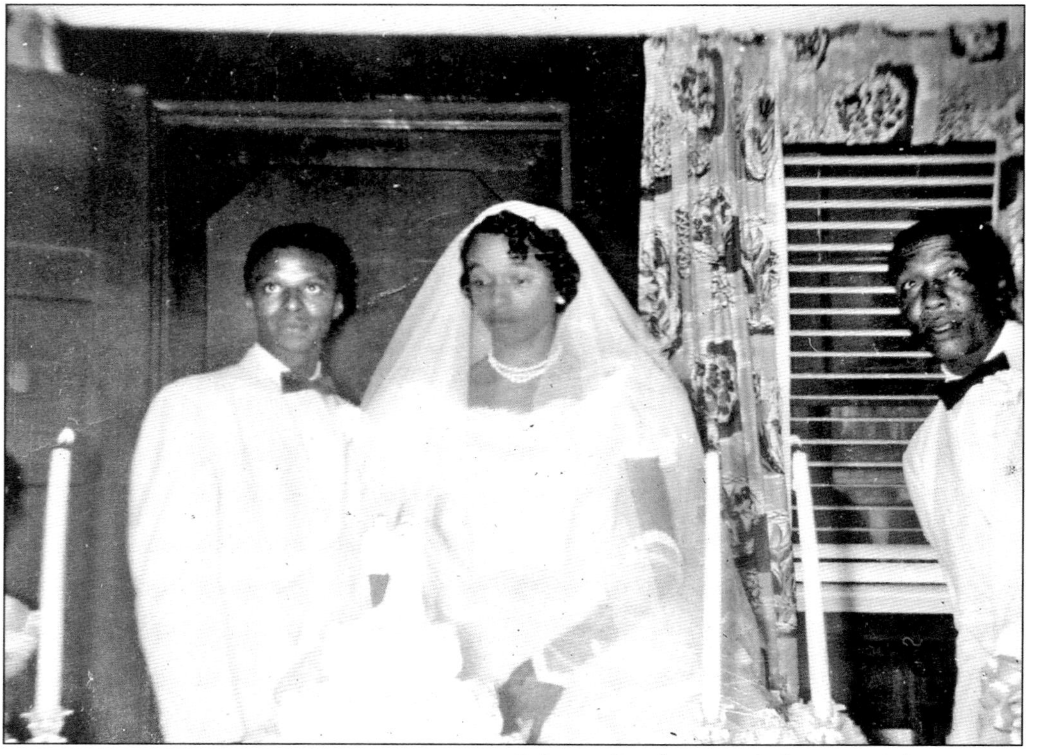

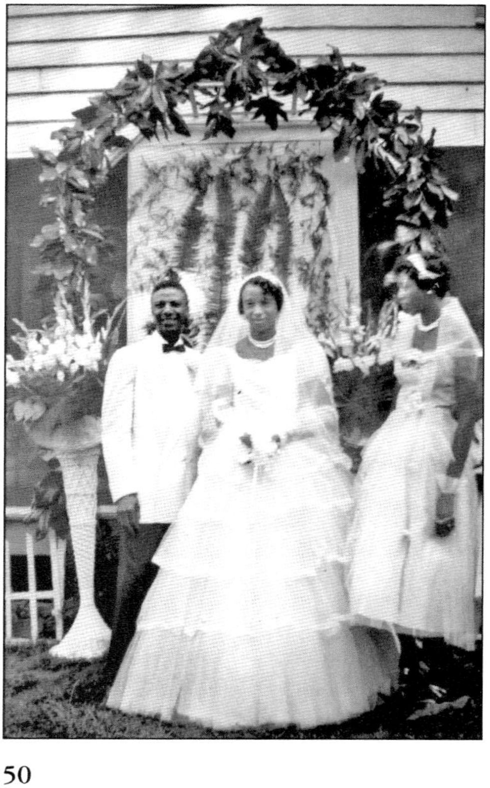

Rebecca Booker married Emory Robinson at the Booker home in 1955. The bride and groom are shown cutting the three-tier cake at the reception, also held in the home. (Courtesy Elzata Brown.)

Rebecca Booker and Emory Robinson are shown with maid of honor Elzata Brown in this 1955 wedding photograph. (Courtesy Elzata Brown.)

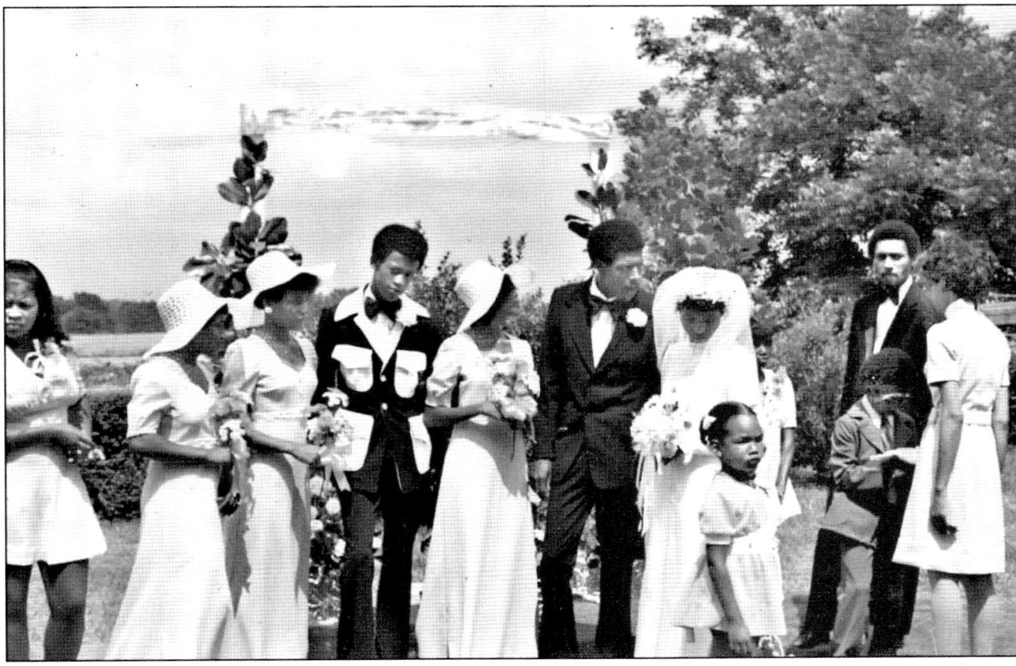

The outdoor wedding of Imogene Booker and Freeman Locklin was held in Madison during the 1970s. (Courtesy Elzata Brown.)

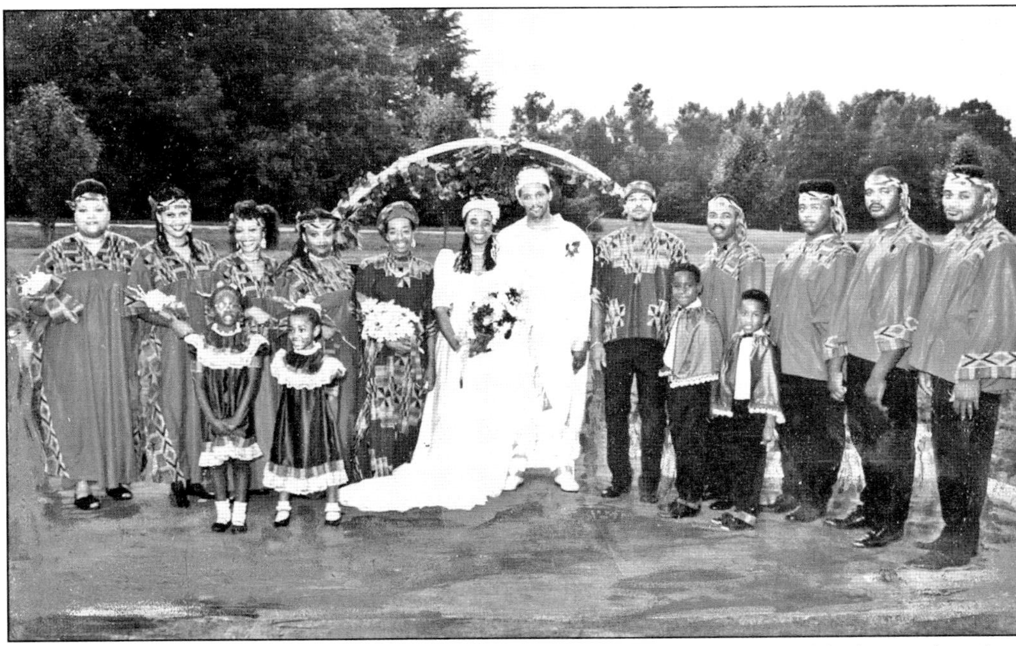

Sherry Butler married William Winchester in an outdoor wedding directed by her godmother, Elzata Brown. Ms. Brown also custom-designed and made the wedding party's Afro-centric attire, with the exception of the bride and groom's outfits. Sherry is the granddaughter of Leegree and Willie Ann Booker of Morgan County. (Courtesy Elzata Brown.)

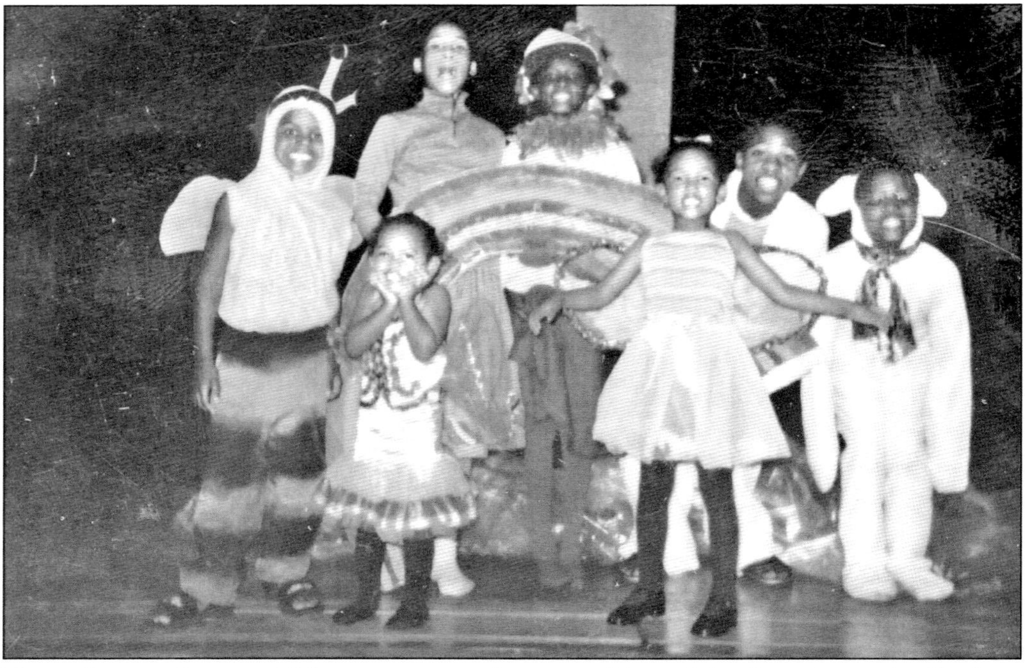

These Morgan County children are presenting a rendition of the Creation at the Madison Missionary Baptist Association Sunday School Congress. (Courtesy Elzata Brown.)

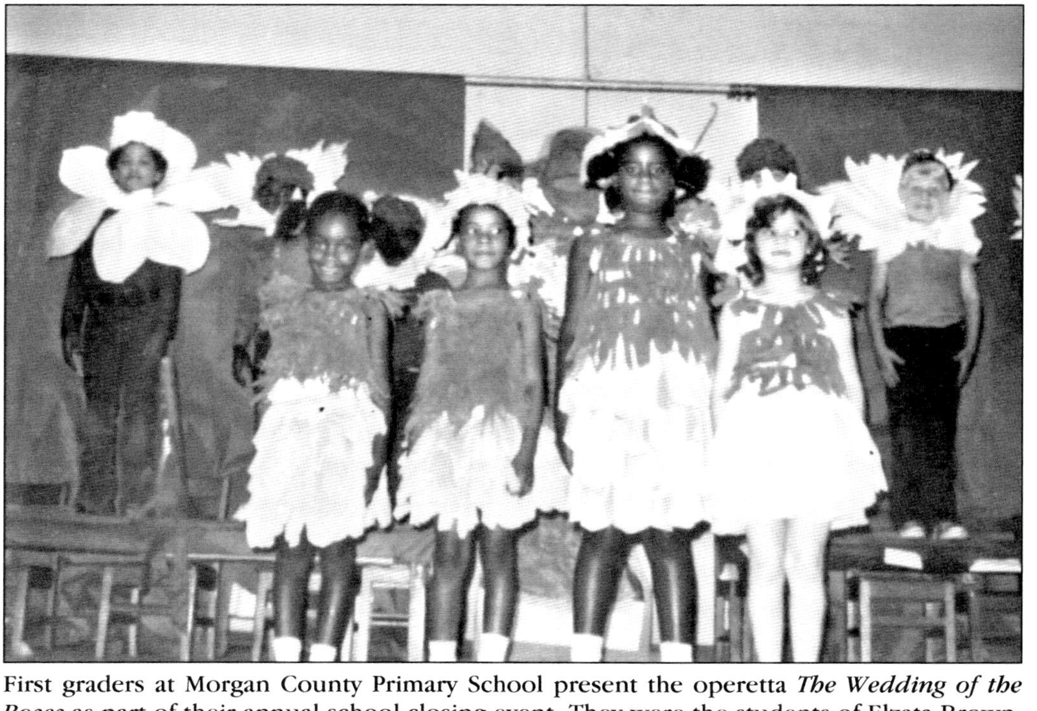

First graders at Morgan County Primary School present the operetta *The Wedding of the Roses* as part of their annual school-closing event. They were the students of Elzata Brown, who directed the operetta and handmade their costumes. (Courtesy Elzata Brown.)

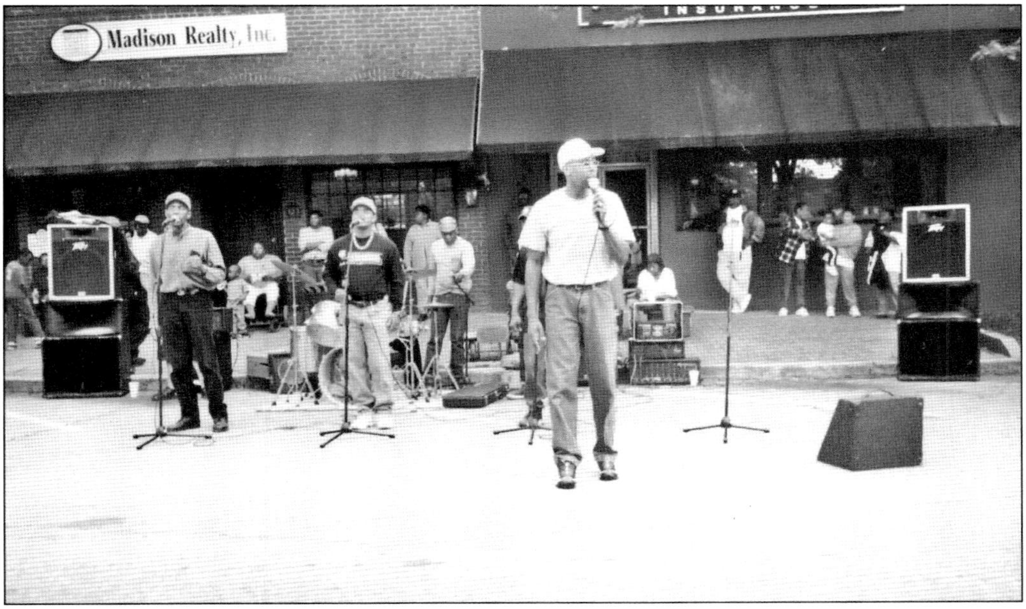

Calvary Gospel Singers perform after the African-American Parade on the square in Madison, *c.* 2000. The crowd enjoyed the quartet-style music made popular during the golden age of gospel music (1955–1963) by national recording artists like the Five Blind Boys, Roebuck Staple and the Staple Singers, and Sam Cooke and the Soul Stirrers. (Courtesy the author.)

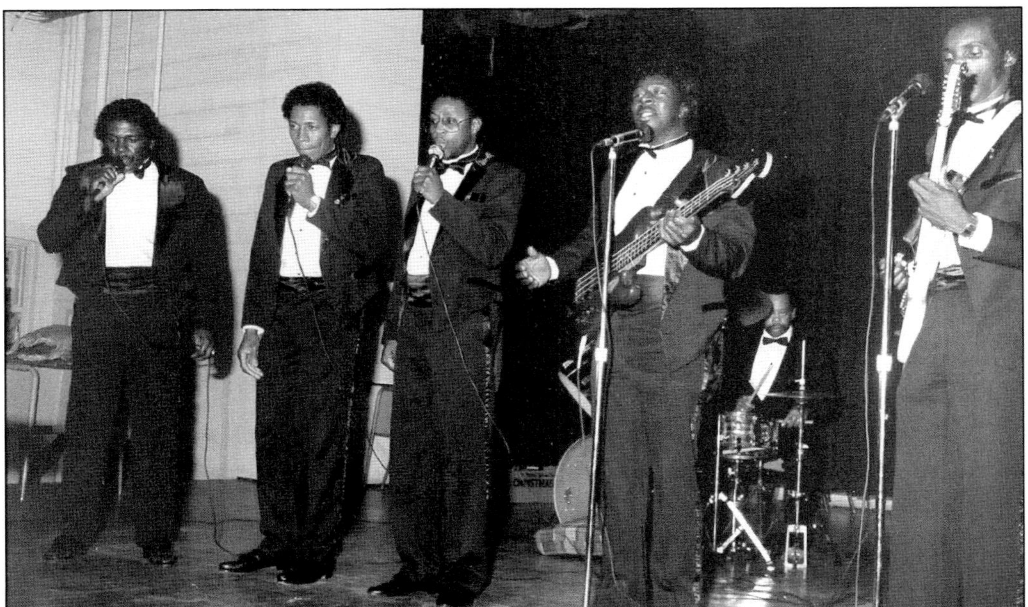

Buckhead Star #213 Masonic Lodge Male Chorus are performing at the Christmas Banquet held at Morgan County Elementary School in 2000. The Masons and Eastern Stars have held the banquet annually since the 1980s. The Eastern Stars are from Star of Amaranth #15 O.E.S. Lodge. (Courtesy Elzata Brown.)

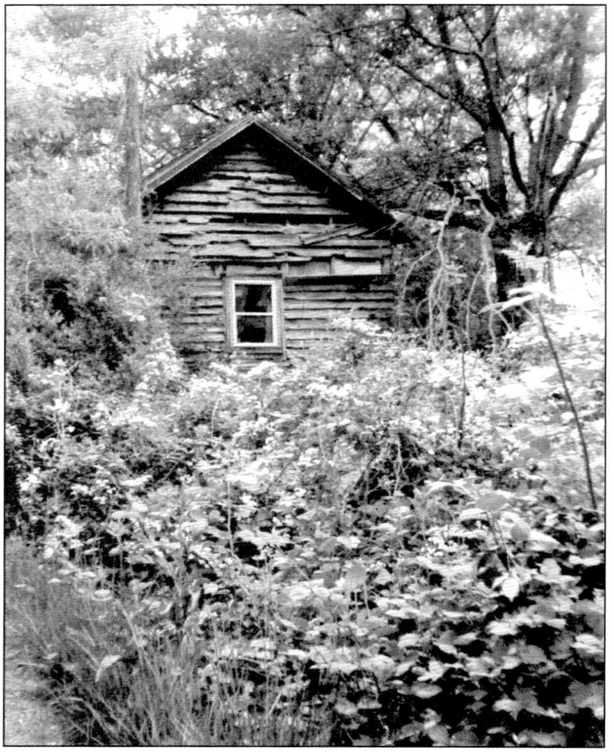

This abandoned house was once a home in the Bostwick neighborhood known as "The Alley." Although older homes are abandoned, newer ones have been built, so that an active neighborhood still remains today. (Courtesy the author.)

The home of Percy and Nettie King Williams on Pearl Street is shown in this winter scene. Mrs. Williams lived to be 97 years old and resided on Pearl Street for 40 years. She cared for the young Peek children, Reginald and Karen, while their parents worked. (Courtesy Minnie Peek.)

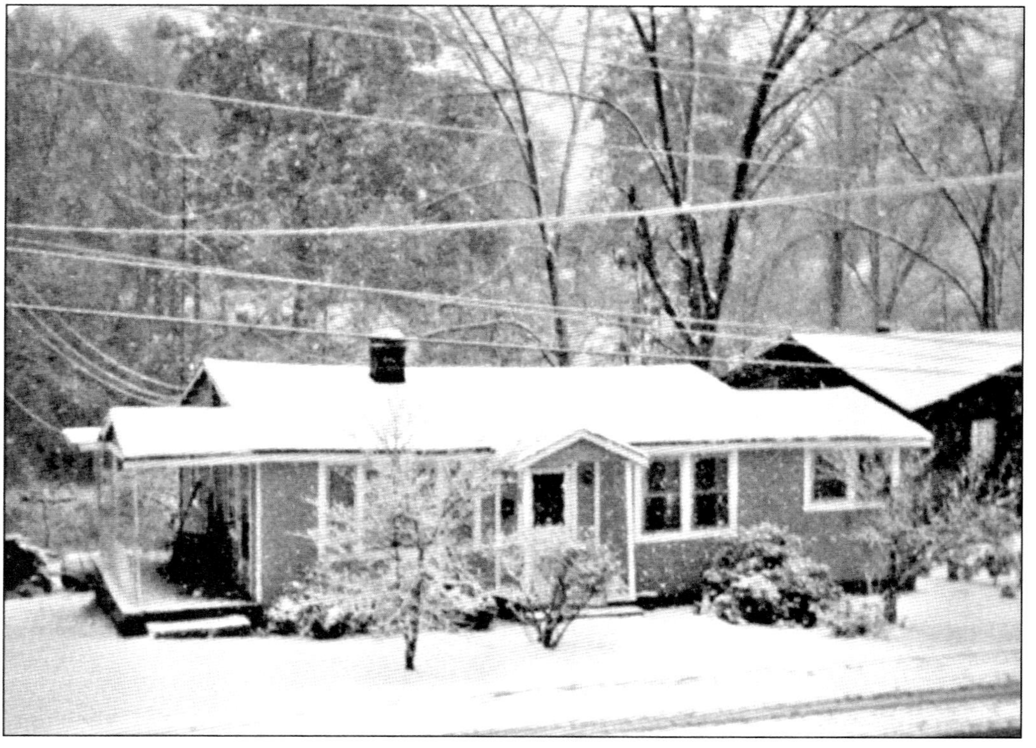

Mozelle Lewis Jordan (1907–1988) and her son-in-law Jack Drake pose in the yard of the Jordan home in 1972. She taught school, farmed, and later was a midwife who delivered many babies in Morgan County. Traditional midwives did more than "catch babies." They were considered healers, public health activists, and community organizers. (Courtesy Annette Drake.)

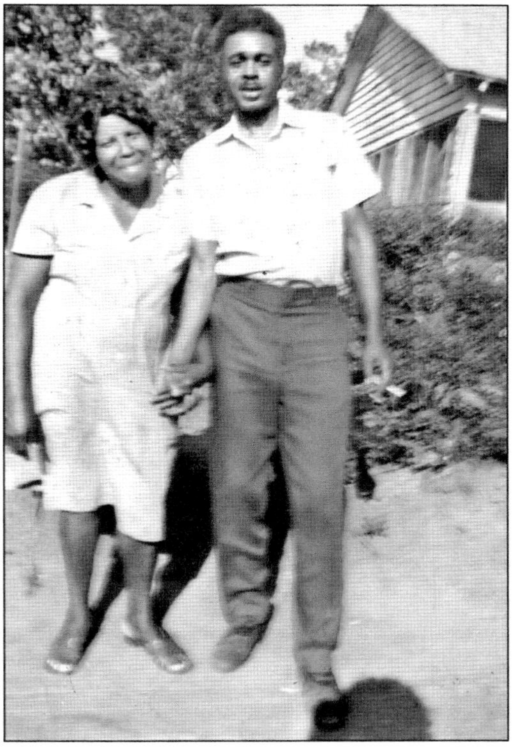

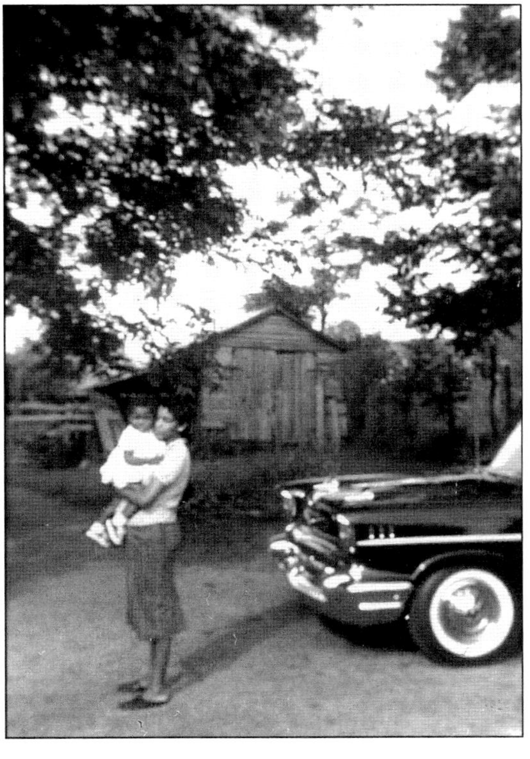

Edith Smith and her baby, Jacquelyn, are shown here in Edith's grandparent's back yard *c.* 1960. (Courtesy Minnie Peek.)

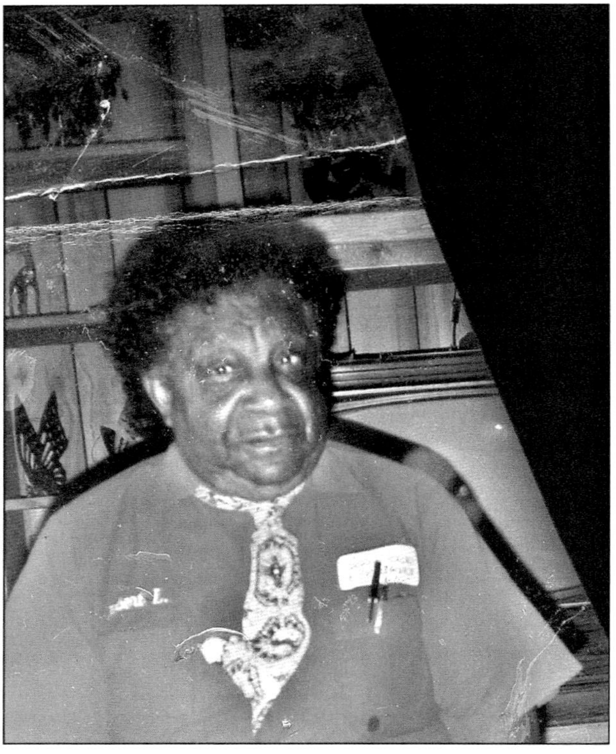

Robert Griffin was born in Greene County and moved to Morgan County around 1930. The family lived on the Tamplin Farm on Bostwick Highway. Mr. Griffin became known as "The TV Doctor." According to verbal lore in the community, he was the first African American employed by Pennington Seed and Feed Company. He did delivery and worked the cash register. (Courtesy Thelma Griffin.)

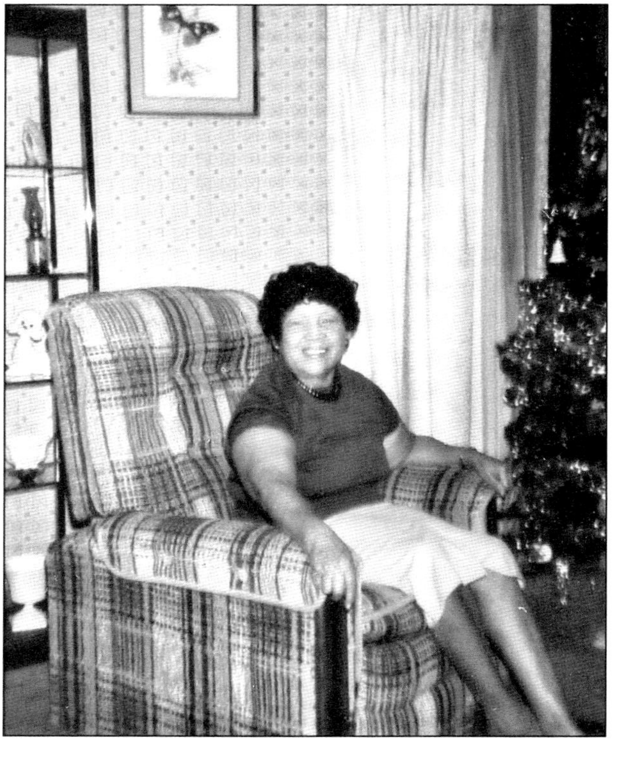

Roberta Kelly Booker is shown in her home in Madison, *c*. 1984. She was a teacher in Morgan County School System. (Courtesy Minnie Peek.)

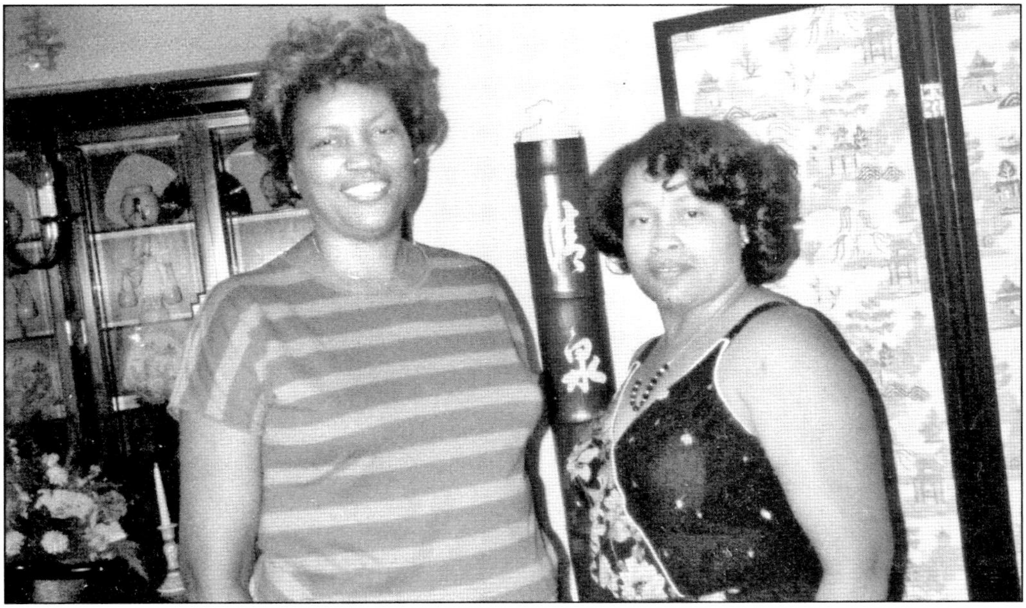

Both Mary Lou Hunter Martina (left) and her sister Jessie Hunter Smith (right) graduated from Pearl High School. Mary Lou graduated in 1957, and Jessie graduated with honors in 1962. Mary Lou moved to Philadelphia after graduating, where she was employed by the federal government. Jessie moved to Atlanta, where she married and raised a son while doing factory work. She moved back to her childhood Morgan County home in 1992 to care for her mother. (Courtesy Jessie Hunter Smith.)

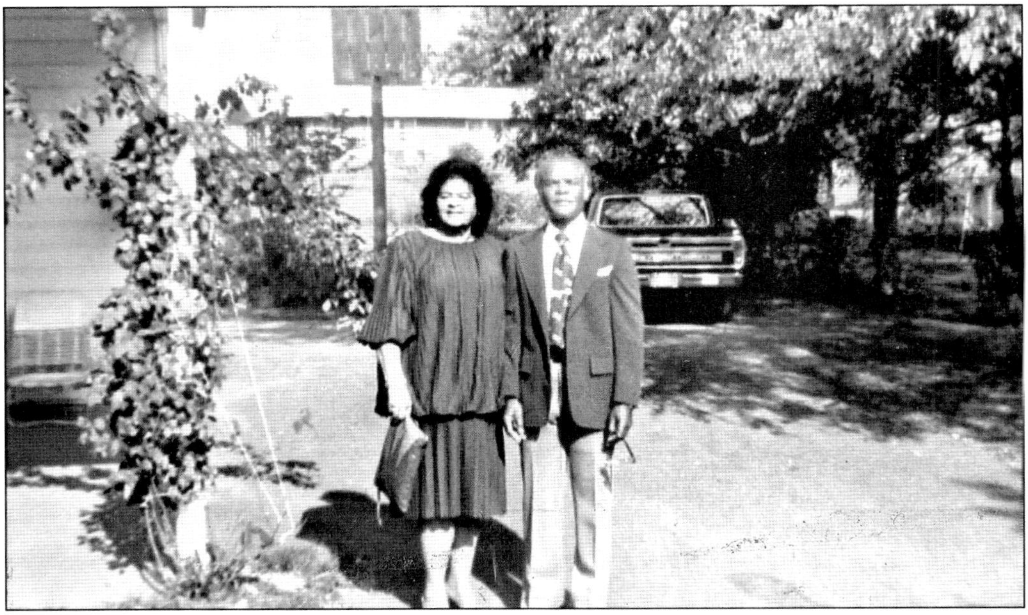

Dorothy Watkins and Lee Oliver are shown in this 1984 photograph. Mrs. Watkins worked at East Inn Motel. She also cooked, cleaned, and cared for the Hall family's children. (Courtesy Minnie Peek.)

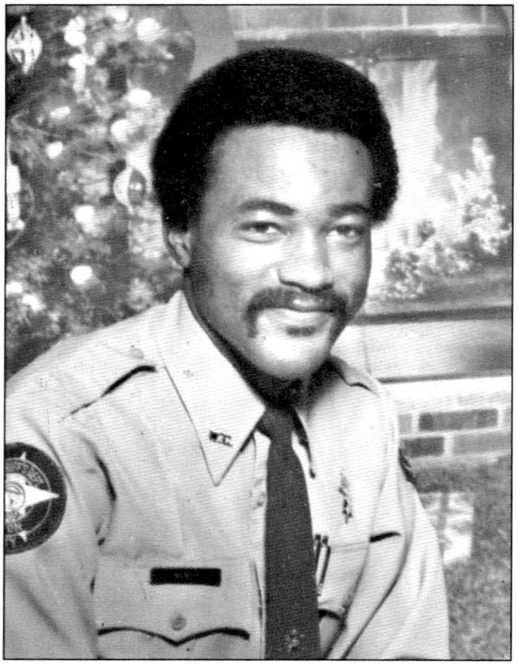

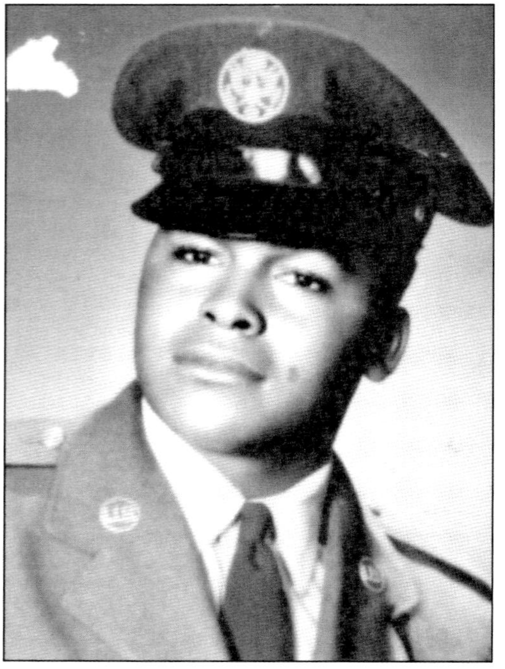

(Left) Drexwell Booker attended elementary and high school in Morgan County. He now lives in nearby Social Circle and works for the Walton County Sheriff Department. (Courtesy Elzata Brown.)
(Right) Legree Booker II served in the United States Air Force after graduating from Morgan County High School in Madison. (Courtesy Elzata Brown.)

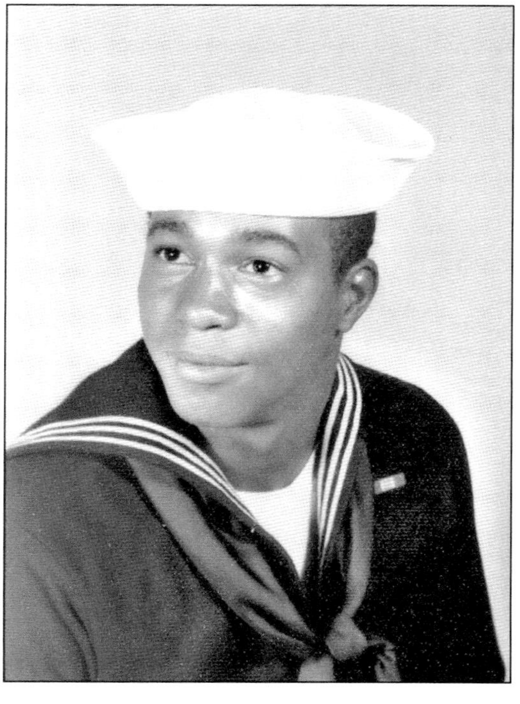

Winfrey "Bro" Booker graduated from Morgan County High School and served in the United Stated Navy. (Courtesy Elzata Brown.)

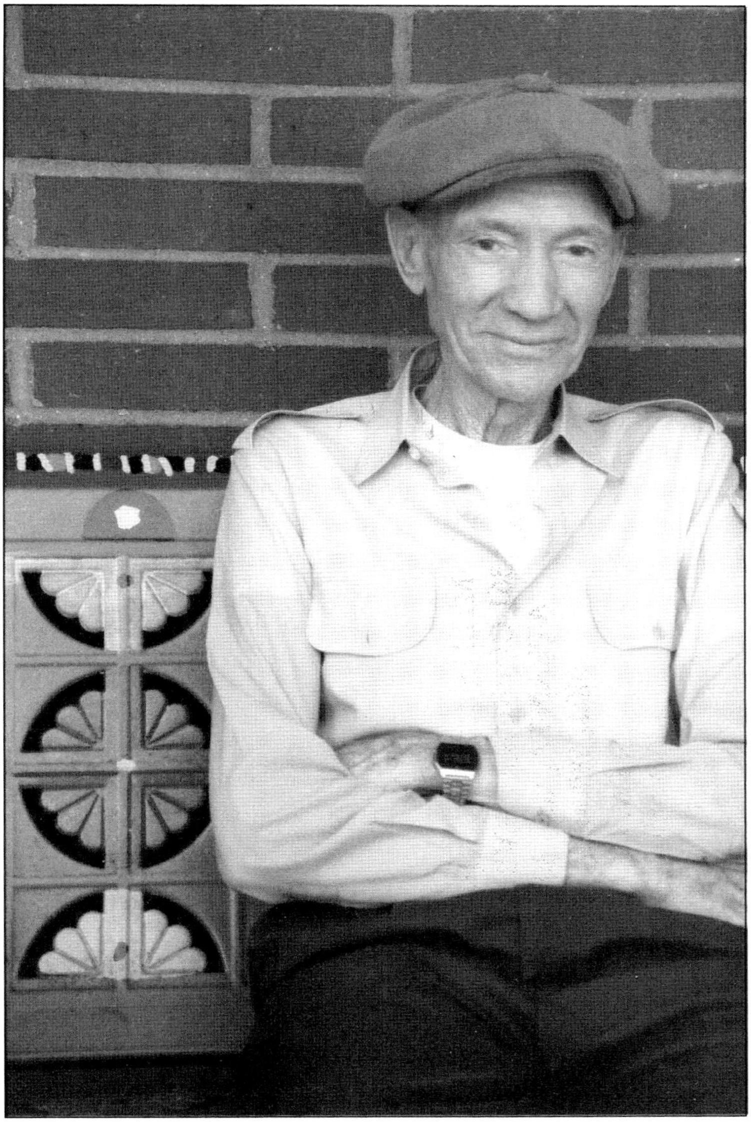

George Andrews (1911–1996) was known as the "The Dot Man" of Madison, because he frequently used dots while beautifying common household items, transforming them into works of folk art. George married Viola Perryman during the Depression, and they lived on a small farm in the Plainview community with their children. George had a hard life of farming and sharecropping to support his family, but he would tell the children stories and draw for them after working hard all day. The Andrews children—Harvey, Benny, Valeria, Raymond, Shirley, Harold, Joe Louis, Johnny, Veronica, and Deloris—were all born in Plainview. The last child, Gregory, was born in Atlanta after Viola and the other children left Morgan County. Although Viola was pregnant when she left, George refused to live—or even spend the night—anywhere except Morgan County. He stopped farming and took a job with the city of Madison in the early 1950s. George later moved to Madison to be closer to his job and friends after the rest of the family moved to Atlanta. His friends called him "Gee." (Courtesy Benny Andrews.)

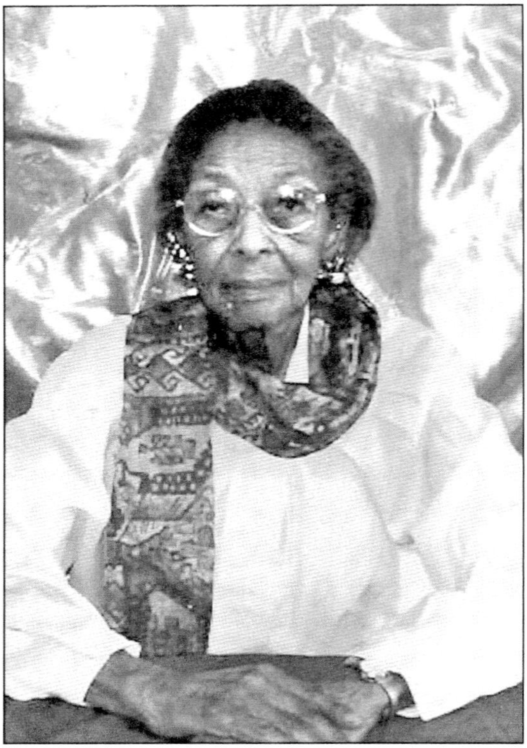

Louise Ingram Shepherd Newberry was the daughter of Mr. and Mrs. Ed Ingram of Madison. She worked as a licensed practical nurse before she retired. She now lives with her daughter, Minnie Peek. (Courtesy Minnie Peek.)

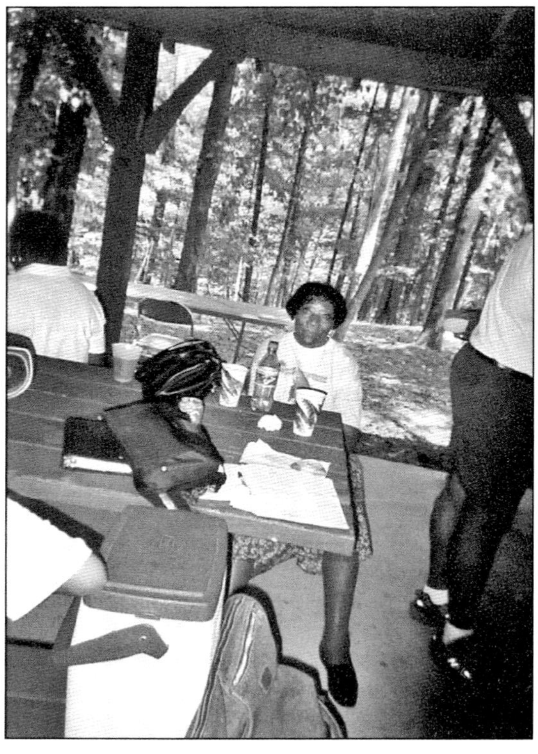

Geneva Hughley is sitting placidly at a family reunion. She is the youngest daughter of Emma Drummond. Many Morgan County families gather for family reunions periodically. (Courtesy Thelma Griffin.)

George Washington White was born in 1906. George attended Barrow Grove and Plainview Schools and finished the seventh grade. He was asked to teach school but turned down the offer. His stepmother taught him to cook, and since he loved cooking, it became his trade. He cooked at the Veterans of Foreign Wars (VFW) for approximately 20 years. George became popular in the area for the delicious barbecue and Brunswick stew he prepared. (Courtesy Minnie Peek.)

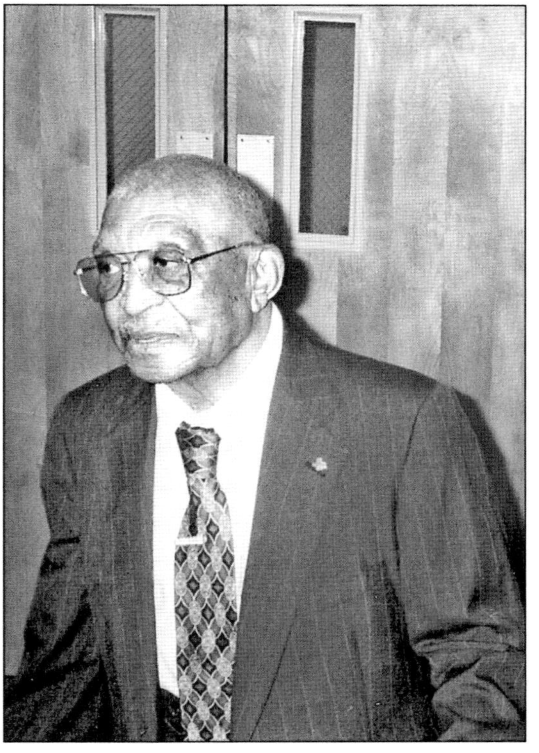

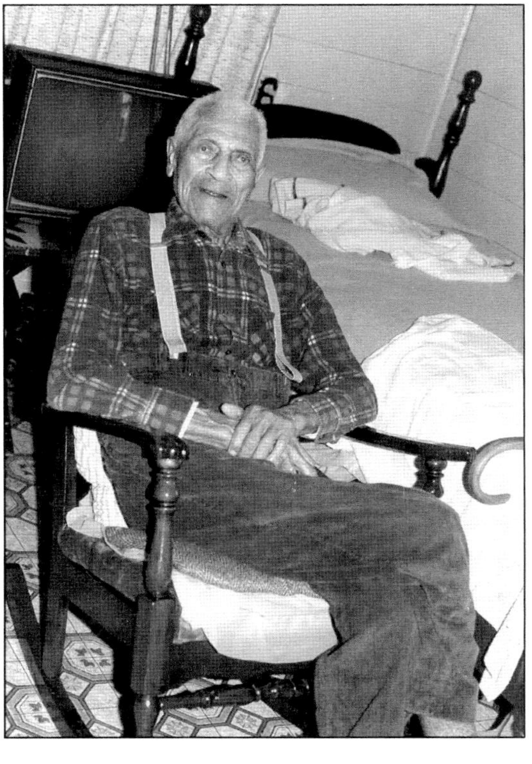

This is Ed Ingram at age 97 in 1985. A farmer and landowner, he often told the story of the "dark day" (the 1900 solar eclipse) when he was working in the field and thought the world was coming to an end. Ed lived in his home on the Greensboro Road until shortly before his death 1987. (Courtesy Minnie Peek.)

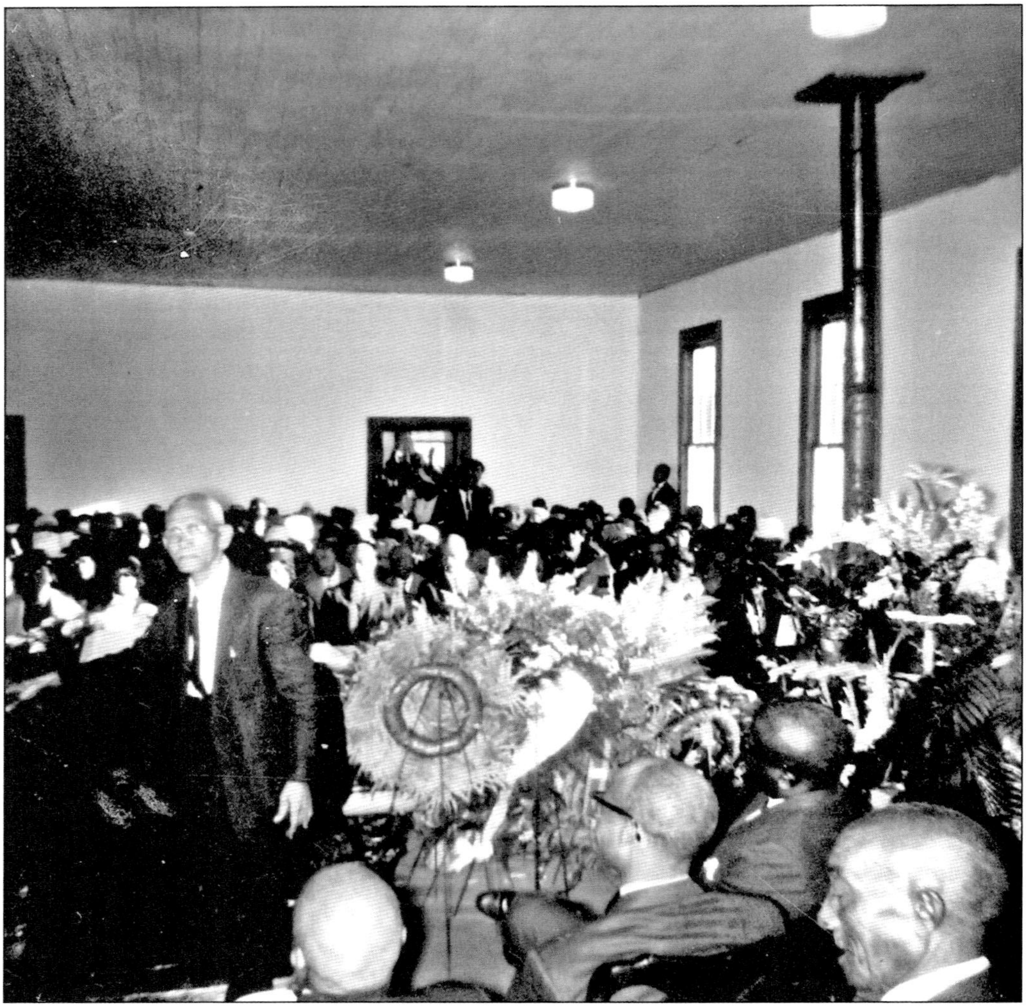

Rev. W.M. Mitchell is shown at the funeral of Willie Ann Booker in 1964. Many family members and long time friends attended the funeral at Mt. Perry Baptist Missionary Church. Reverend Mitchell was the pastor of the church during the later 1940s and early 1950s. (Courtesy Elzata Brown.)

Three

UPON THIS ROCK
Our Churches, Where We Worship

Upon this rock I will build my church; and the gates of hell shall not prevail against it.
Matt. 16:18 (KJV)

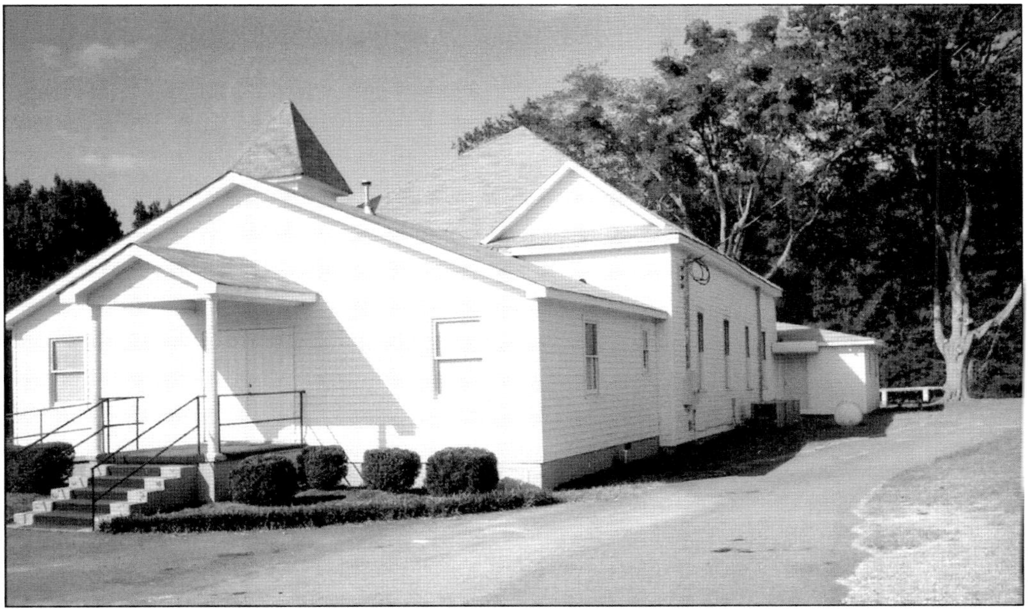

Smyrna Baptist Church, located in Buckhead, was organized in 1870 and rebuilt in 1907 under the leadership of Rev. D.C. Bracy. Prior to the Civil War, blacks and whites in the Buckhead community worshipped together at the Sugar Creek Baptist Church, but the African-American members left Sugar Creek Baptist Church in 1867 and formed their own the congregation. Smyrna Baptist Church was one of the churches pastored by Rev. W.M. Mitchell during the 1940s and early 1950s. Other pastors included Rev. J.H. Hensley and Rev. F.D. Clark, who served for 35 years (1963–1998). The current pastor is Rev. H. Heard. (Courtesy the author.)

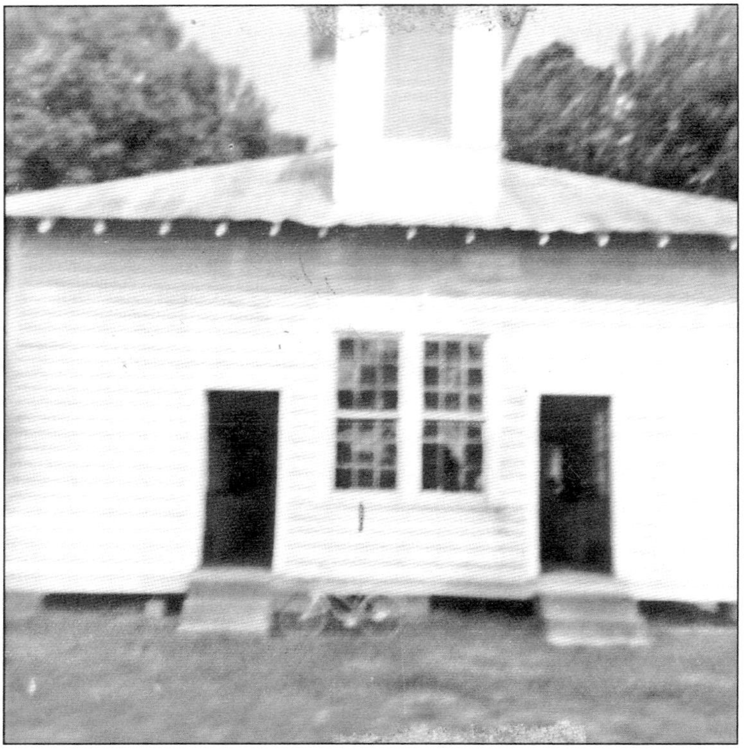

Jackson Grove Missionary Baptist Church, seen *c.* 1973, was organized in 1902. After the church was constructed, the school that had been on the property since 1897 was moved into the sanctuary. Rev. John Daniel, Reverend Shorter, Rev. J.W. Bennett, Rev. James Day, and Deacon Milledge Moore were present at the organizing service. Other pioneers of the church were Deacon and Sister A. Bell, Sister Dora Taylor, and Deacon G.A. Scott. (Courtesy Dora Peeks Boswell.)

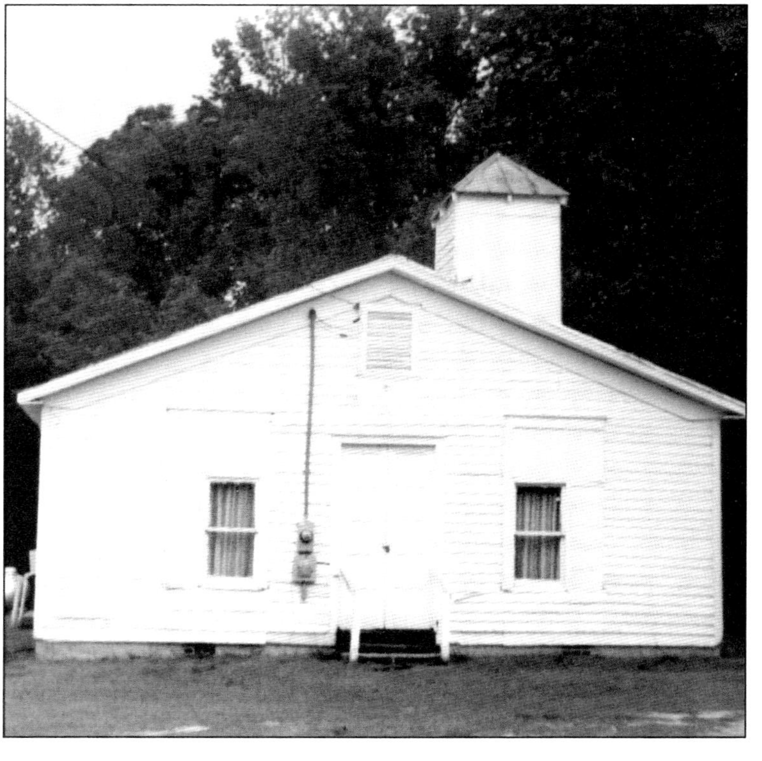

The exact year Sweet Home Baptist Church was established is not known, but the church was re-located to its current location around 1918. The Bostwick congregation was led by Rev. Charlie Jackson for 72 years. The current pastor is Rev. John Hyman. (Courtesy the author.)

Saint Paul African Methodist Episcopal Church, located 811 Fifth Street in Madison, was built in 1881. The original structure is still in use today. Rev. John M. Cargile and trustee Harrison Harris were present when Anna G. Johnston granted the land for the church in 1871. The cornerstone was laid with Bishop Dickerson and Jabez C. Campbell presiding in 1882. (Courtesy the author.)

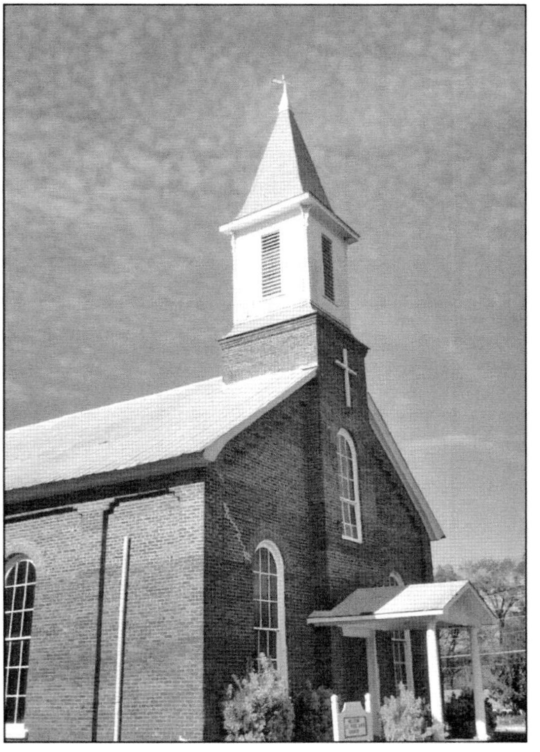

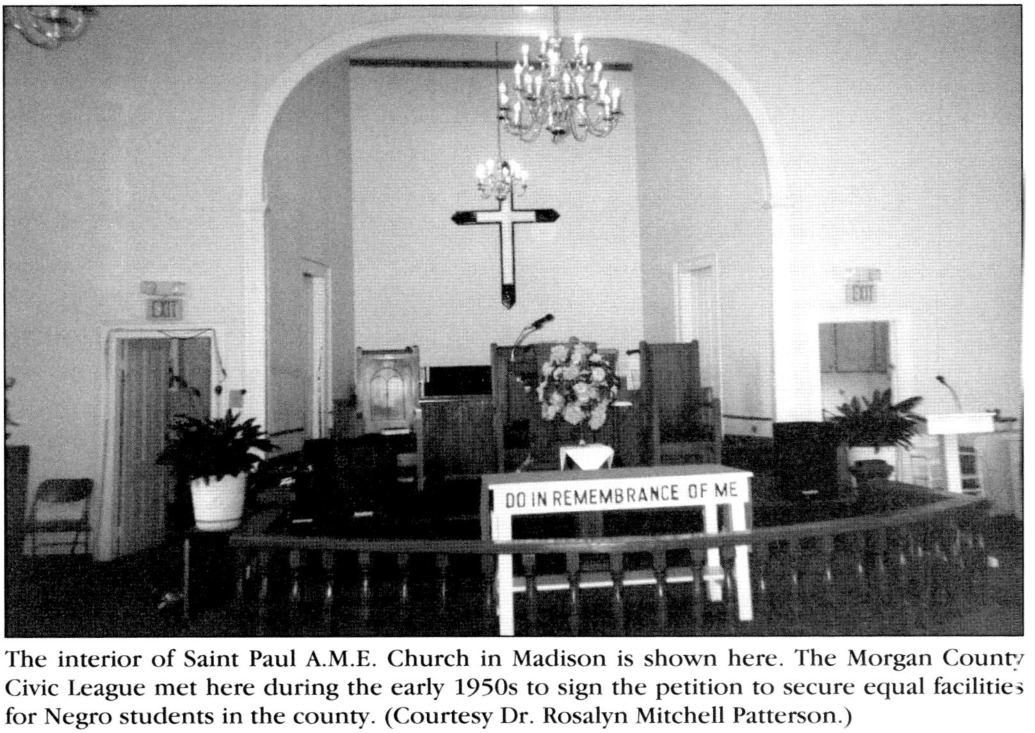

The interior of Saint Paul A.M.E. Church in Madison is shown here. The Morgan County Civic League met here during the early 1950s to sign the petition to secure equal facilities for Negro students in the county. (Courtesy Dr. Rosalyn Mitchell Patterson.)

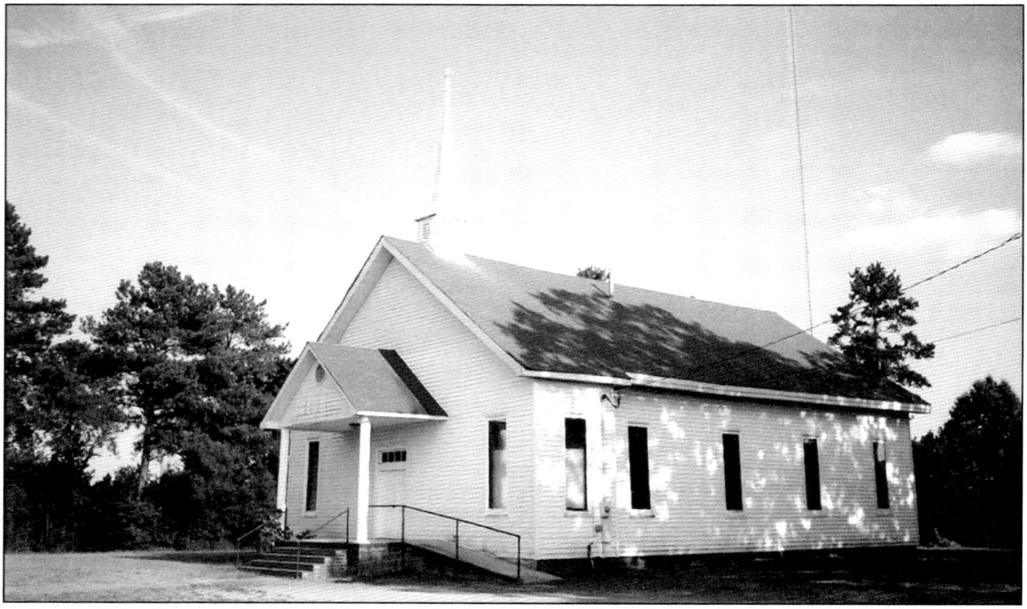

Bethlehem Baptist Church was organized on October 20, 1877, by Reverend Harrison. It was rebuilt under the leadership of Rev. A.J. Brown as pastor and A.J. Jones, secretary. (Courtesy the author.)

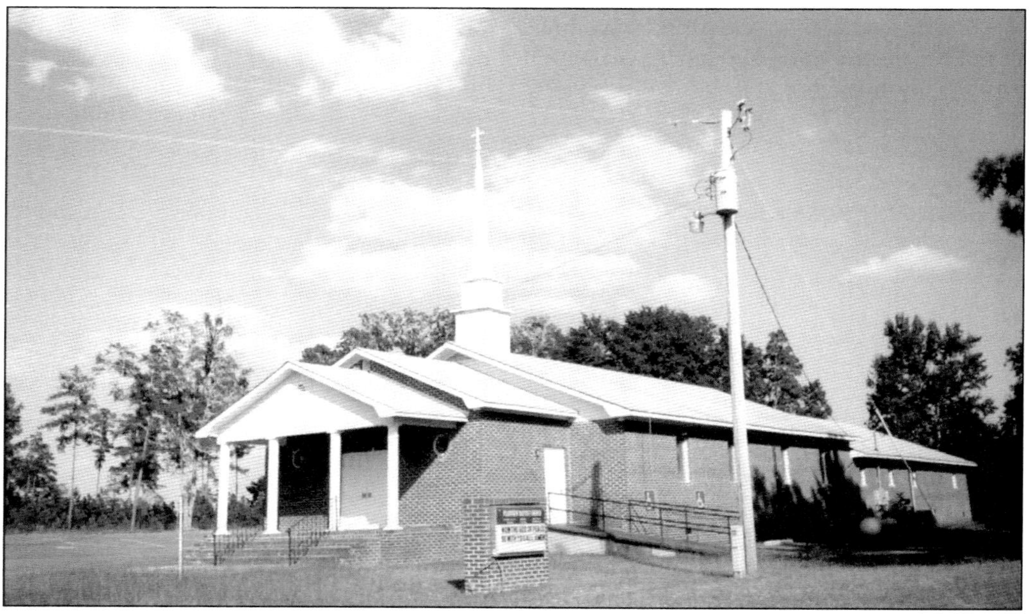

Plainview Baptist Church was organized on April 17, 1898, by Rev. W.B. Charleston. Rev. G.W. Buggs was presiding on July 4, 1916, when the church building was erected. The deacons at that time were G.C. Williams Jr., Lorenza Paschal, Job E. Williams, Donald Harris, Ward Crew, William Bell, Benjamin Williams, and Mrs. A. Winder Clark. Landowner and businesswoman Anna Charleston donated the lumber for the original church building. (Courtesy the author.)

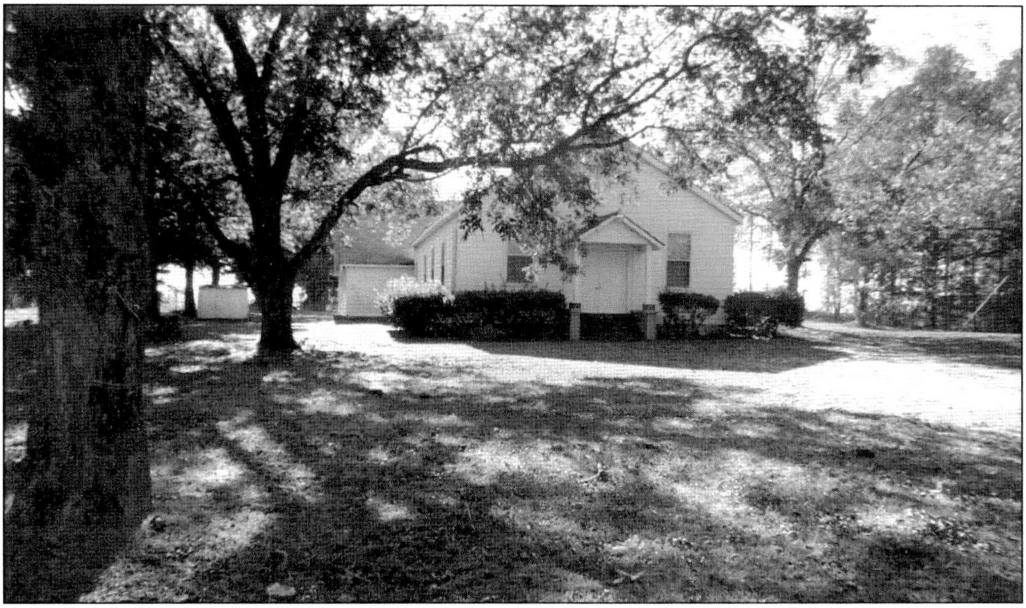

Gresham Grove Baptist Church creates a pastoral scene, nestled in the shadows of pecan trees on Hardeman Mill Road in Bostwick. The current pastor is Bishop L. Donte Smith; Deacon Roger Calloway is chairman of deacons. (Courtesy the author.)

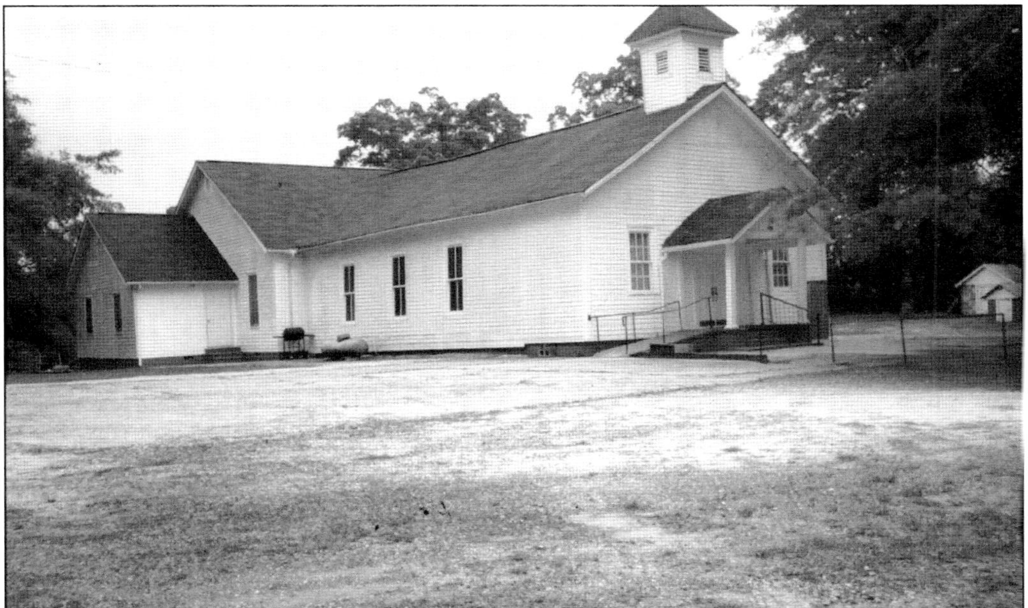

Flat Rock Baptist Church's cornerstone reads "Flat Rock Baptist Church was built and organized in 1890 on Sandy Creek near a large flat rock. After the church burned, Flat Rock was rebuilt and moved January 1910 on Bostwick Highway 83 by Rev. Price. It was remodeled as it stands today on 8 acres of land by Rev. Baker May 1977." A new building was constructed in 2004. (Courtesy the author.)

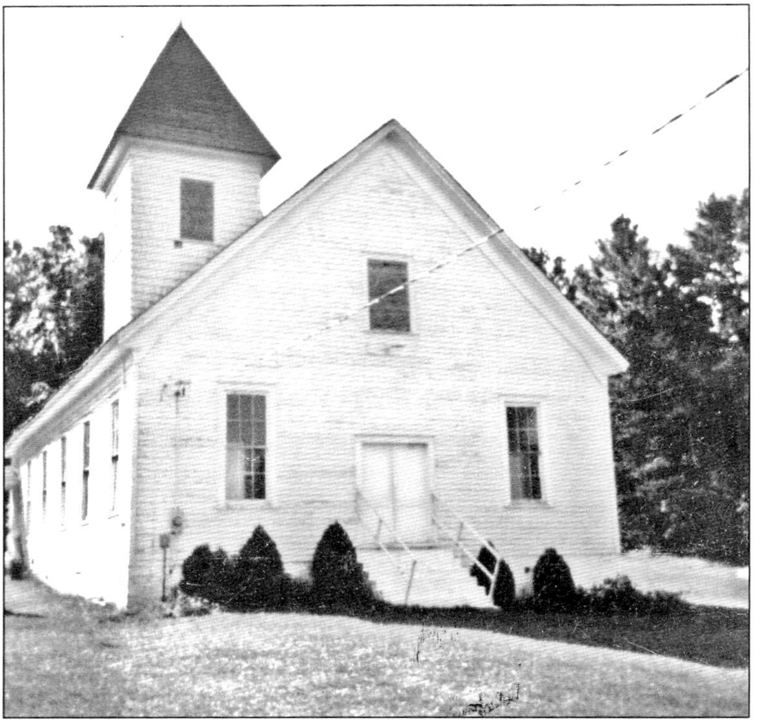

Mt. Perry Missionary Baptist Church was established under a bush arbor in 1870. A wooden structure was built sometime later, which was destroyed by fire twice. The current vernacular structure, with its front-end gable and a side tower featuring a six-over-six window treatment, was built around 1920. Located at 2920 Price Mill Road, the church's first pastor was Rev. Bob Williams. The current pastor is Rev. Lemuel O. Billingsley. (Courtesy Elzata Brown.)

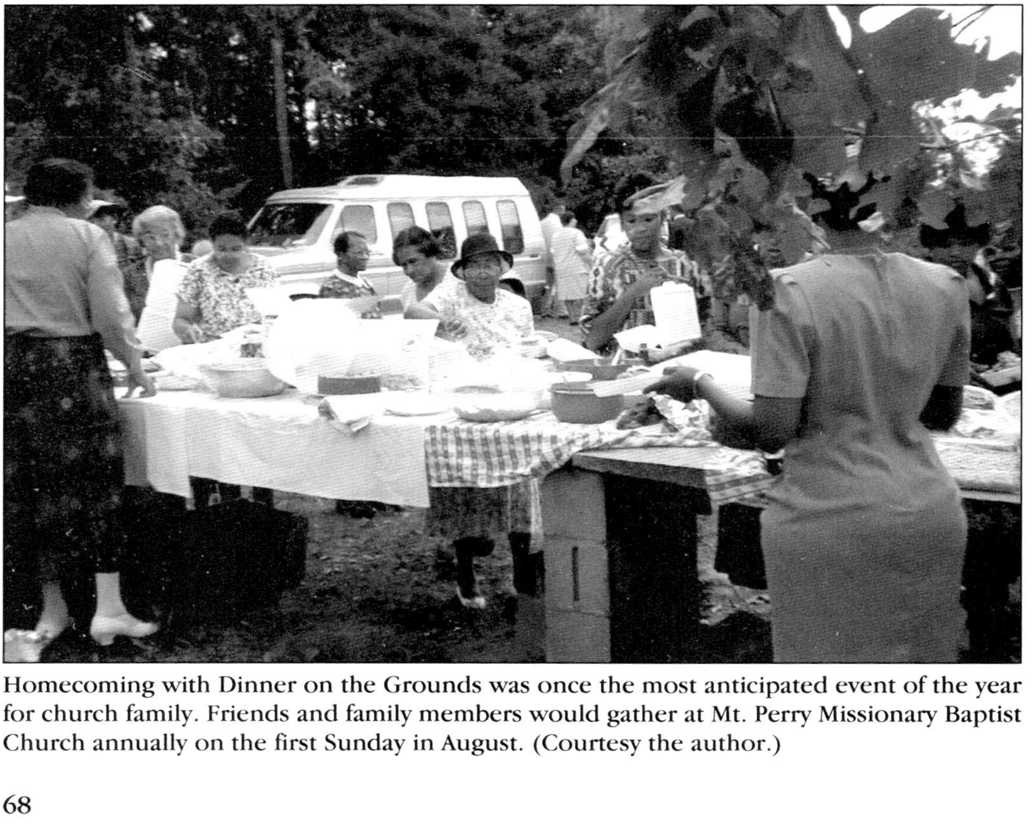

Homecoming with Dinner on the Grounds was once the most anticipated event of the year for church family. Friends and family members would gather at Mt. Perry Missionary Baptist Church annually on the first Sunday in August. (Courtesy the author.)

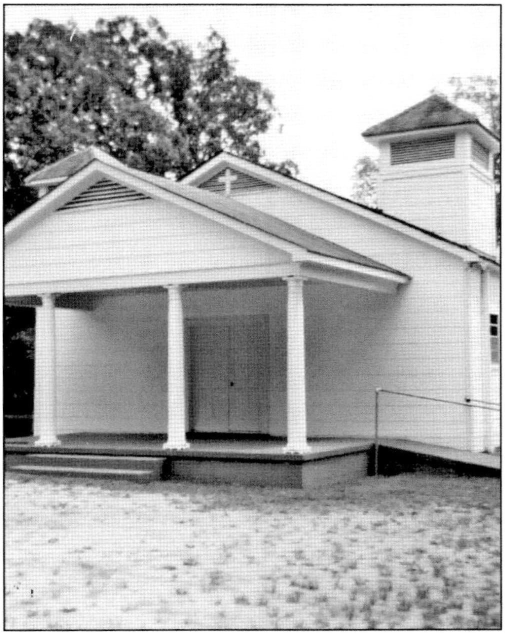

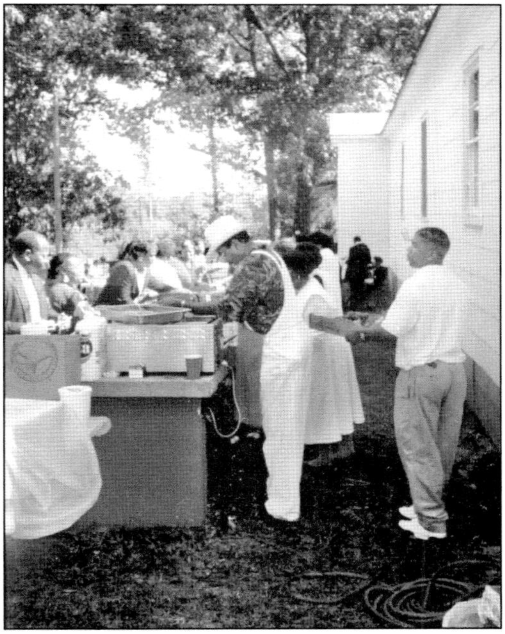

(Left) Wallace Grove Baptist Church, located in Rutledge, was organized in 1901. Four deacons from area churches helped to build this church—N. Durden from Thankful Baptist Church, J. Clark from New Enon Baptist Church, and B. Russell and J. Brown from Indian Creek Baptist Church. (Courtesy Geraldine Cooper.)
(Right and below) Family and friends of Wallace Grove Baptist Church are shown here on Homecoming Day. Dinner on the Grounds is an enduring tradition at the church. (Courtesy Geraldine Cooper.)

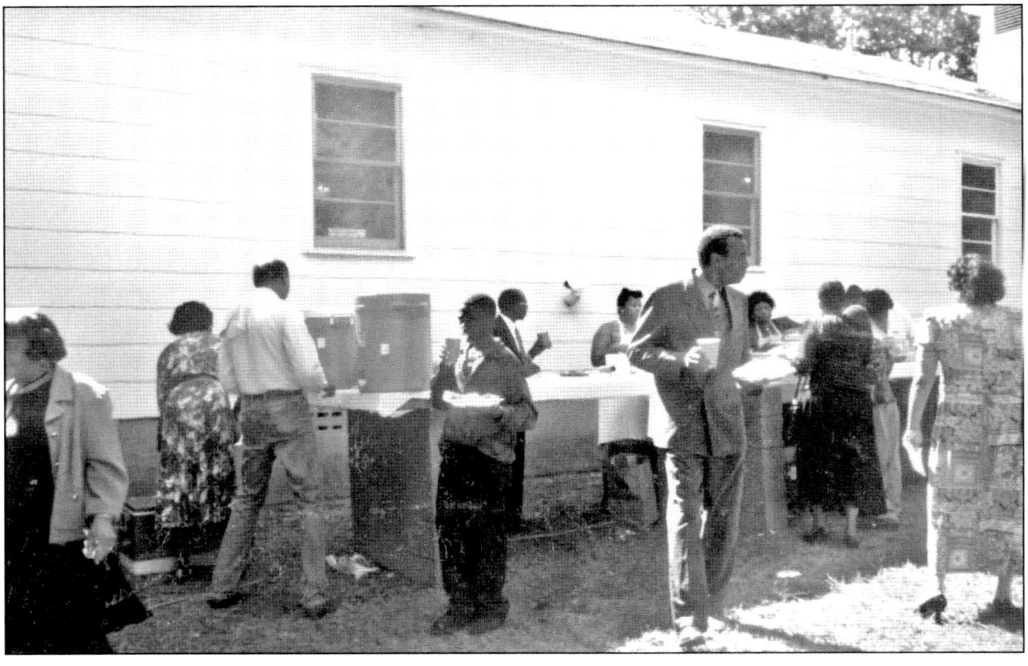

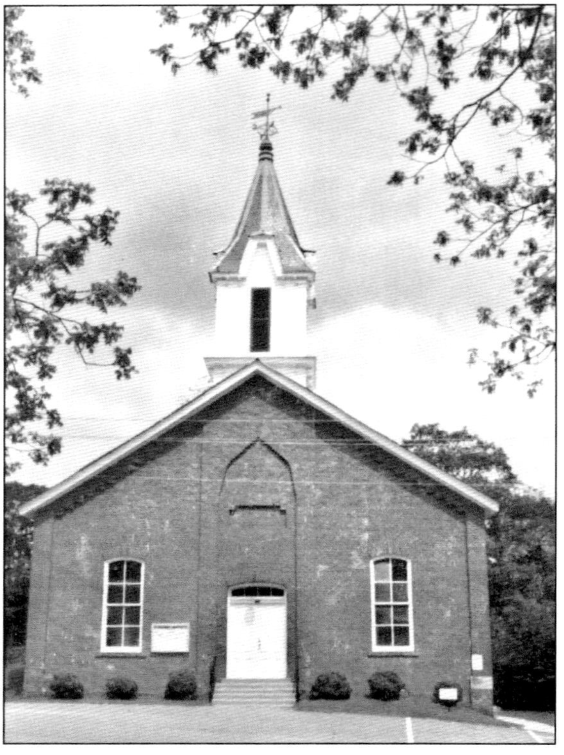

Calvary Baptist Church, located at 324 Academy Street in Madison, is one of the county's oldest African-American churches. The first church was organized in 1833, and the current structure was built during the 1870s. (Courtesy Mildred Bass.)

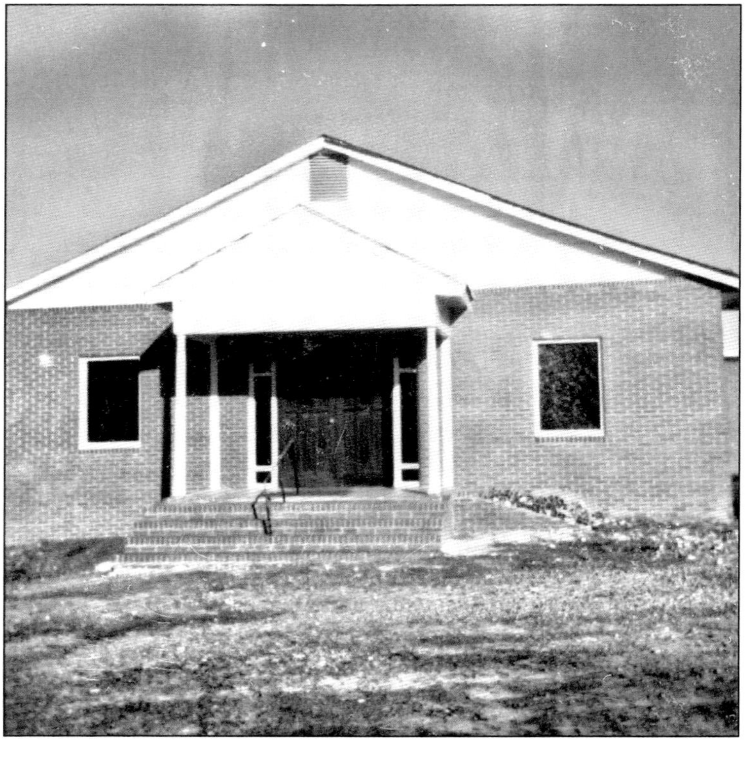

Morgan County Church of Christ was organized in 1960, when I.V. White began meeting with family and friends for Bible class in his father's home. The class grew, and the group began to meet in the Springfield Masonic Hall. The church is now housed in a modern facility on Seven Island Road, on land purchased from Mary Booker for $1.00. Brother Ruben T. Walker has been the minister since 1979. (Courtesy Minnie Peek.)

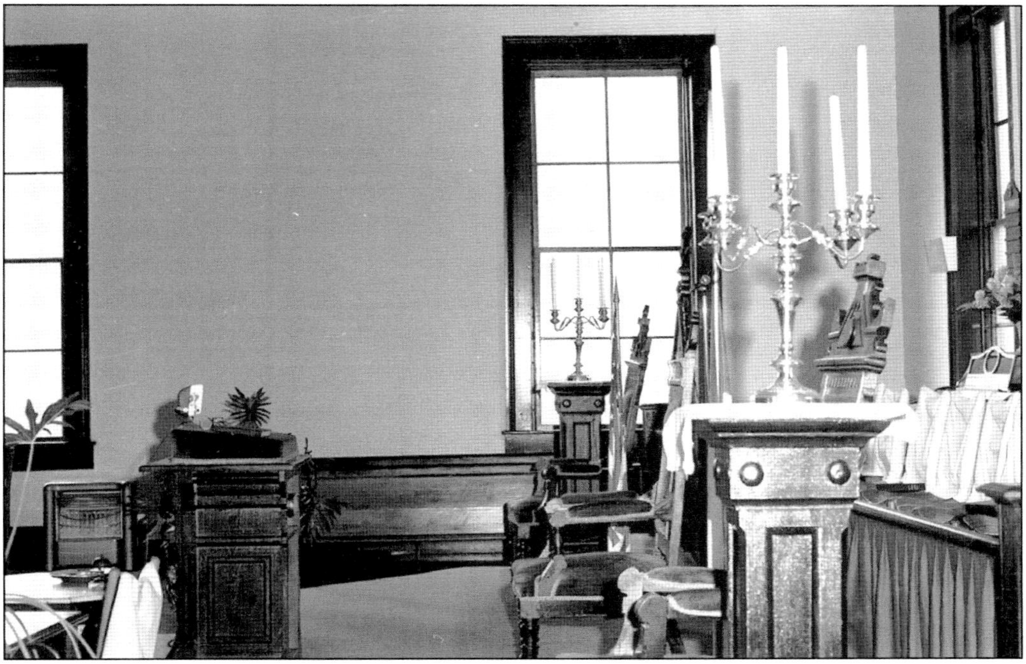

The interior of Calvary Baptist Church, *c.* 1976, is shown here. The sanctuary of this church was used to hold commencement for Pearl High School's Class of 1953. (Courtesy Mildred Bass.)

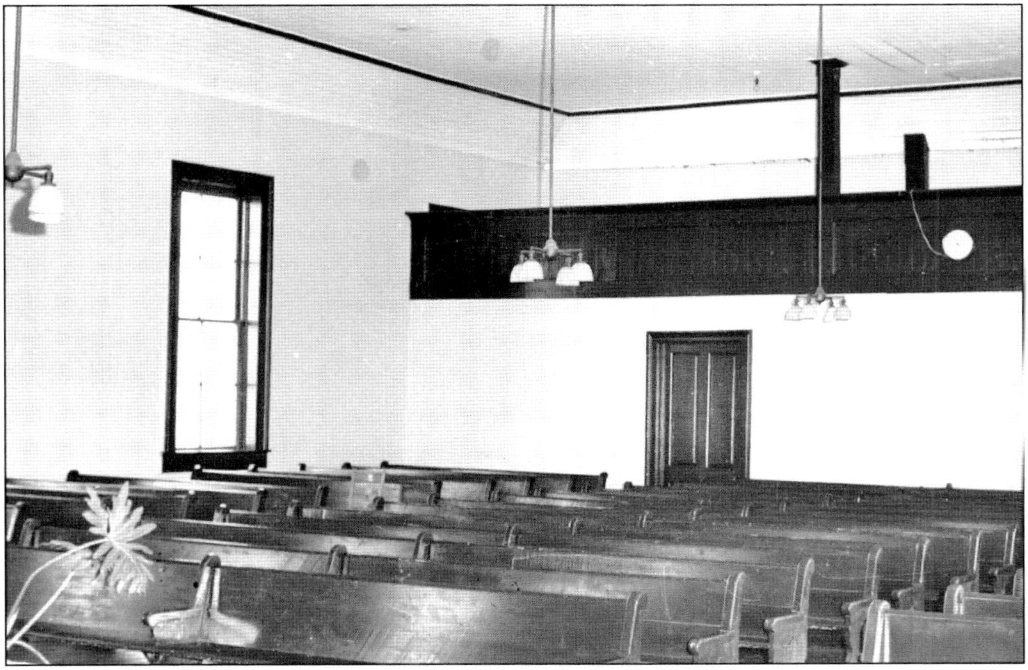

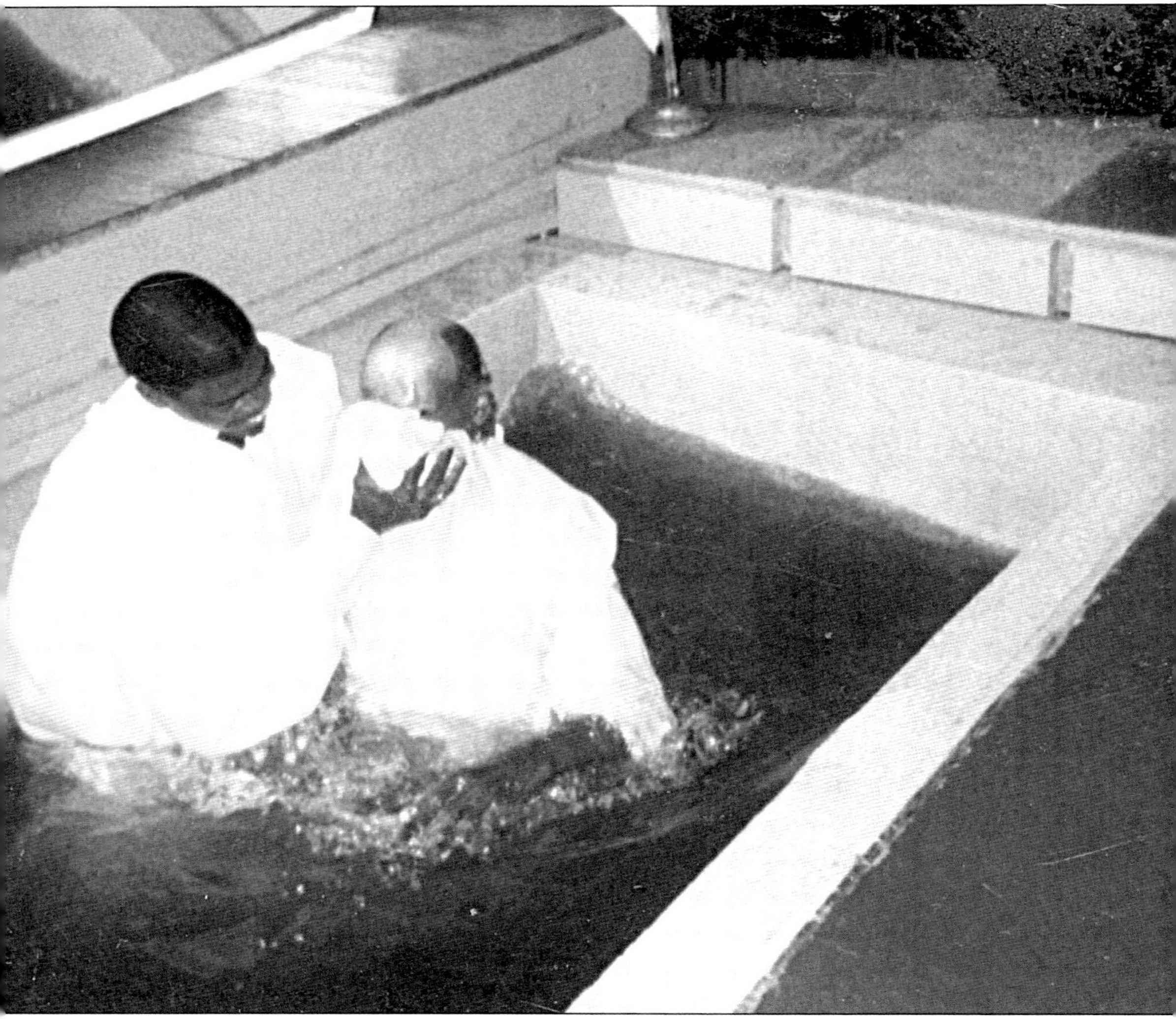

Albert Booker is shown being baptized on Labor Day by Reverend Billingsley. *c.* 1990. (Courtesy Elzata Brown.)

Four

Our Family Album

The image of self and the image of family are reciprocally interdependent.
N. Ackerman

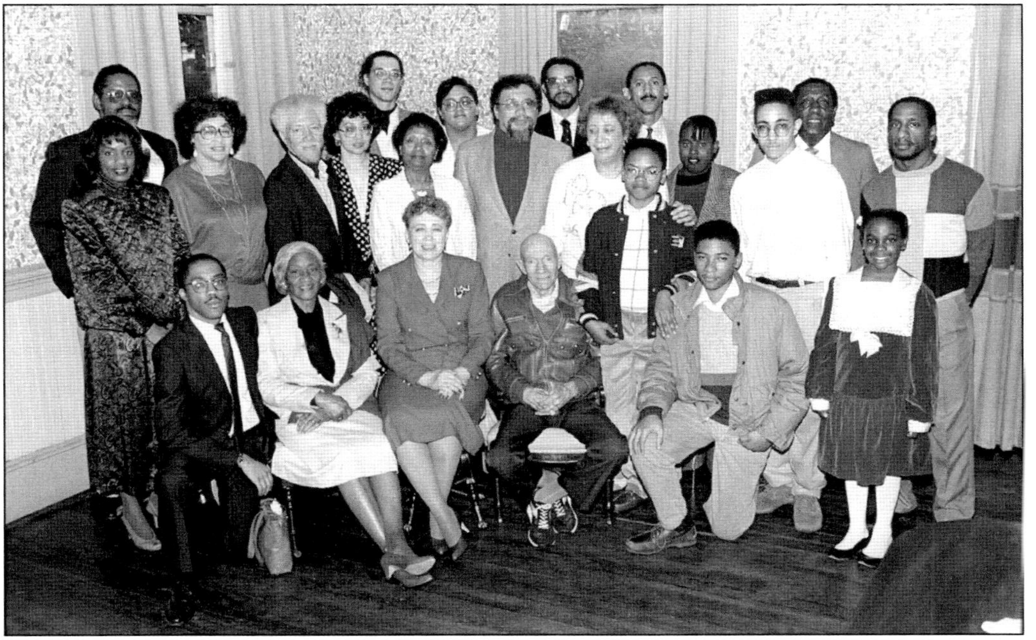

The Andrews family is one of Morgan County's most well-known families. Among them are writer Viola Andrews (front row, second from the left); George Andrews, the Dot Man (front row center); internationally known artist Benny Andrews (second row third from left); and award-winning author Raymond Andrews (second row center). They gathered for this 1990 photograph at the Morgan County Cultural Center in Madison. (Courtesy Benny Andrews.)

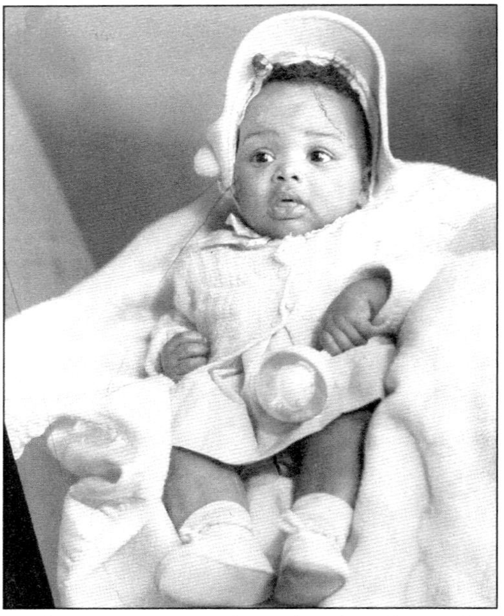

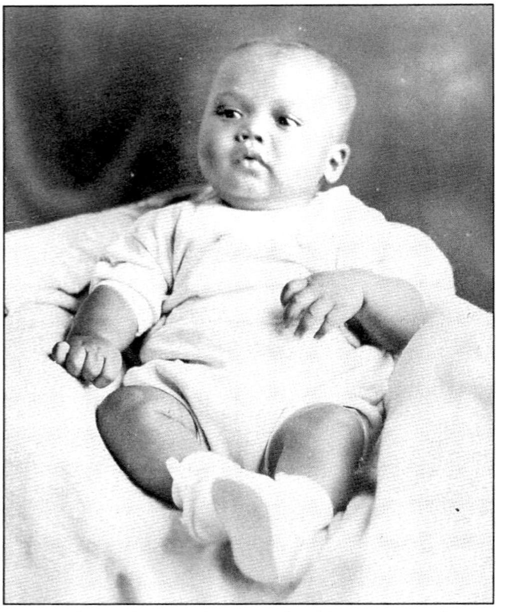

(Left) Imogene Booker, the daughter of George and Ruth Booker, is holding a rattle in this *c.* 1955 postcard photograph. She is the only daughter of Ruth and George Booker of Morgan County. (Courtesy Elzata Brown.)
(Right) Maxwell Booker is the subject of this 1951 photograph. Maxwell is the eldest son of Joseph and Ruby Booker. (Courtesy Elzata Brown.)

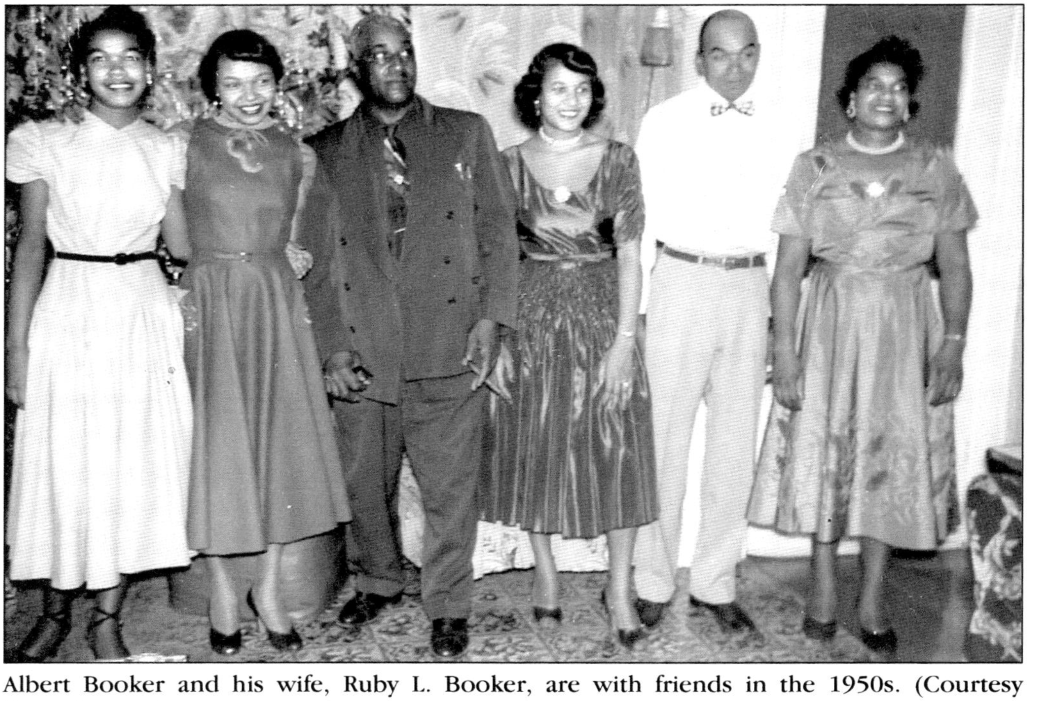

Albert Booker and his wife, Ruby L. Booker, are with friends in the 1950s. (Courtesy Elzata Brown.)

Four generations of the Ingram family are represented here. Louise Newberry (center) holds Ethan Reginald Warrior, and behind Louise are Karen LaWuane Warrior (left) and Minnie Peek (right). (Courtesy Minnie Peek.)

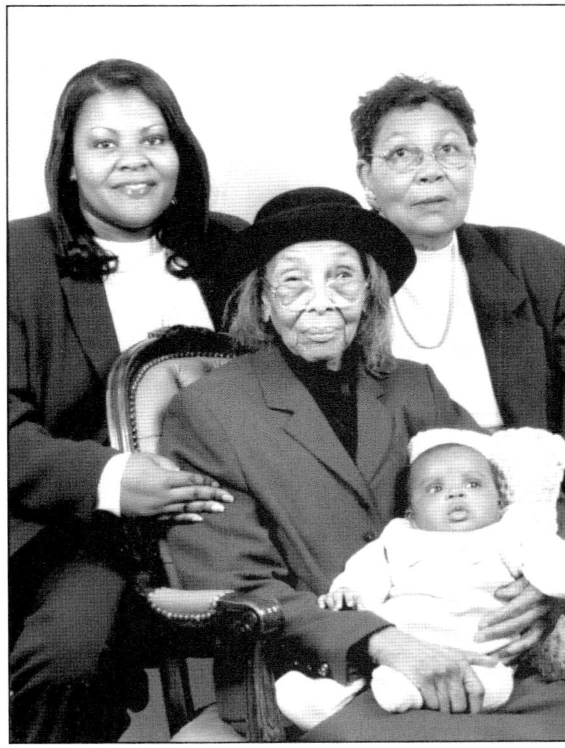

Eddie Ingram is shown with his granddaughter, Minnie Peek, and two great-granddaughters, Karen Peek and Jacqueline Shepherd, who is holding a great-great-grandchild. (Courtesy Minnie Peek.)

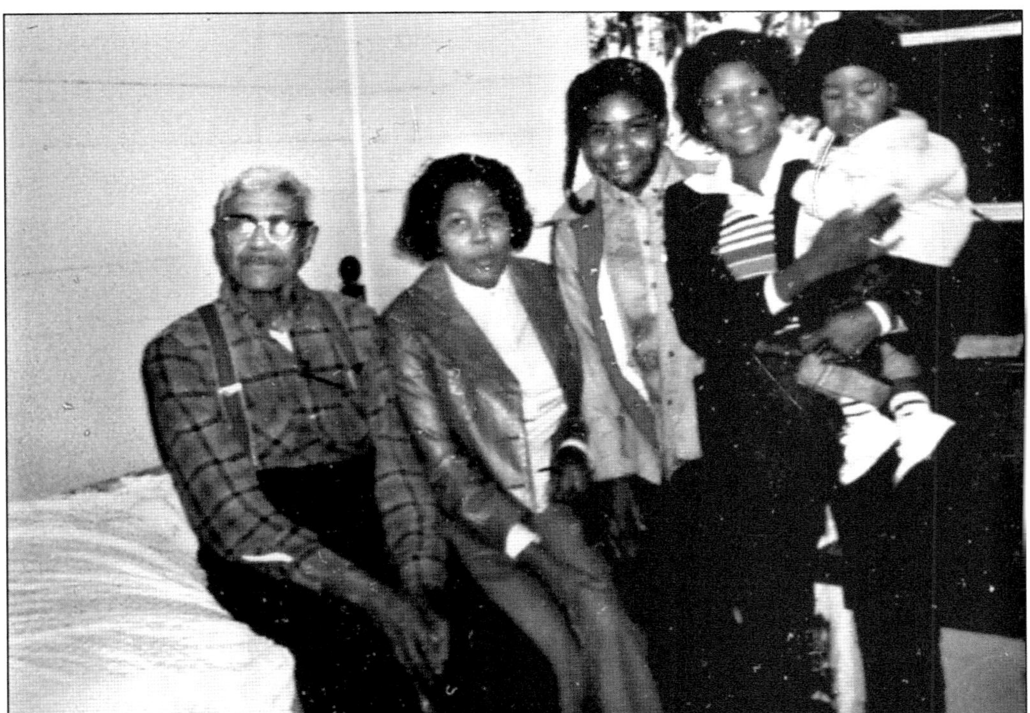

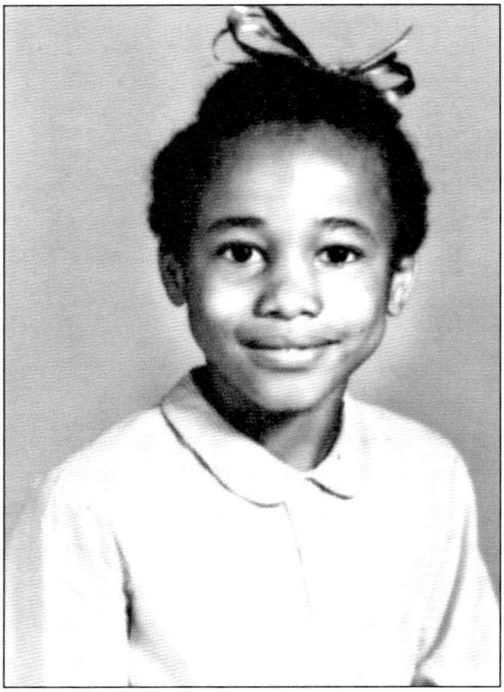 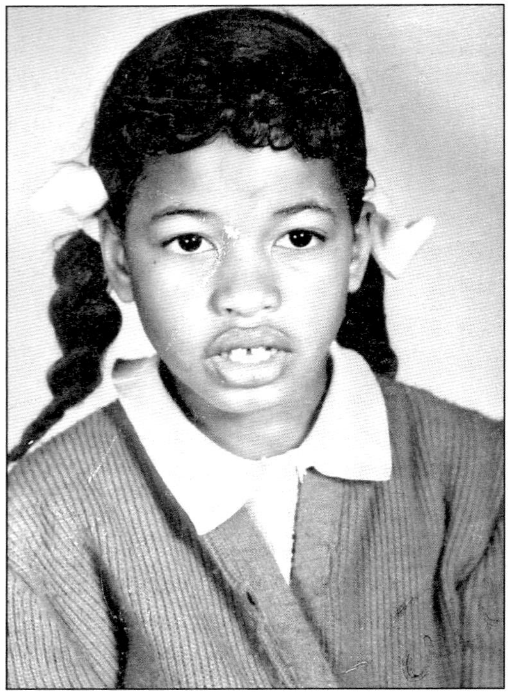

(Left) Princilla Booker, the daughter of Joseph and Ruby Booker, was a student a Pearl Elementary School when this school photograph was taken. (Courtesy Elzata Brown.) *(Right)* Vallee Trina Booker was an elementary school student in this 1960s photograph. After high school, she joined the military. (Courtesy Elzata Brown.)

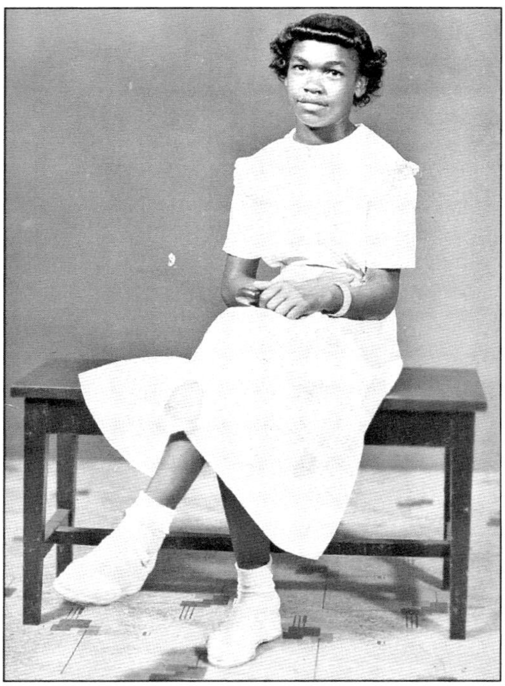

Alberta Booker, daughter of Albert and Ruby Booker, wears a hairstyle popular *c.* 1950 that features bangs and curls. The hair was pressed with a straightening comb and then curled with marcel wax and a curling iron. Madam C.J. Walker made this revolutionary method of hair care popular. (Courtesy Elzata Brown.)

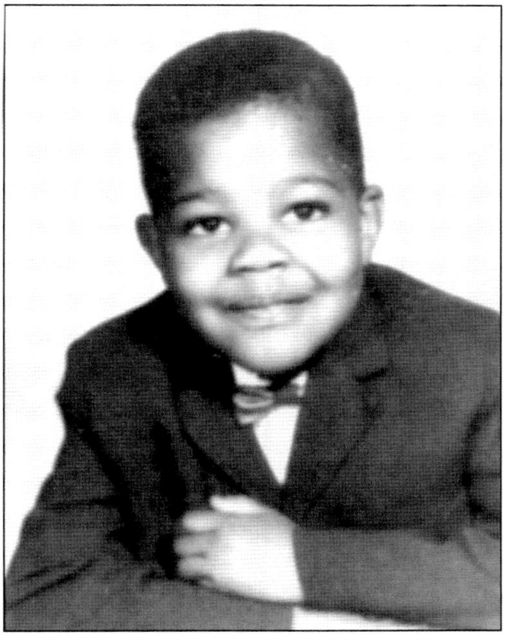 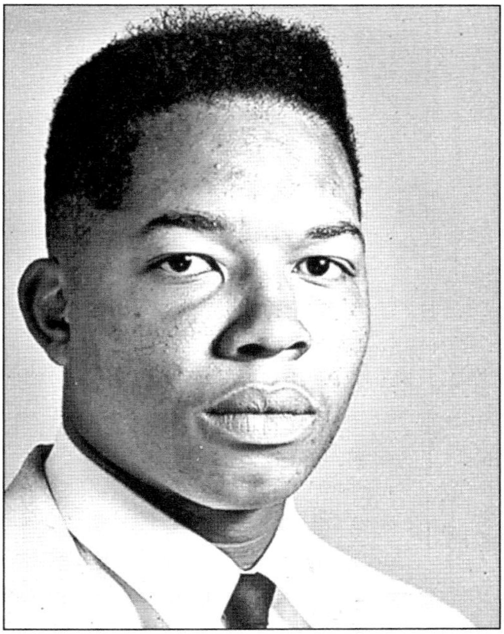

(Left) Reginald Dwayne Peek, seen *c.* 1967, is the son of Minnie and Reginald Peek of Madison. After graduating from Morgan County High School, Reginald began a career in the United States Air Force. (Courtesy Minnie Peek.)
(Right) Amos Jones is the son of Sam and Salina Jones of Madison. The Jones family has a strong tradition as farmers and landowners in Morgan County. Amos's brother, Horace, works for the sheriff's department in Morgan County. (Courtesy Elzata Brown.)

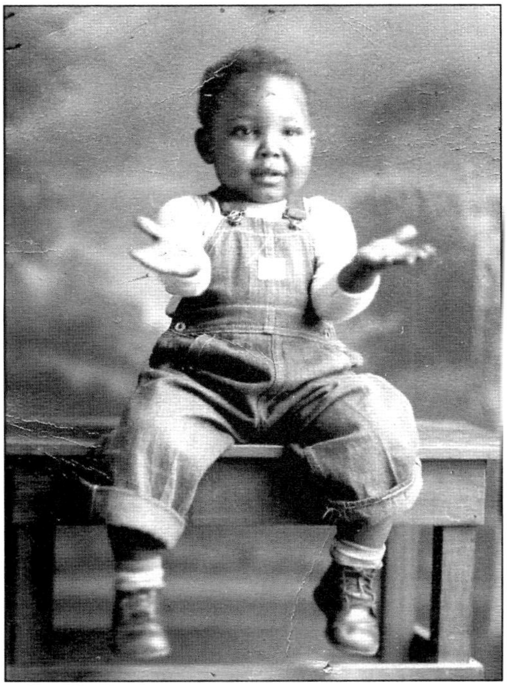

This photograph of Norris Robinson was taken *c.* 1951. Norris lived with his uncle Huel and aunt Tessie Robinson in Bostwick until he was seven years old.

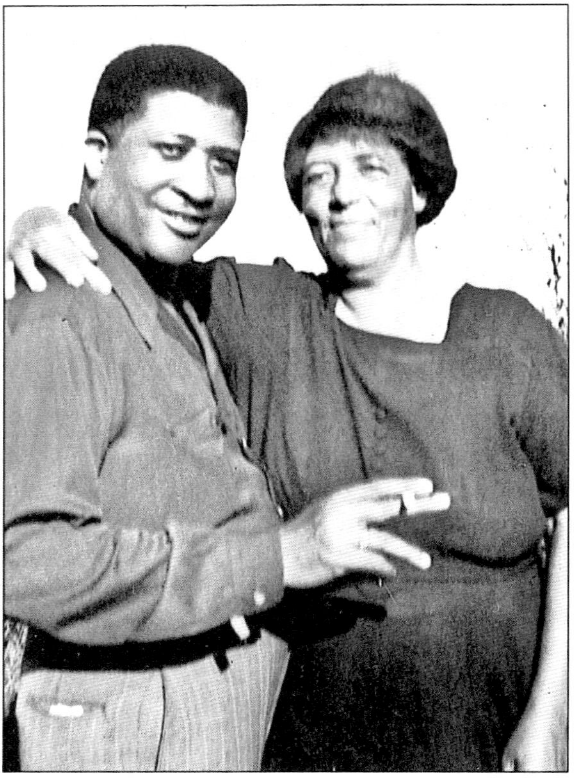

"Ma" Minnie Collier Shepherd and John Shepherd are shown here. (Courtesy Minnie Peek.)

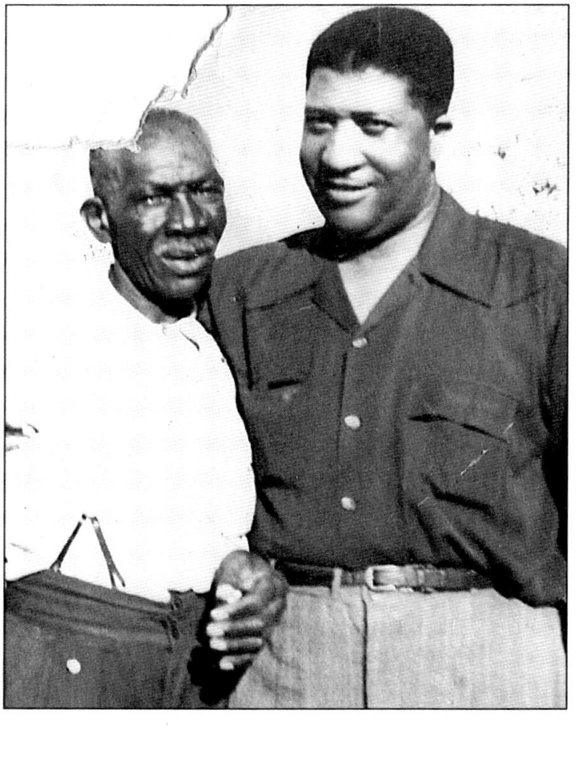

"Pa" Ben Shepherd and John Shepherd are shown here. (Courtesy Minnie Peek.)

Fannie Mae Brown was married to Horace Brown and is the daughter of Emma Drummond. (Courtesy Thelma Griffin.)

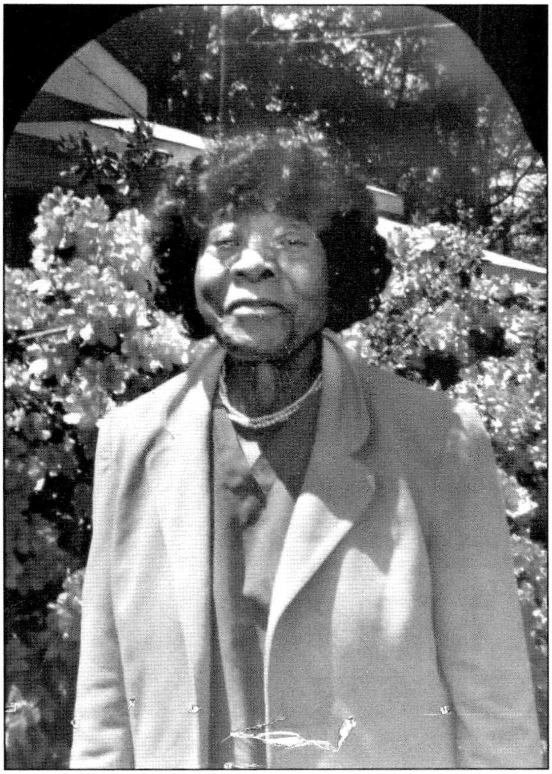

Sarah Weems Murray was the wife of brick mason and respected landowner Harold Murray. The Murrays moved to Morgan County in 1931 during the Depression. They had 12 children, two of whom died when they were very young. Two daughters, ministers Wauline Baptiste and Doris Booker, currently live in Madison; son Rev. W.H. Murray is the owner of Ole Murray's in Madison, where food is cooked from scratch. (Courtesy Wauline Murray Baptiste.)

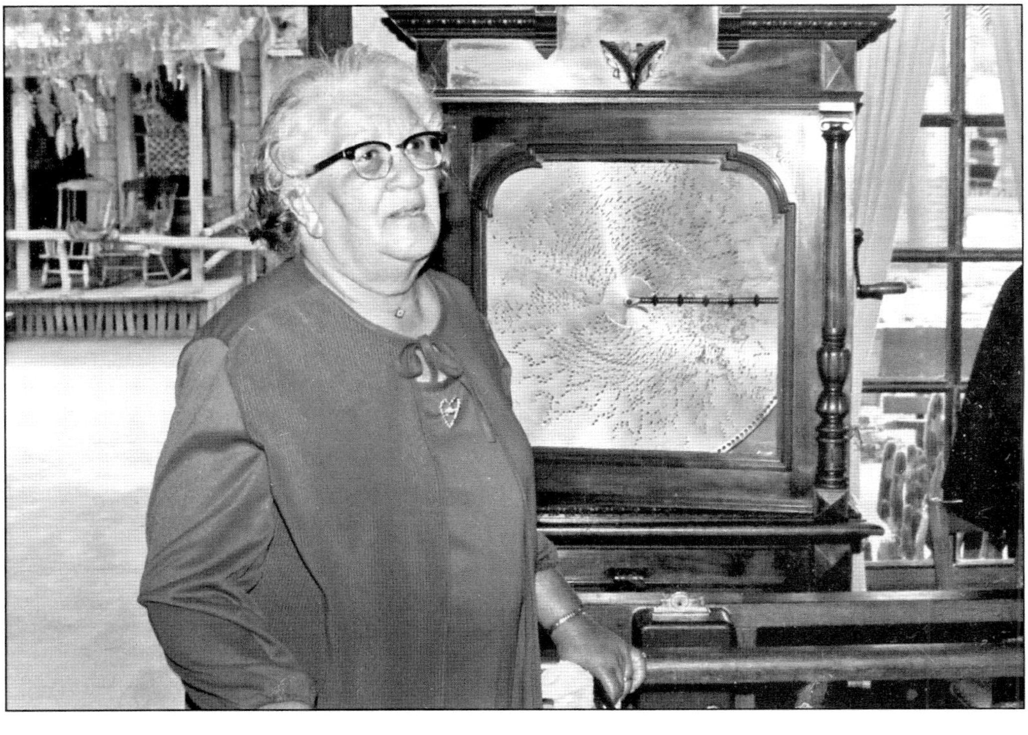

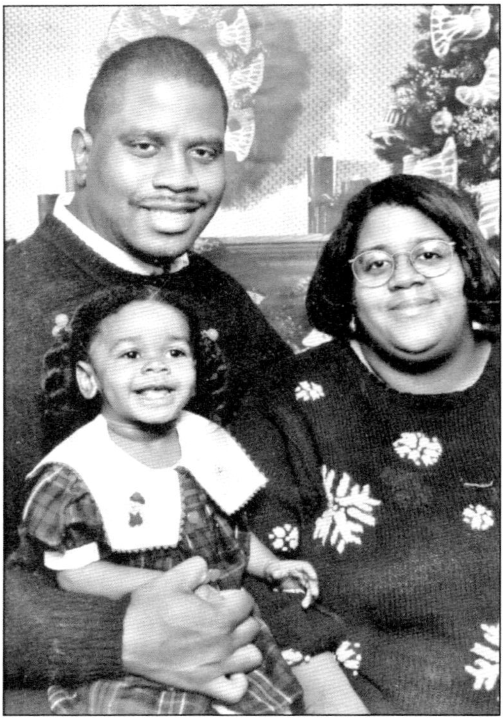

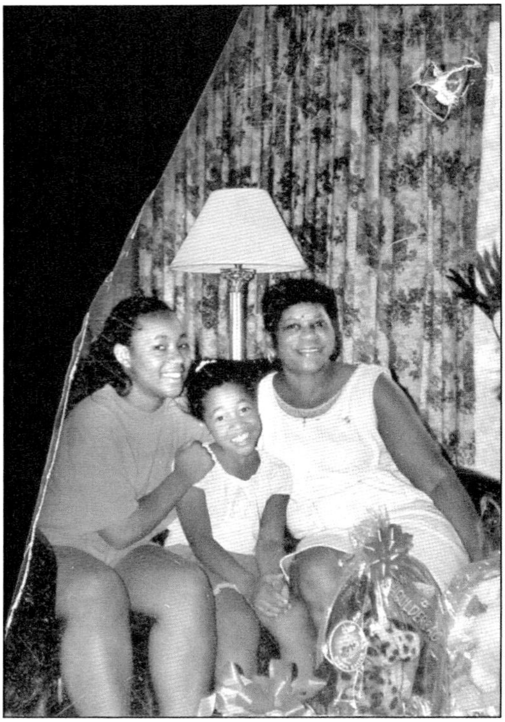

(Left) This is a family photo of Stacy, Denise, and Mallory Johnson. (Courtesy Thelma Griffin.)
(Right) This is Emma Drummond Johnson and her daughters. (Courtesy Thelma Griffin.)

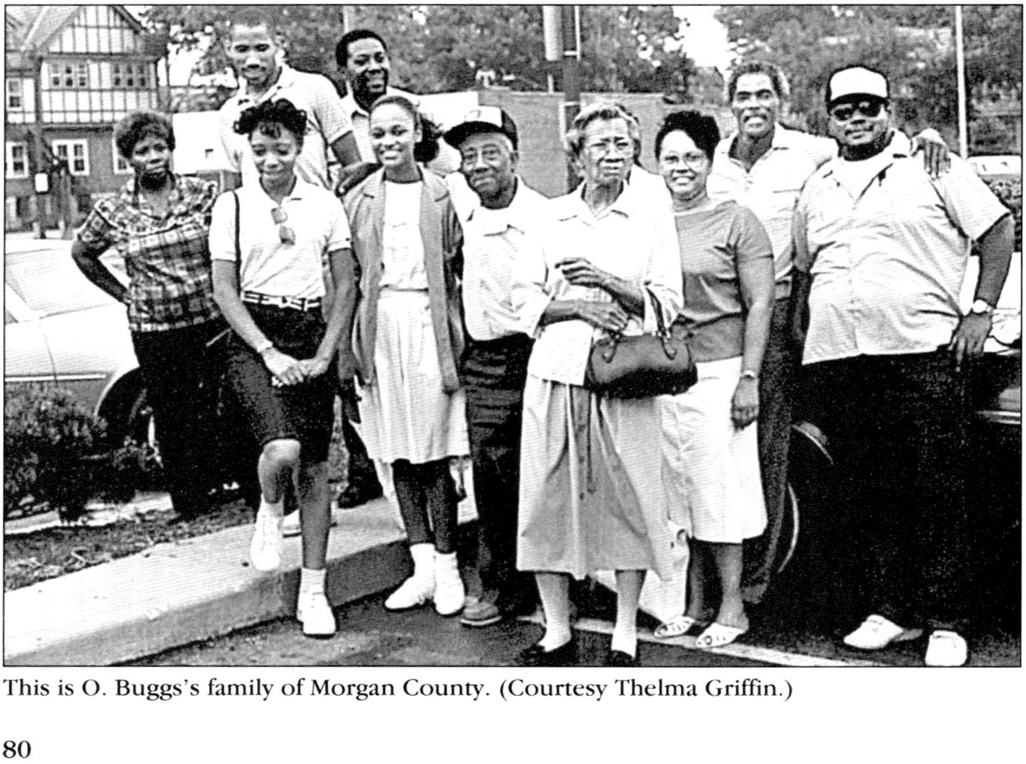

This is O. Buggs's family of Morgan County. (Courtesy Thelma Griffin.)

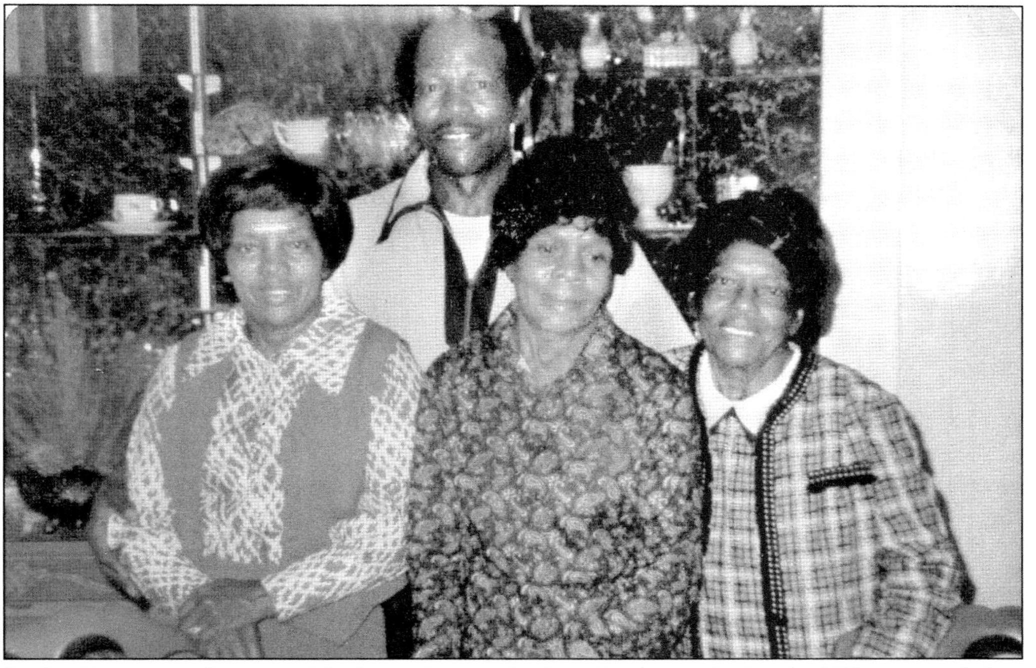

Susie Evans is shown with her sisters, Lorine Beale and Carrie Wilson, and her brother, Augusta Standfield, in Mrs. Evans's home. Their hometown is Buckhead. (Courtesy Elzata Brown.)

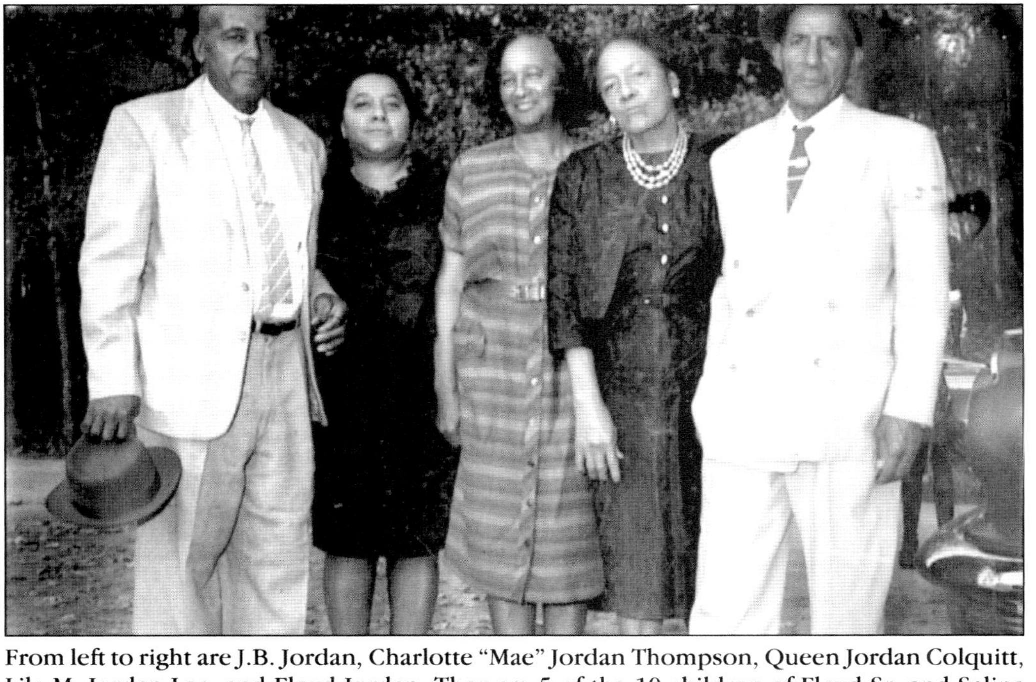

From left to right are J.B. Jordan, Charlotte "Mae" Jordan Thompson, Queen Jordan Colquitt, Lila M. Jordan Lee, and Floyd Jordan. They are 5 of the 10 children of Floyd Sr. and Salina Love Jordan of Morgan County. (Courtesy Annette Drake.)

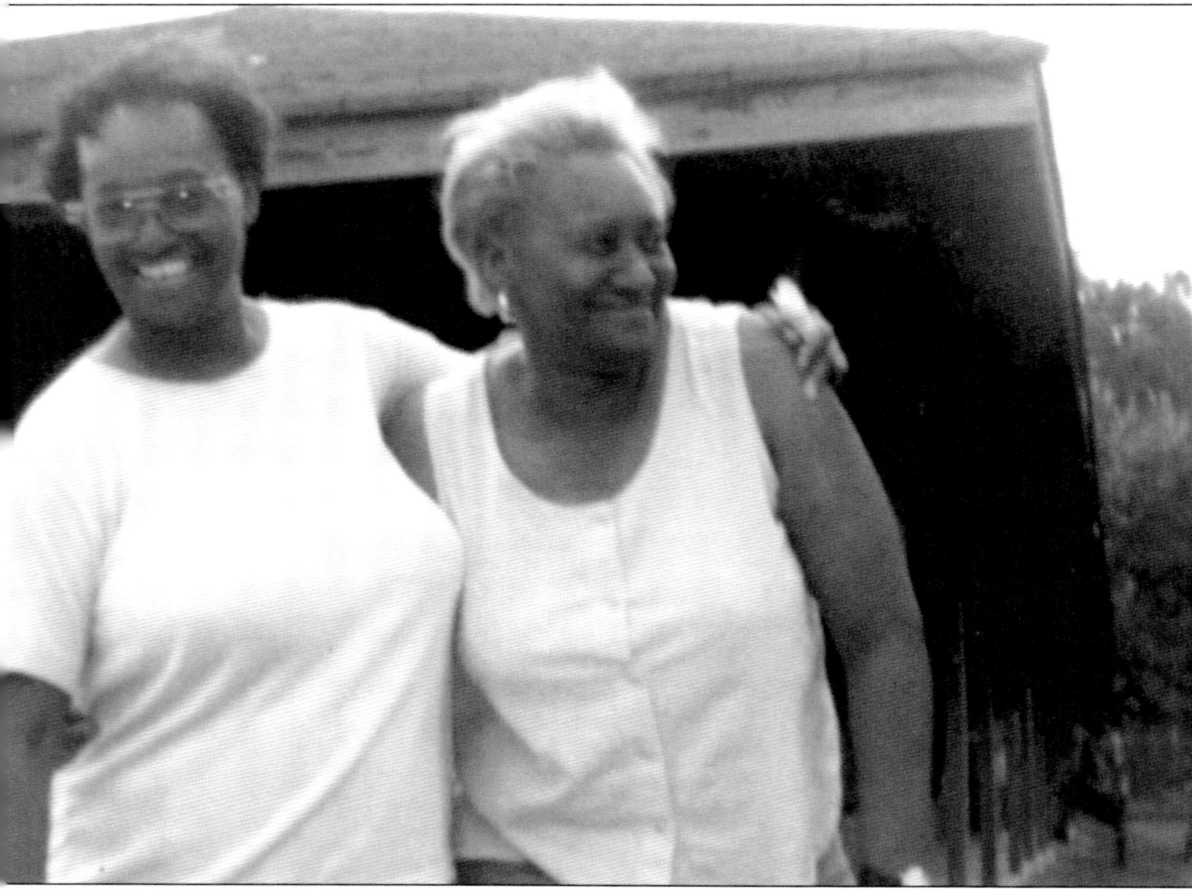

Sisters Marilyn Colquitt Neal and Clara Colquitt Hunter enjoy a few laughs at the family reunion. (Courtesy Annette Drake.)

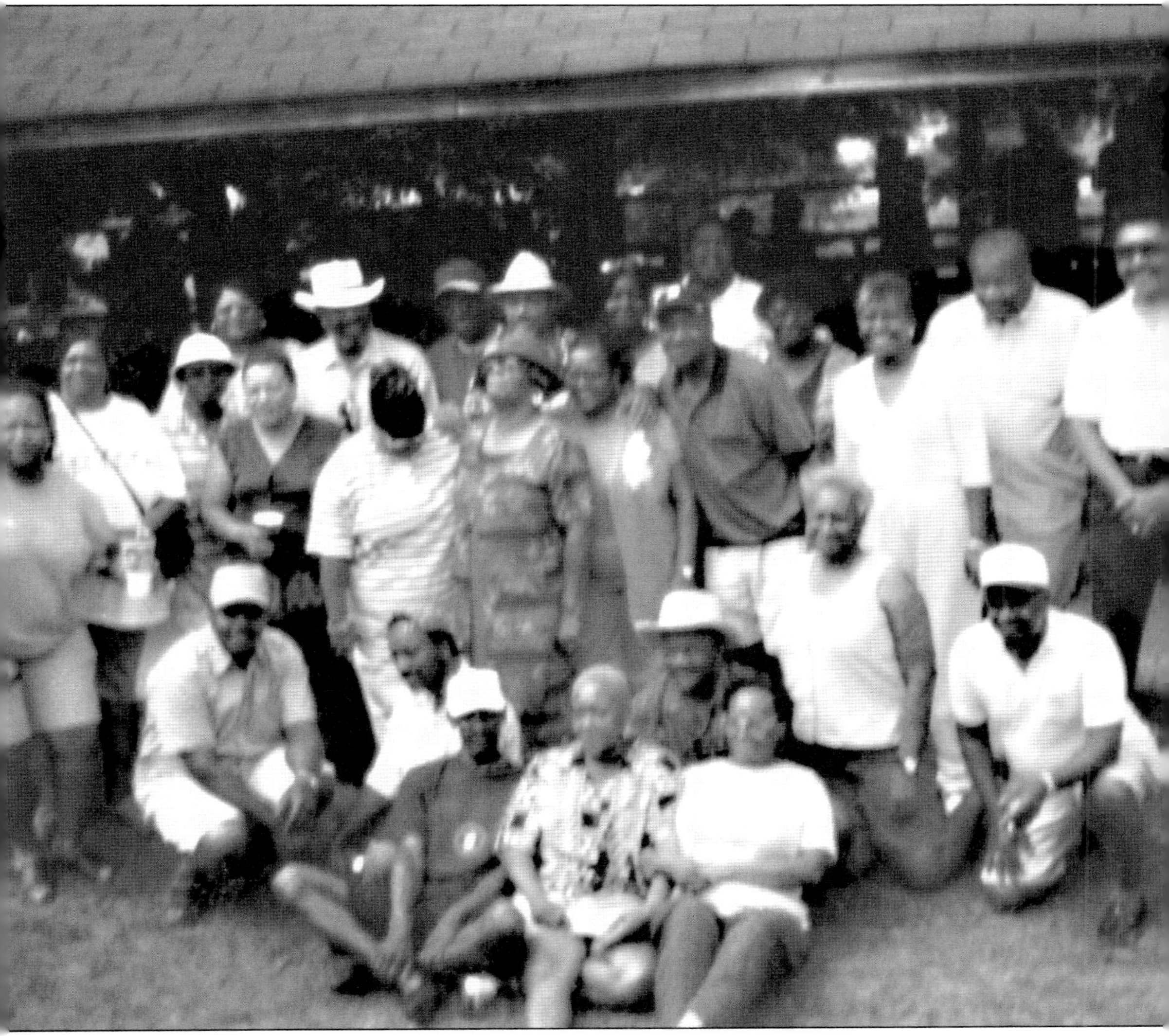

The Jordan family reunion brings generations of the Jordan family together. (Courtesy Annette Drake.)

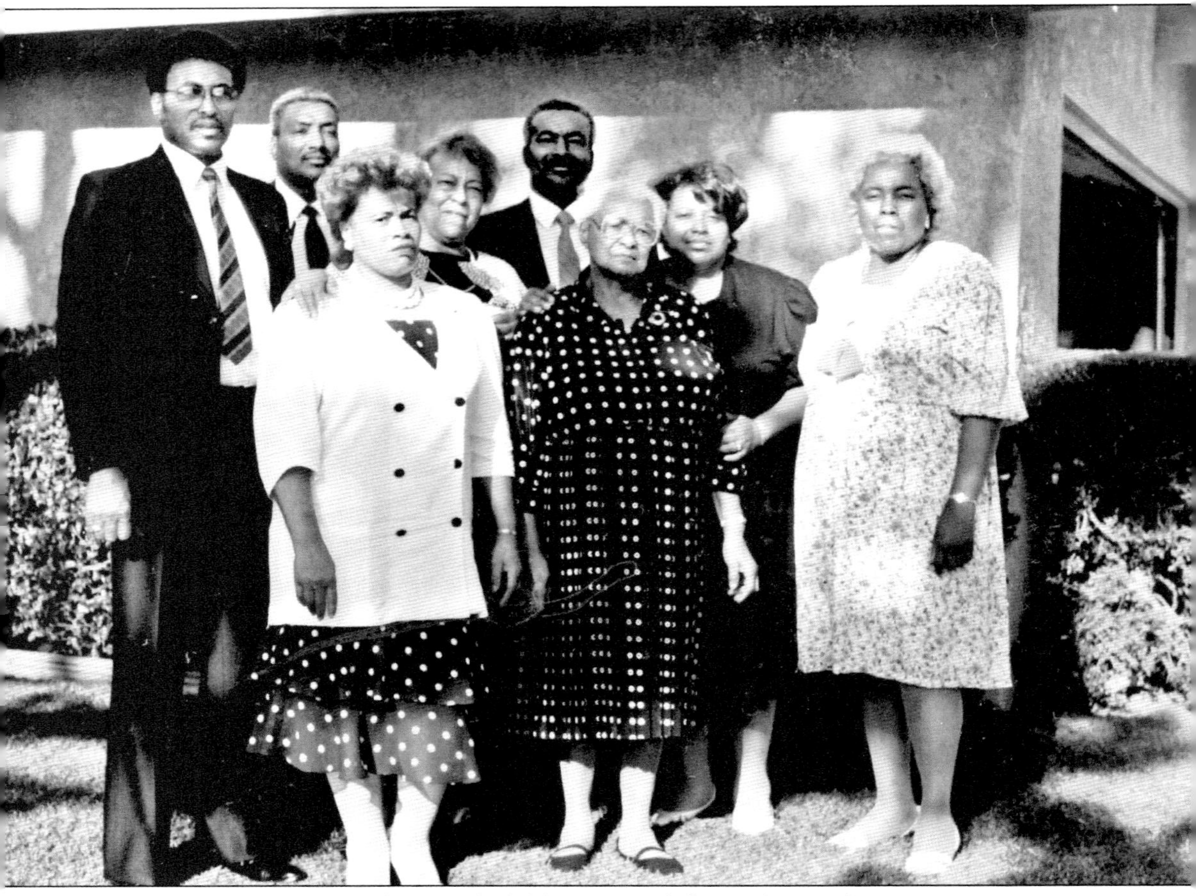

Mary Lou Hunter is shown here with children. From left to right are (front row) Jessie Hunter Smith and Mary Lou (1905–1994); (back row) Eddie Lee Hunter, Verlen Hunter, Virginia Hunter Robertson, Claude Hunter, Gloria Jean Hunter Glenn, and Margaret Furlow. The family lived on a farm on Sandy Creek Road, where the 11 children grew up. Their father was Rance Hunter (1898–1970). (Courtesy Jessie Smith.)

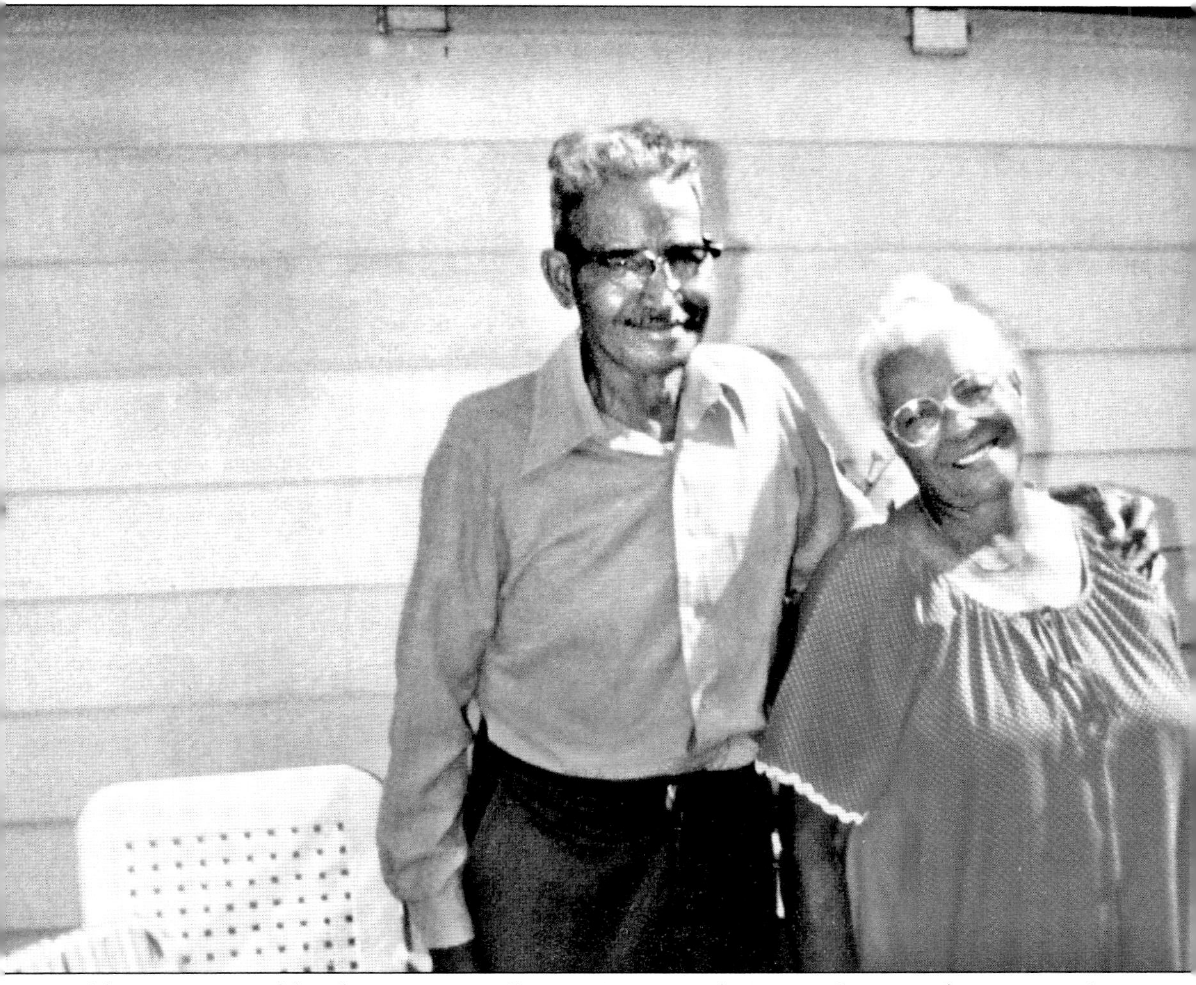

This is sister and brother Mary Lou Garrett Hunter and Morgan Garrett, who grew up in Morgan County. Their parents were Charlotte and Louis Garrett. Morgan joined the army and served in World War II; Mary Lou married and raised her family in Morgan County. (Courtesy Jessie Hunter Smith.)

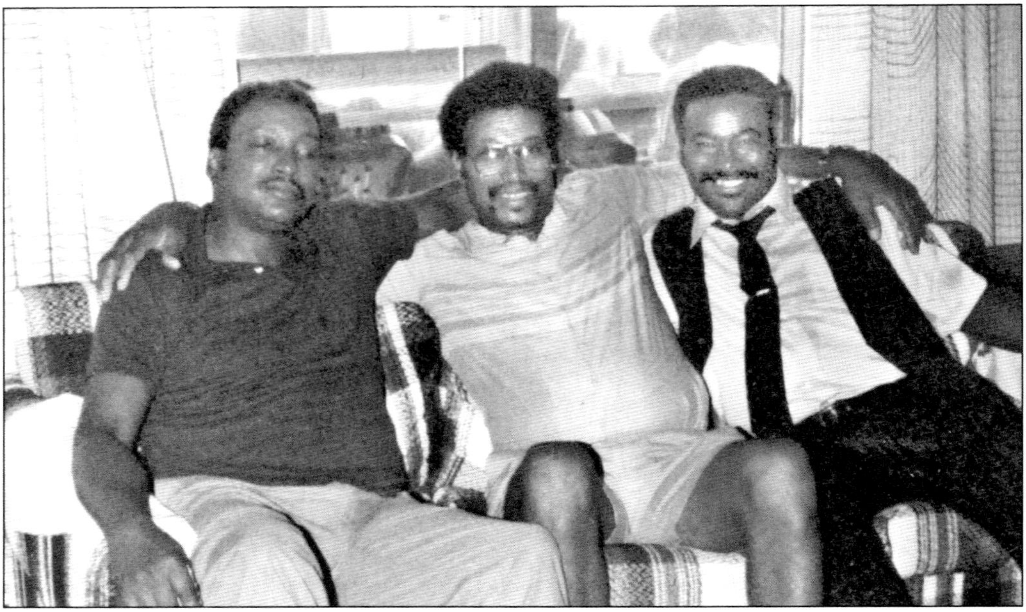

Verlen, Eddie Lee, and Claude Hunter are the brothers shown here, from left to right. They are the sons of Mary Lou and Rance Hunter. Eddie now lives in Jacksonville, Florida, while the other two brothers now live in Atlanta. (Courtesy Jessie Hunter Smith.)

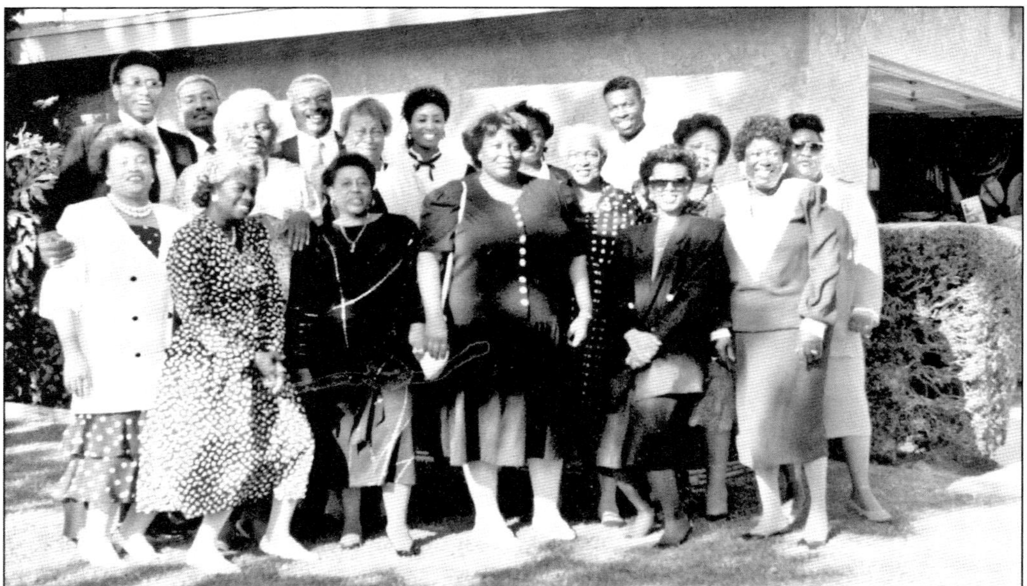

This 1990 family photograph of the Hunter family features, from left to right, (front row) Jessie Hunter Smith, Mary Ruth Hunter, ? Hunter, Gloria Jean Hunter Glenn, Cathy Hunter, and Evelyn Hunter; (middle row) Margaret Hunter Furlow, Virginia Hunter Robertson, Mary Lou Hunter (mother), Tyree Hunter, and ? Hunter; (back row) Eddie Lee Hunter, Verlen Hunter, Claude Hunter, unidentified grandchildren, and an unidentified daughter-in-law. (Courtesy Jessie Hunter Smith.)

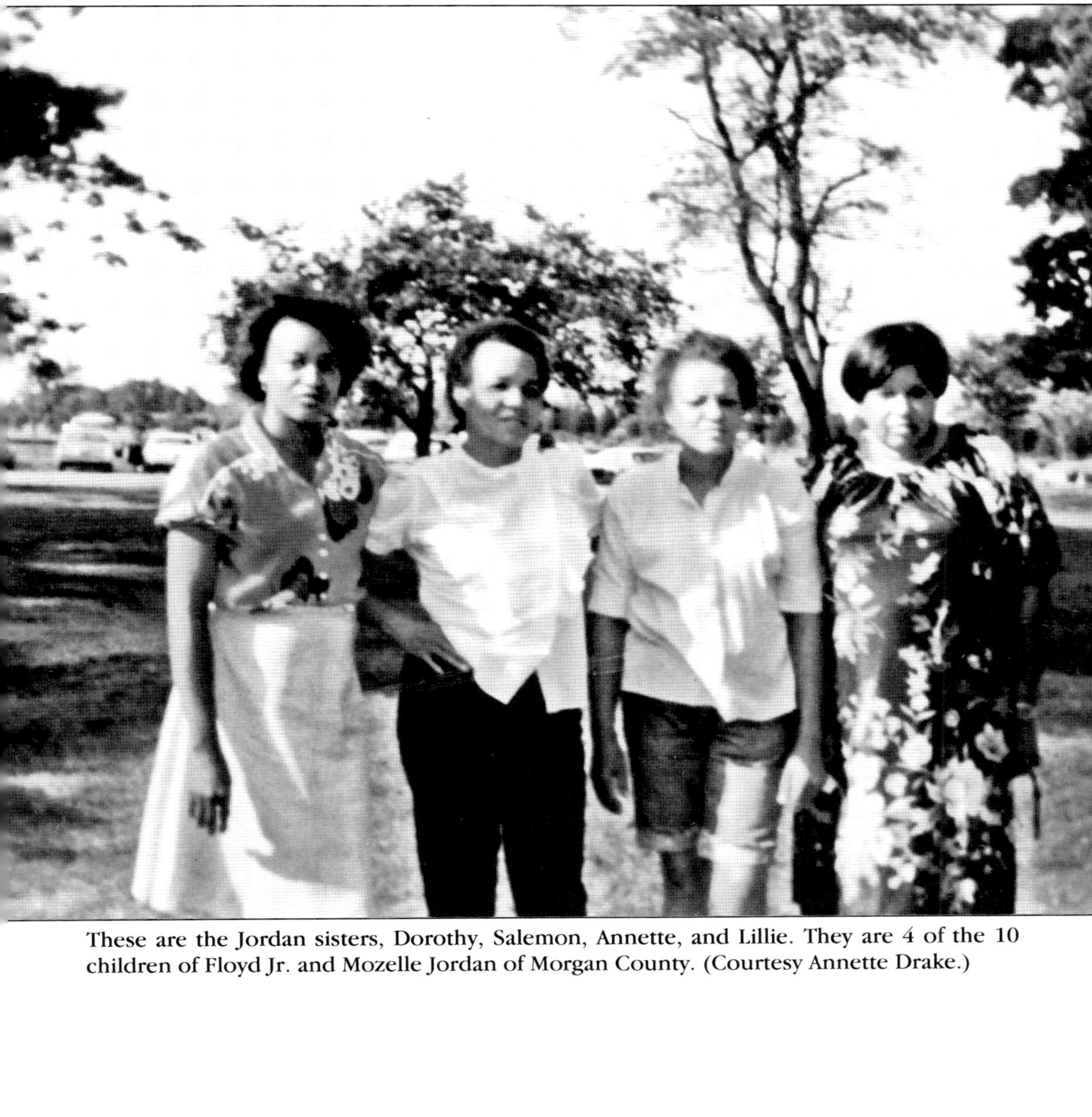

These are the Jordan sisters, Dorothy, Salemon, Annette, and Lillie. They are 4 of the 10 children of Floyd Jr. and Mozelle Jordan of Morgan County. (Courtesy Annette Drake.)

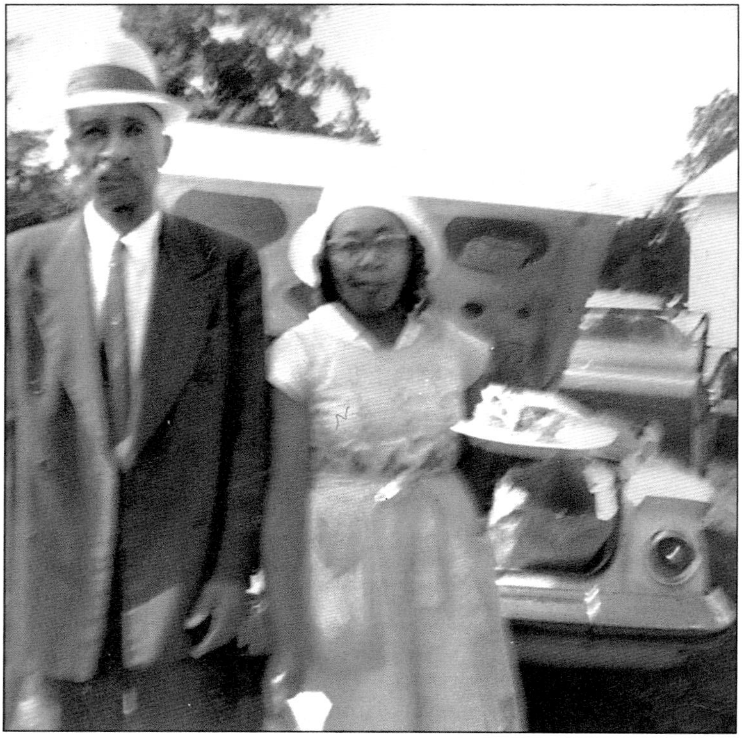

Huel and Tessie Robinson lived on a farm in Bostwick until 1956. They are shown on Homecoming Day at Mt. Perry Missionary Baptist Church. (Courtesy Tessie Robinson.)

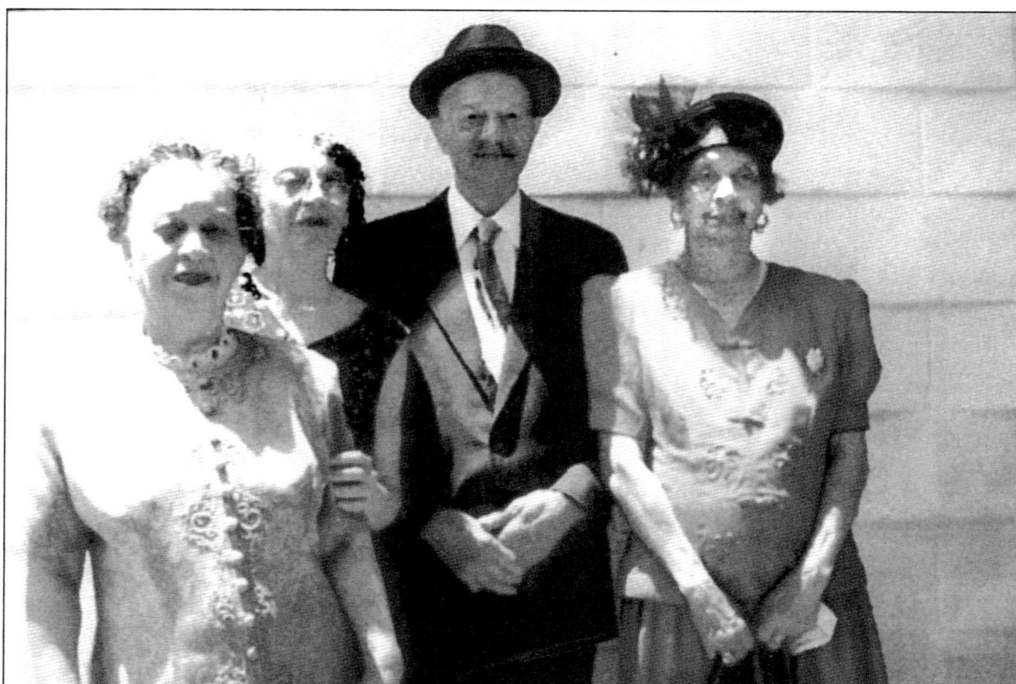

From left to right are Susie Perriman, Gracie Bell Perriman Wright, Paul Perriman, and Essie Mae Perriman. Generations of this family have lived in Buckhead. (Courtesy Minnie Peek.)

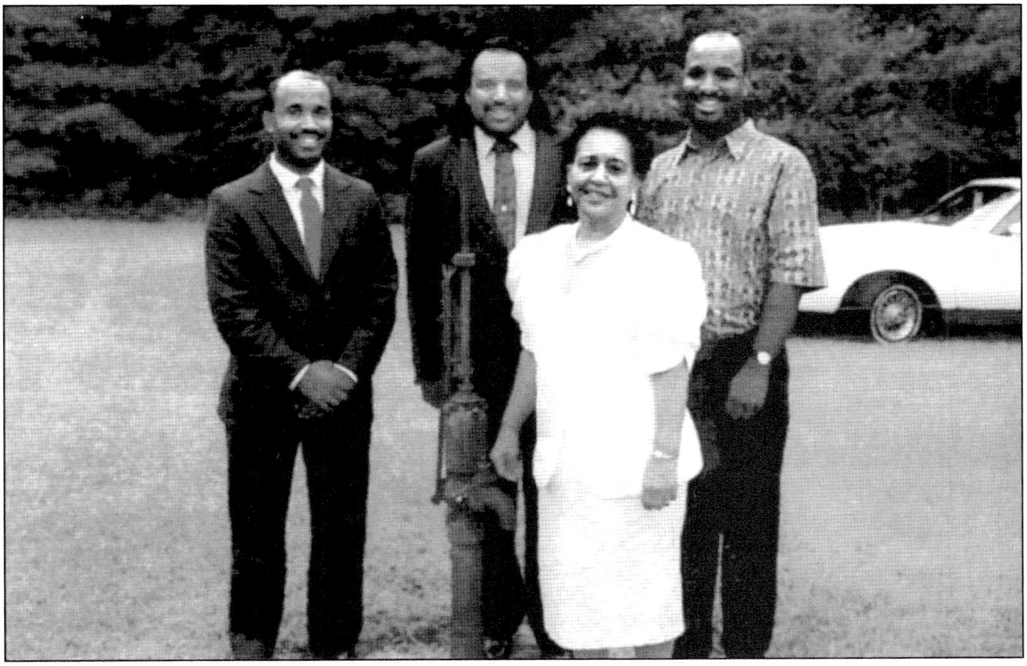

Shown here are Kenneth, Sammie, Paul, and Susie Perriman. (Courtesy Minnie Peek.)

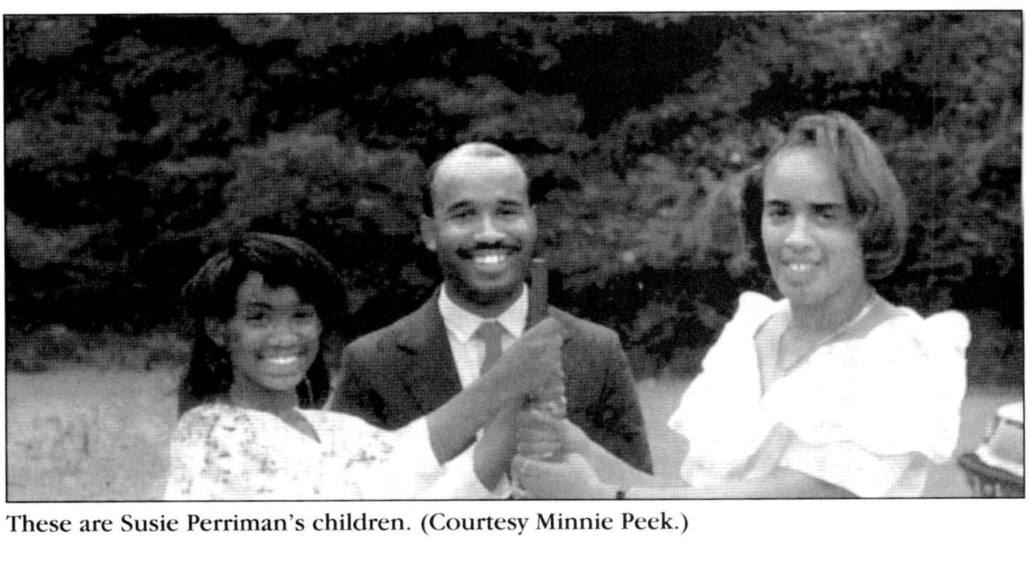

These are Susie Perriman's children. (Courtesy Minnie Peek.)

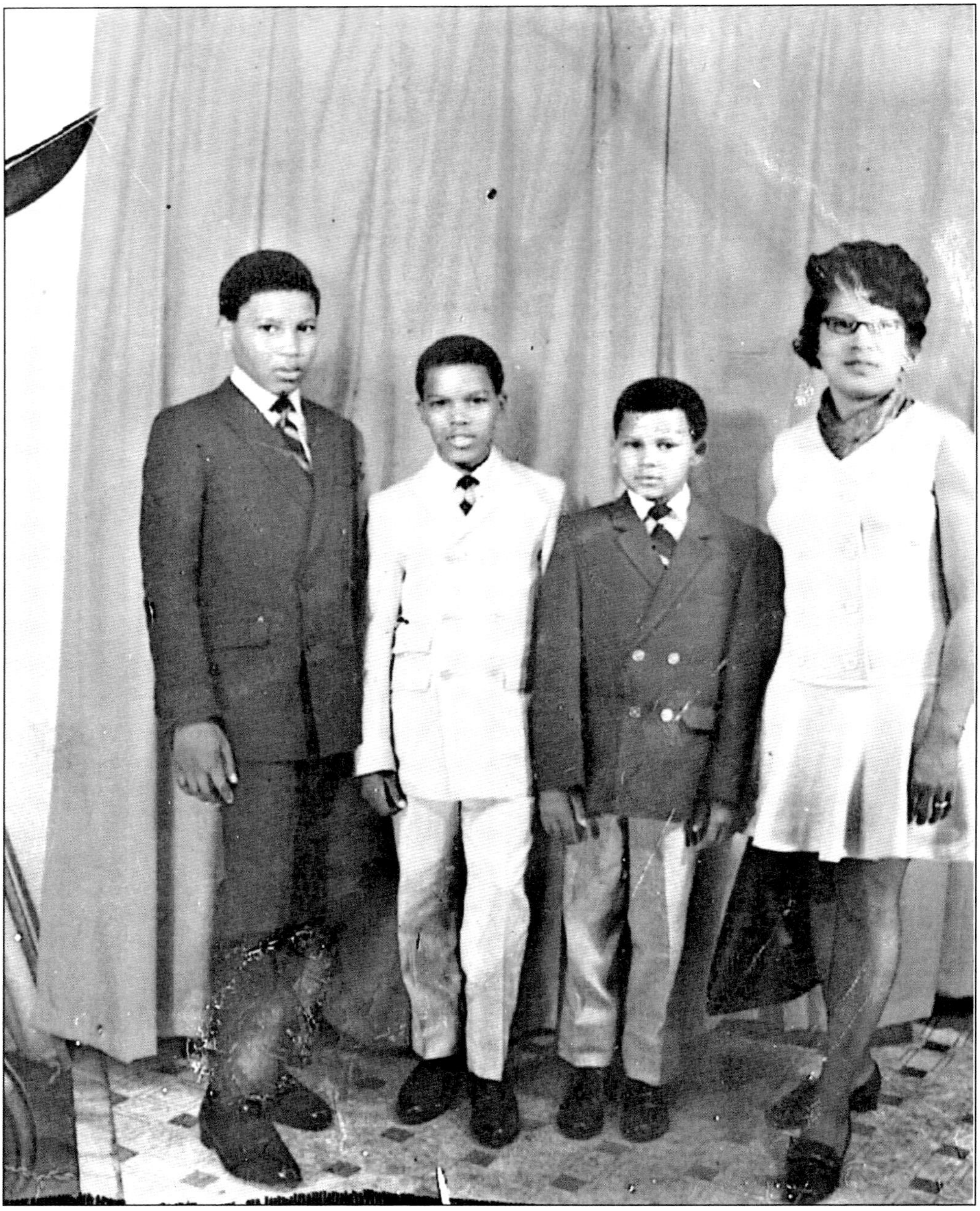

Carrie Rollin Chambers, seen *c.* 1960s, left Madison after graduating from Pearl High School in 1953. She became a beautician and later a licensed practical nurse in Atlanta. Carrie maintained ties with the Morgan County community by visiting family and friends. She also continued to attend Bethlehem Baptist Church with her children, from left to right, Percy Lee, Terry LaBronze, and John Wesley Chambers. The boys also enjoyed spending part of their summer vacation with their grandparents in Morgan County. (Courtesy Carrie Chambers.)

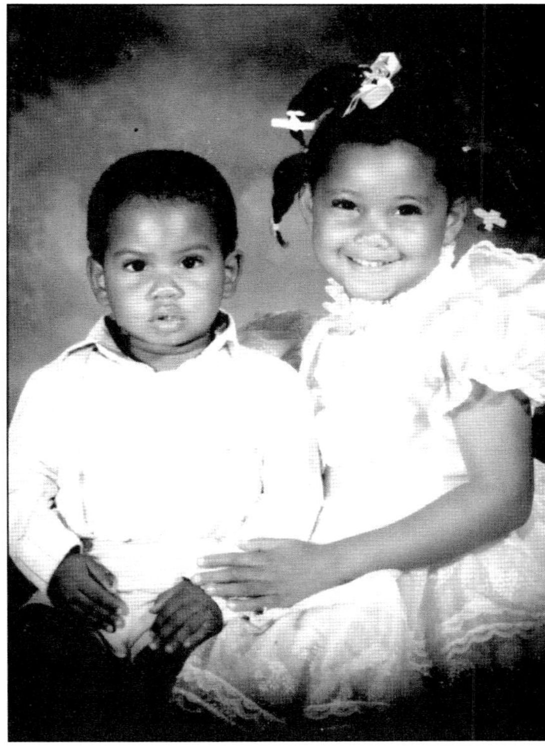

Jaylin and Jasmine Chambers, seen *c.* 1988, are the great-grandchildren of Albert and Julia Rollin and grandchildren of Carrie Rollin Chambers of Morgan County. Jaylin participated in the Youth Challenge Program at Georgia Army National Guard Academy. Jasmine studied theatre and marketing at Georgia State University. (Courtesy the author.)

Alreca Chambers, pictured here *c.* 1991, is the great-granddaughter of Albert and Julia Rollin, oldest granddaughter of Carrie Rollin Chambers, and daughter of Sharon Chambers of Morgan County. She has completed studies at Georgia State University and Howard University to become an occupational therapist. She is shown here with her uncle Jay. (Courtesy the author.)

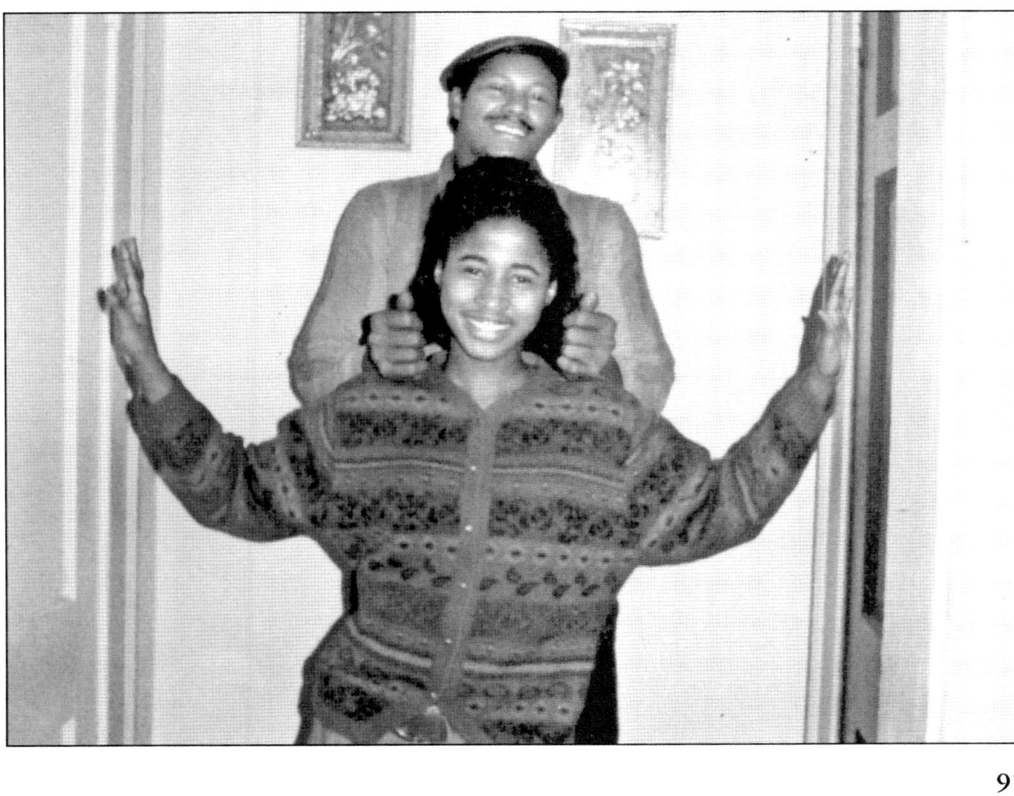

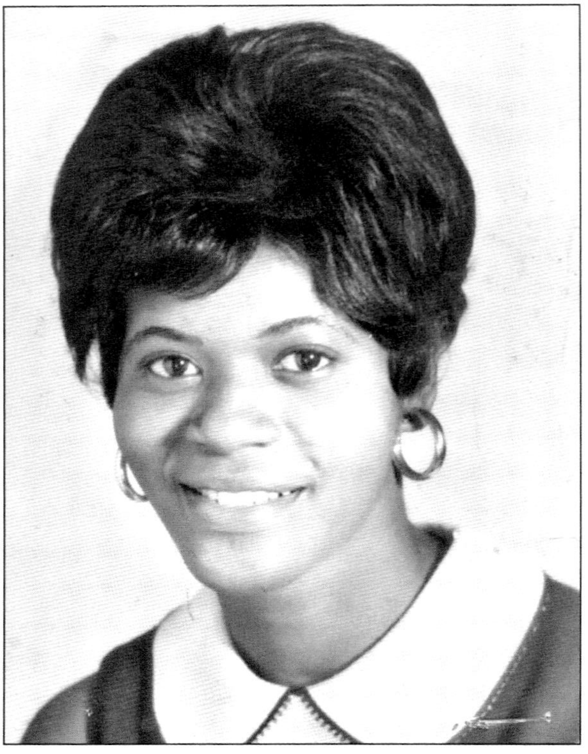

This is Joyce Elizabeth Griffin of Morgan County. She graduated from Savannah State College, married Marion Dingle, and has two daughters, Jocelyn and Miriam. She was a high school social studies teacher. (Courtesy Thelma Griffin.)

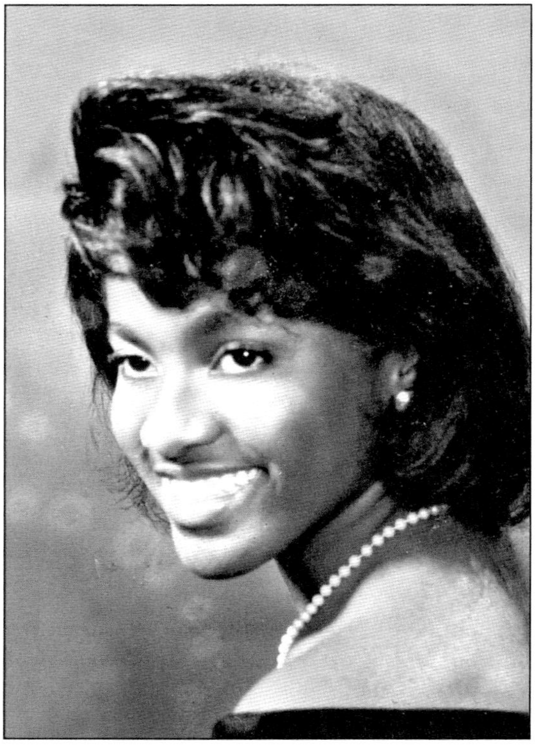

Jocelyn Dingle is the youngest daughter of Joyce and Marion Dingle. This is her 1988 class photograph. (Courtesy Thelma Griffin.)

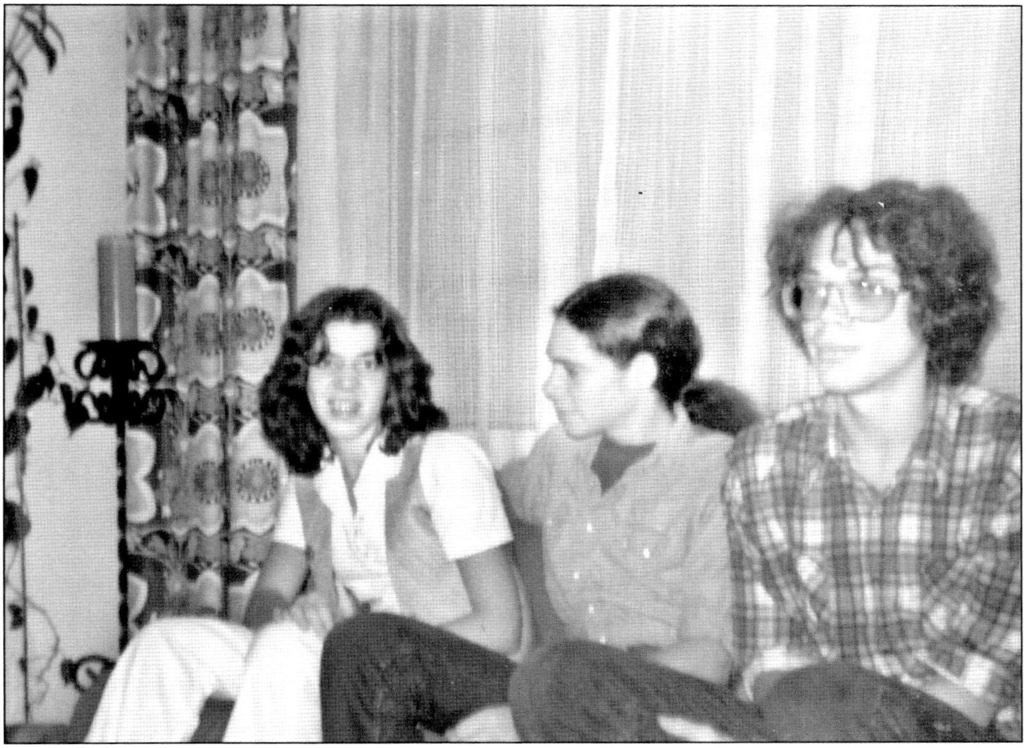

Julia, Thomas, and Christopher Andrews are the children of Benny Andrews of Morgan County. (Courtesy Benny Andrews.)

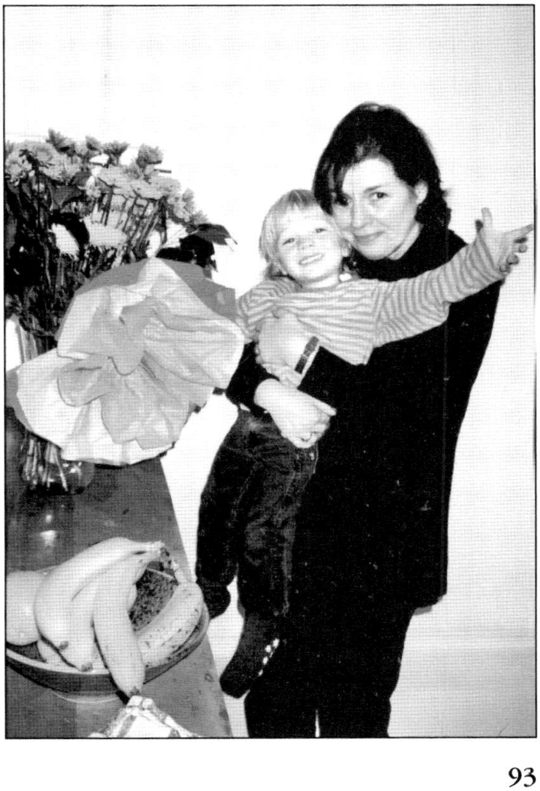

This is Benny Andrews's wife NeNe Humphrey and their grandson Casey Andrews. (Courtesy Benny Andrews.)

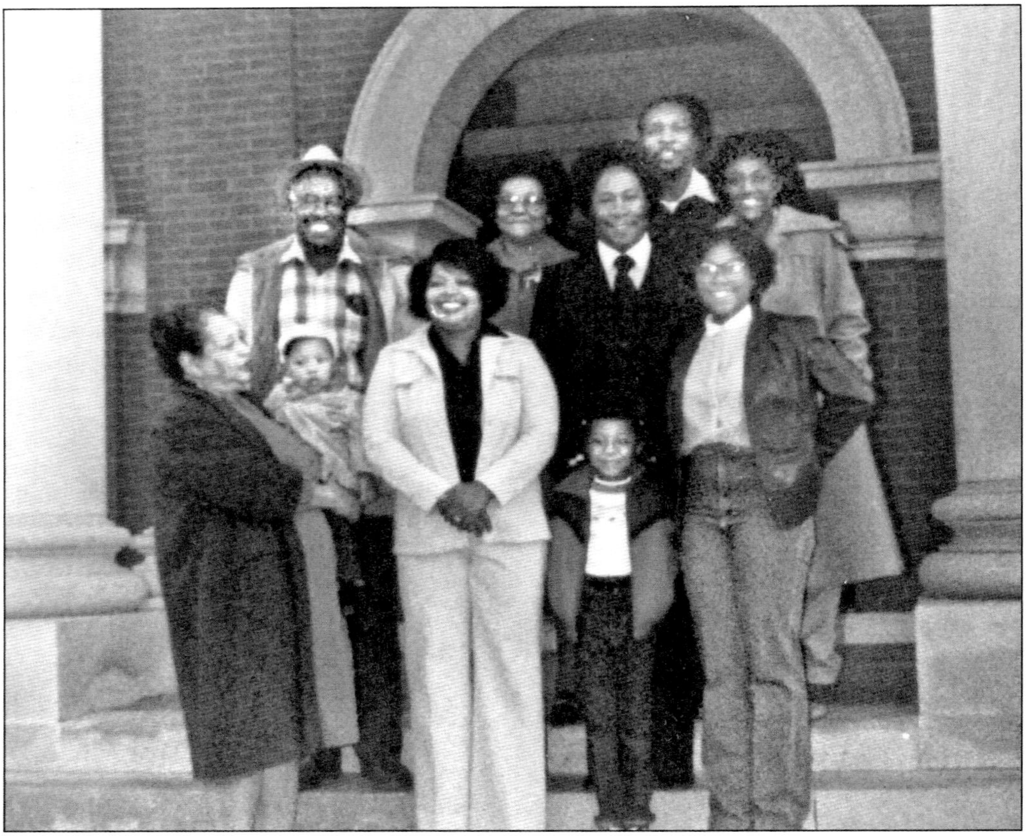

The Butler family is, from left to right, (front row) E.M. Neal, Walter Curtis Butler III, Laura Butler, Celeste Butler, and Lavelle Butler; (middle row) Walter Curtis Butler Sr., Hattie Mae Butler, Walter Curtis Butler Jr., and Lavorne Dorsey; (back row) James Edwards. (Courtesy Laura W. Butler.)

Five

Our Community Leaders and High Achievers

To honor past achievements is to inspire future ones.
Author unknown

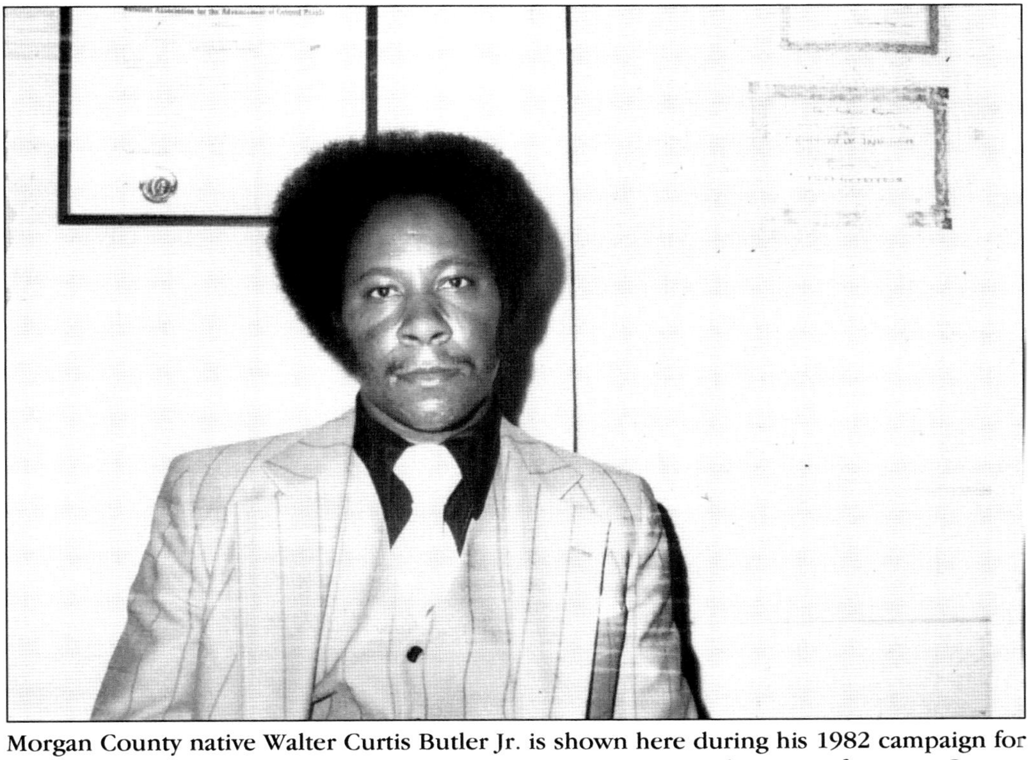

Morgan County native Walter Curtis Butler Jr. is shown here during his 1982 campaign for Morgan County Commissioner District 1. He now serves as vice-chairman of Morgan County Board of Commissions, having been a county commissioner for 21 years. (Courtesy Laura W. Butler.)

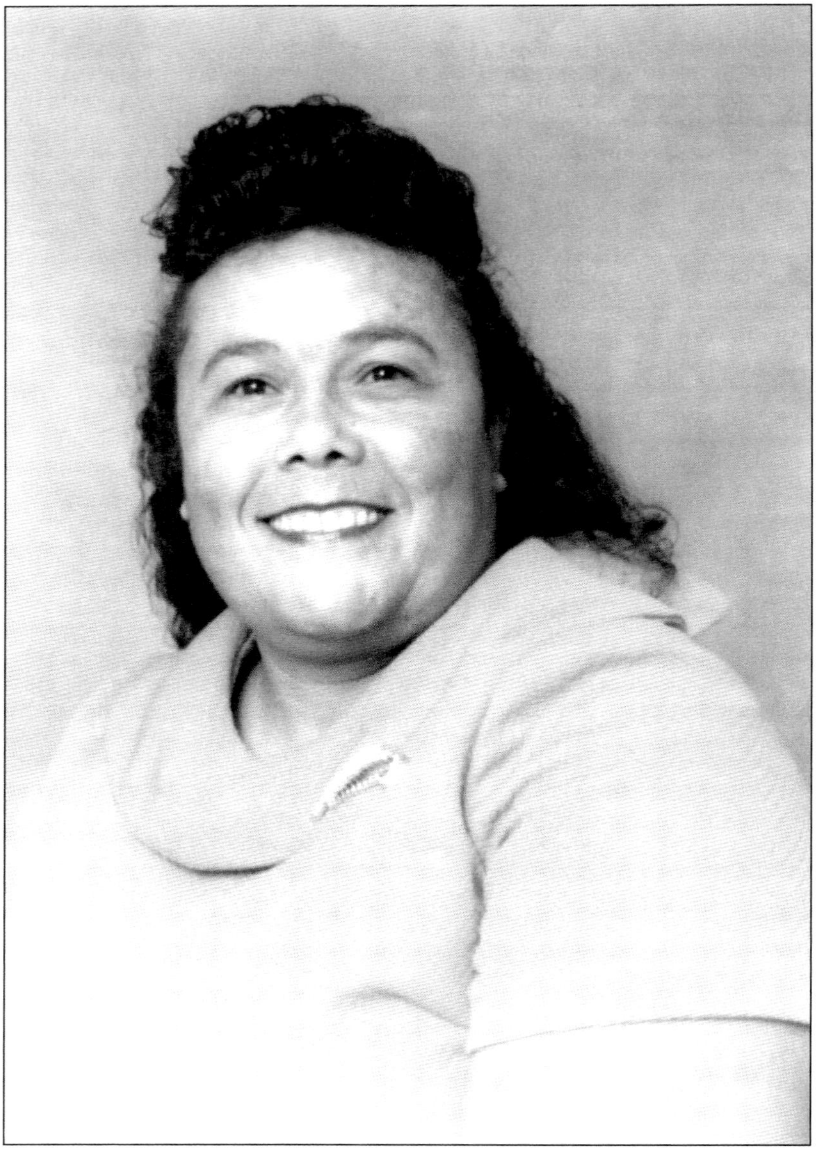

Marie Bass Martin is a well-known educator in Morgan County. After attending Morgan's public schools, she received a bachelor's degree from Savannah State College and a master's degree in education from Atlanta University, and she did advanced studies at Columbia University. She has held positions in Morgan's and surrounding counties' school systems at the elementary and high school level, and she was a Jeanes Supervising Teacher, principal of Pearl High and Elementary School and Morgan County Primary School, and curriculum director. Additionally, she has served on evaluation committees for a number of counties, the Governor's Task Force Committee on Education, and the Georgia Textbook Committee. She was named Teacher of the Year in 1957 and listed in the 1982–1983 edition of *Who's Who in the South and Southwest*. She has been a member of many organizations in the community, served the community in various capacities, and received many other honors. (Courtesy Marie Bass Martin.)

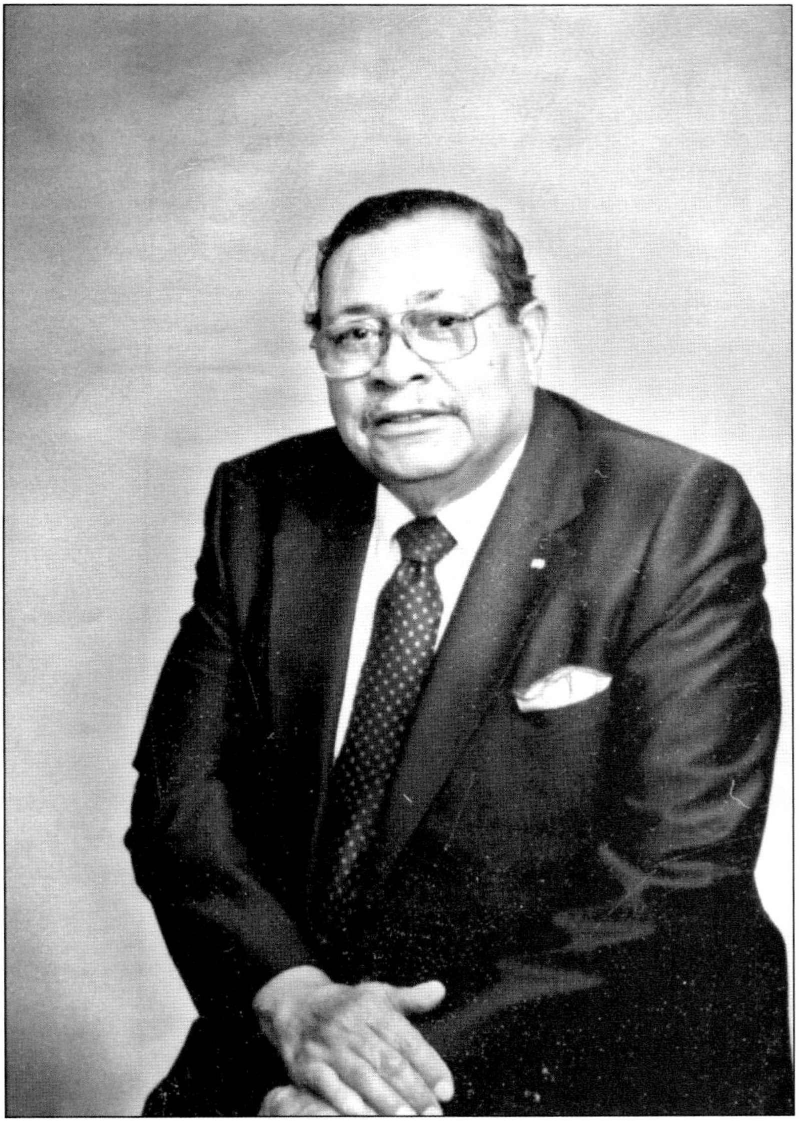

Martin L. Bass Jr. (1919–1997) was one of Morgan County most distinguished citizens. He was born in Morgan County to Martin L. Bass Sr. and Corrine Wyatt Bass. His extensive professional career included being an insurance agent from 1935 to 1942; service in the United States Army from 1942 to 1946, where he advanced from a private to first sergeant; and jobs as a licensed real estate salesman starting in 1948 and as a licensed broker starting in 1951. He became the first African-American appraiser-reviewer in the United States while employed by the Detroit Regional Office of the Veterans Administration. Later, Liberian president William V.S. Tubman appointed him Honorary Consul of the Republic of Liberia for Michigan. Mr. Bass was a loyal member and ordained deacon of Calvary Baptist Church. He and his devoted wife Mildred—a retired teacher from Detroit, Michigan—moved back to Madison after retiring in 1989 and were among the founders and major contributors of the Morgan County African-American Museum. He received many awards and honors in the church and community during his life. (Courtesy Mrs. Mildred Bass.)

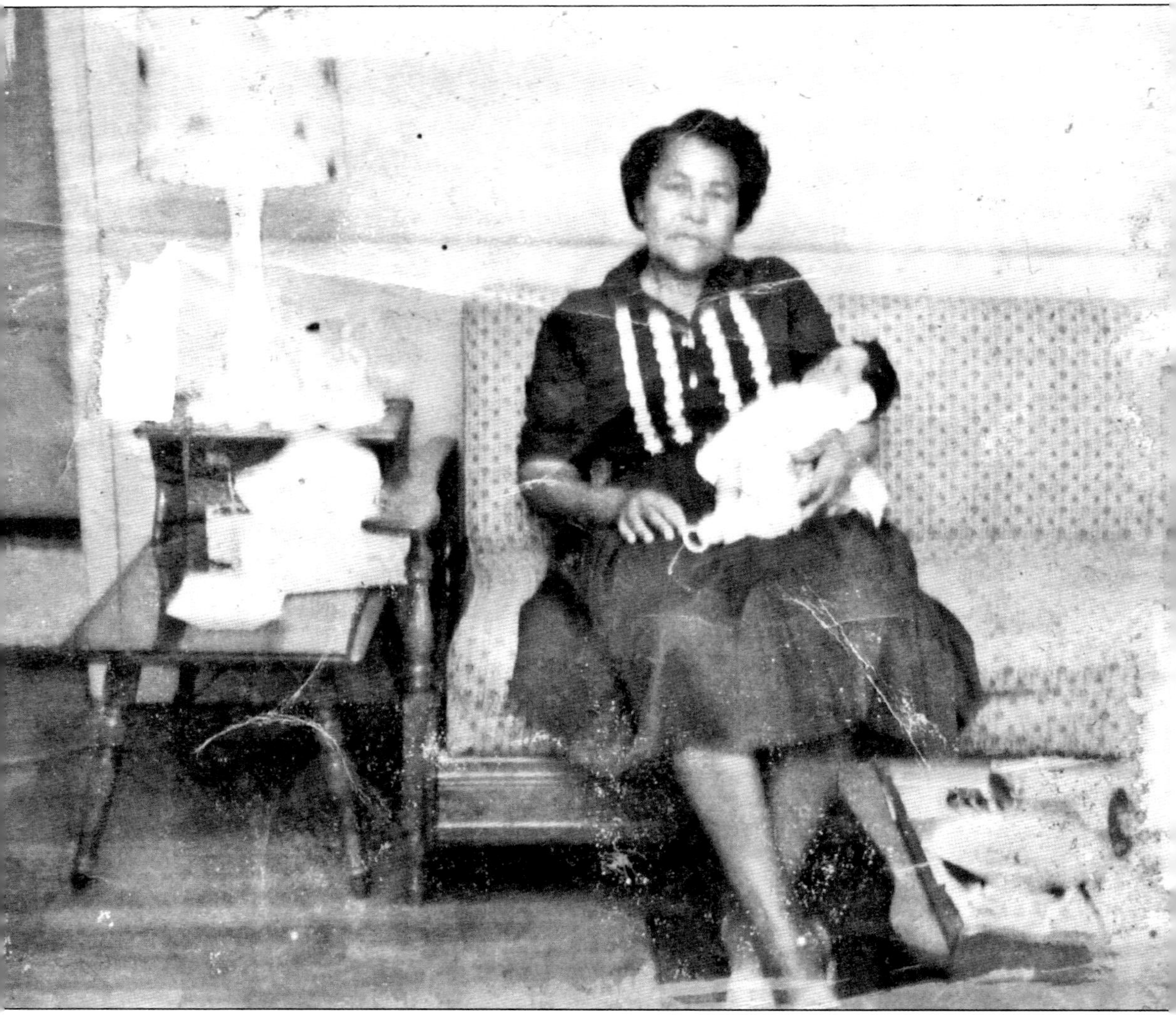

Sarah G. Alford is shown holding her first grandchild, Pamela Lynn Boswell, in 1961. Born in 1912, only three years after the NAACP was organized, she was a civil-rights pioneer and has been honored with a gift of a lifetime membership by the Morgan County branch. Mrs. Alford stood up for equality and social justice during the 1960s, when others would not. Working with Walter Curtis Butler Jr. and the NAACP, her efforts led to the hiring of African-American police officers and city personnel. Mrs. Alford worked for the Morgan County branch of the NAACP as its secretary for many years. She was an insurance agent for Pilgrim Life Insurance before becoming one of the early female agents for Atlanta Life Insurance Company. Mrs. Alford has been honored numerous times in the community. She still lives in Madison at the age of 92 and is a faithful member of Jackson Grove Baptist Church, where she was clerk for 35 years and president of the women's department for 50 years. (Courtesy Dora Peeks Boswell.)

Elzata V. Brown is a retired teacher and community activist. A member of Mt. Perry Missionary Baptist Church and the Madison Missionary Baptist Association and a lifetime member of the NAACP, she founded the African-American Parade and Festival in 1989. A matron of the Star of Amaranth, No. 15 Order of Eastern Star and a member of Moore's Ford Memorial Committee, she works on the scholarship committees of both organizations. (Courtesy Elzata Brown.)

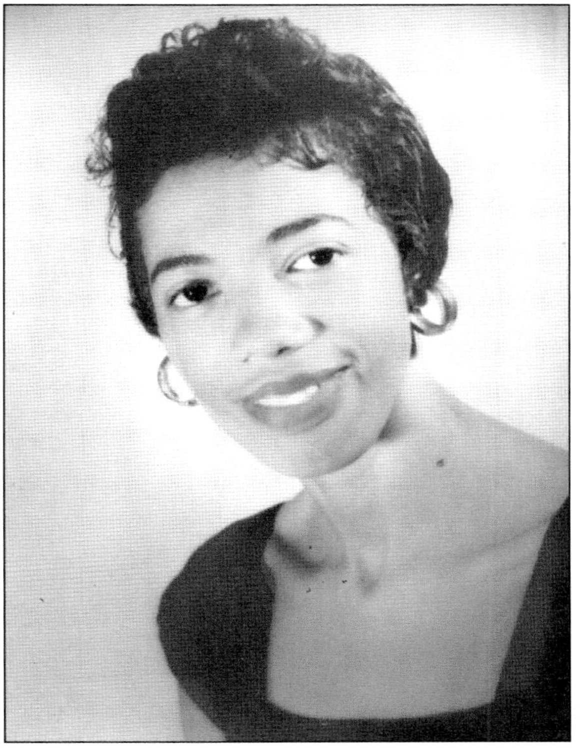

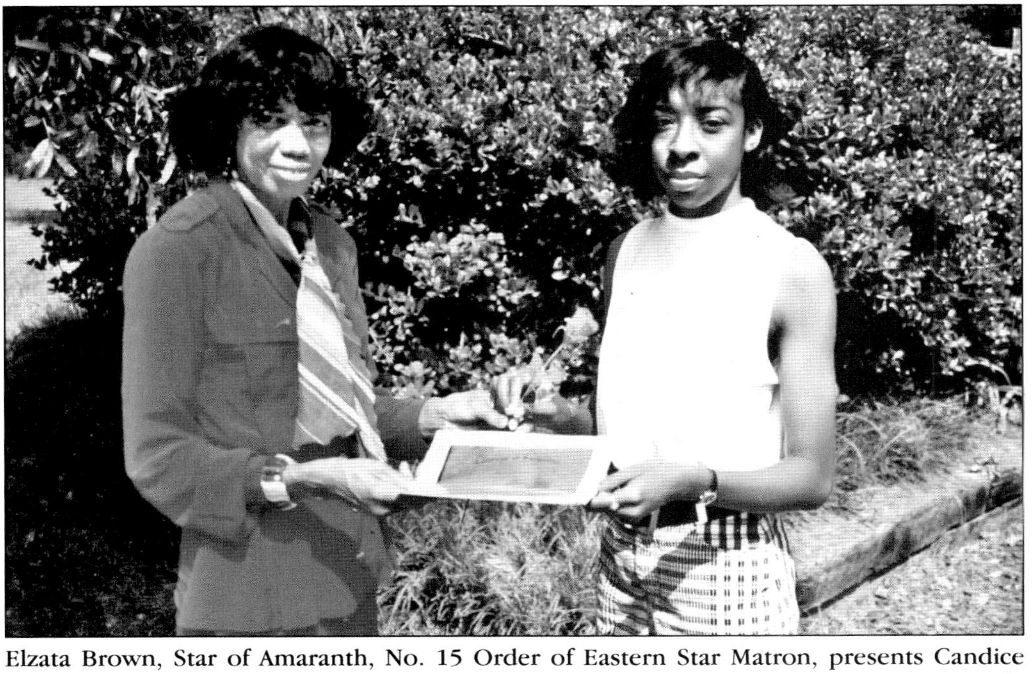

Elzata Brown, Star of Amaranth, No. 15 Order of Eastern Star Matron, presents Candice Jones a scholarship for college. Ms. Brown is well known throughout the region, especially for her work with young people. (Courtesy Elzata Brown.)

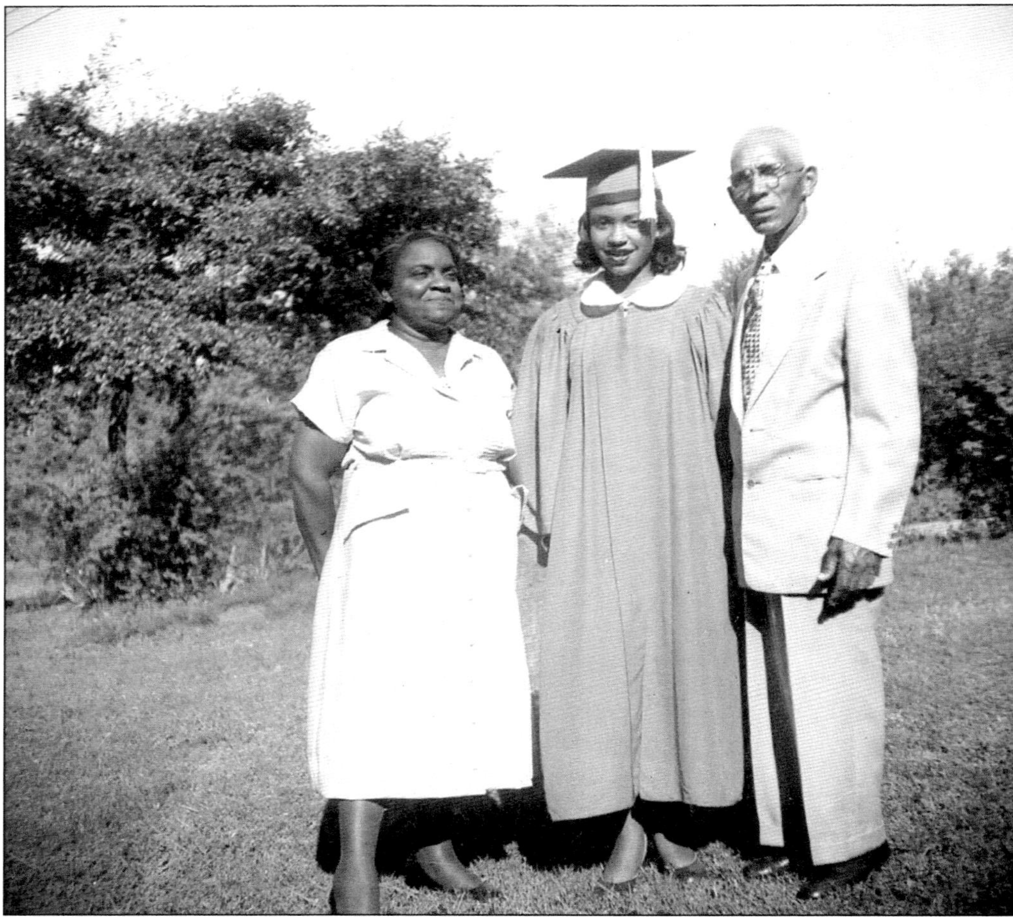

Rosalyn Victoria Mitchell is shown with her parents, Rev. Walter Melvin Mitchell and Hazeltine Jones Mitchell, in front of their home at 111 Whitehall Street in Madison, after graduating from Pearl High School 1954. Her father, who was chairman of the Civic League of Morgan County and the pastor of three churches and moderator of the Madison Missionary Baptist Association, organized local landowners to petition for the new modern high school for African Americans. Her mother, a registered nurse and schoolteacher, started the first nursery school for African Americans. Dr. Rosalyn Mitchell Patterson now lives in Atlanta and continues to carry on the legacy of service to humanity established by her parents in Morgan County. She is an ordained minister, technical writer, research scientist, and educator. She has a long list of honors, awards, accomplishments, and publications. Dr. Patterson was formerly a professor of biology at Spelman College and Atlanta University, as well as department chair of the latter. She is currently an Environmental Protection Agency scientist. (Courtesy Dr. Rosalyn Mitchell Patterson.)

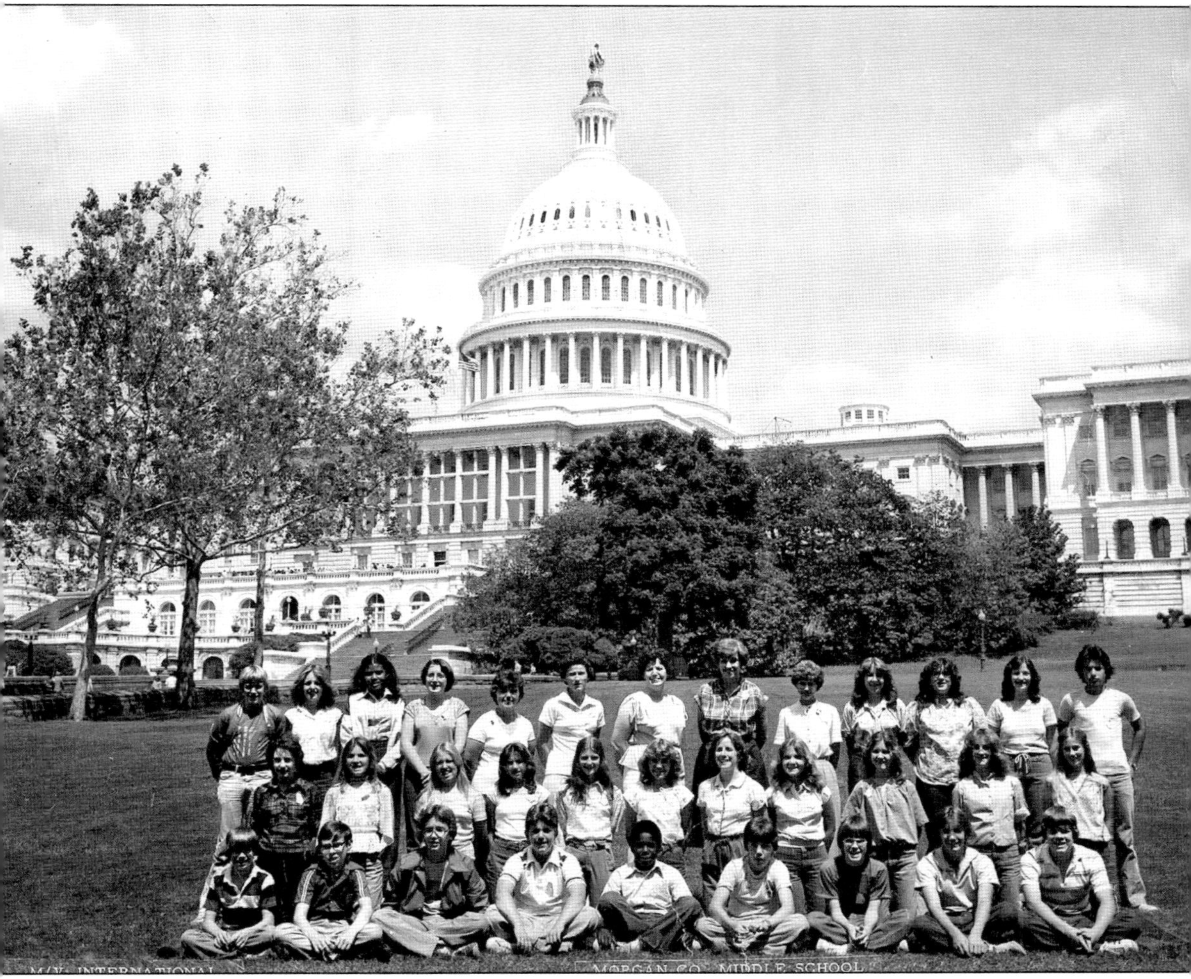

The enrichment class of Morgan County Middle School in 1979 included Karen LaWuane Peek (back row, third from left) and James Lett (middle, front row). Students were selected because of academic excellence in the classroom and test scores. After graduating from Morgan County High School, Karen received a bachelor of science degree in psychology from Howard University, a master's degree in city planning from Georgia Institute of Technology, and a doctorate in business administration from Nova Southeastern University. James Lett joined the military. (Courtesy Minnie Peek.)

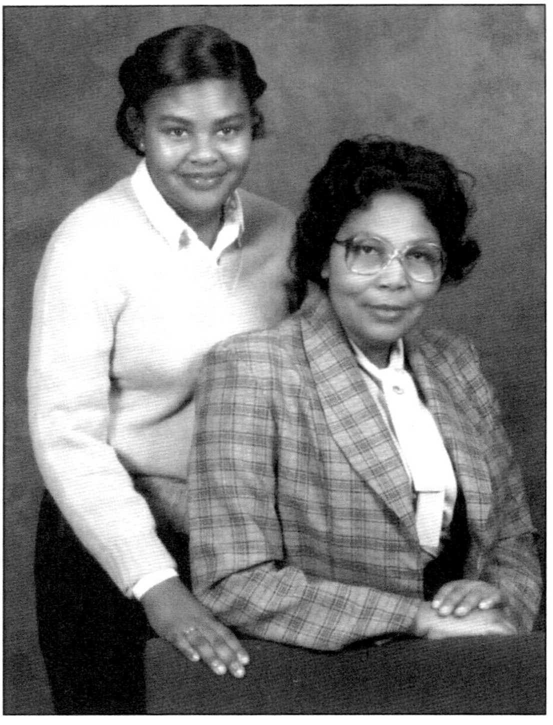

Minnie Peek earned a master's degree in science education from the University of Georgia. She is a member the Georgia Science Teacher Association, Georgia State Board of Hearing Aid Dealers and Dispensers, Morgan County African-American Museum, Morgan County Landmarks, and Morgan County Church of Christ. Her daughter, Dr. Karen L. Peek Warrior, works for the federal government as director of the Atlanta North Service Center. (Courtesy Minnie Peek.)

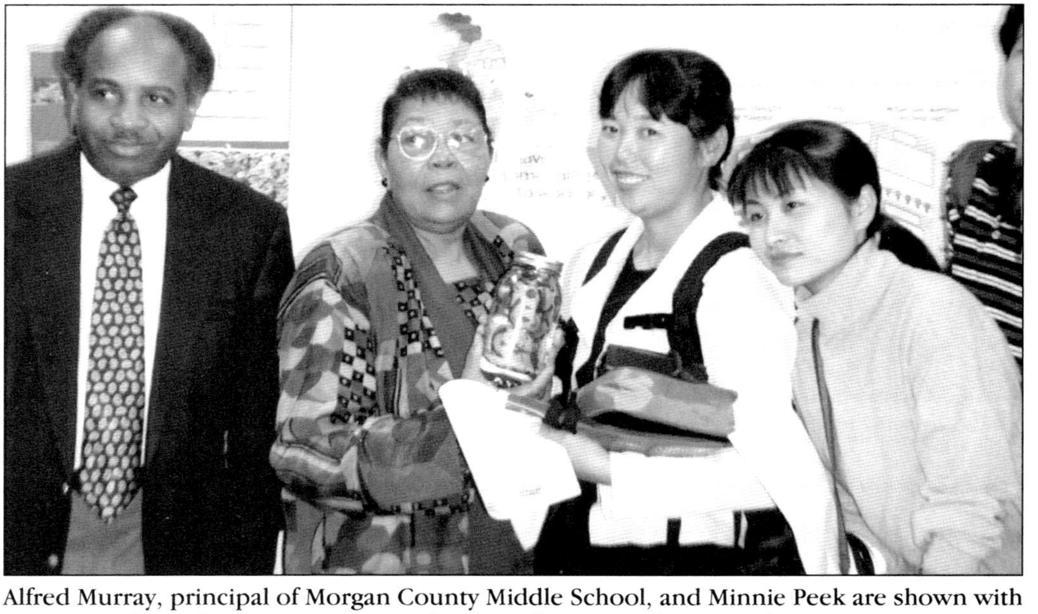

Alfred Murray, principal of Morgan County Middle School, and Minnie Peek are shown with visiting students from Japan. Mrs. Peek was well respected as a teacher in Morgan County. Many students have learned science and been inspired to excel because of her love for the subject and her dedication to teaching. Murray, once Mrs. Peek's student, is currently assistant principal at Morgan County High School and the pastor of Pleasant Grove Baptist Church. (Courtesy Minnie Peek.)

When Minnie Peek retired from teaching, the family celebrated by going on a cruise together. Minnie had taught at schools in Madison, Forsyth, and Watkinsville, including her alma mater, Pearl High School, as well as Morgan County Middle School. She was also among the first African-American teachers at Oconee High School when schools integrated there in 1966. From left to right are Minnie Peek, Bernice Sherrod, Dexter Warrior, Karen Warrior, and Charles Warrior, with Ruby Warrior in the center. (Courtesy Minnie Peek.)

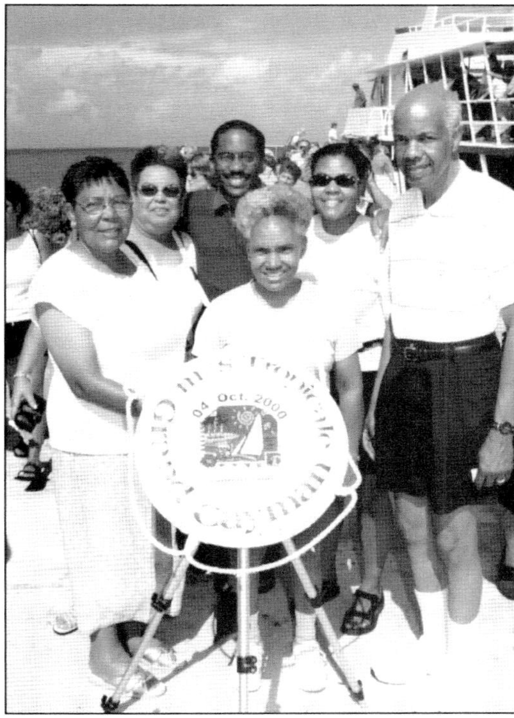

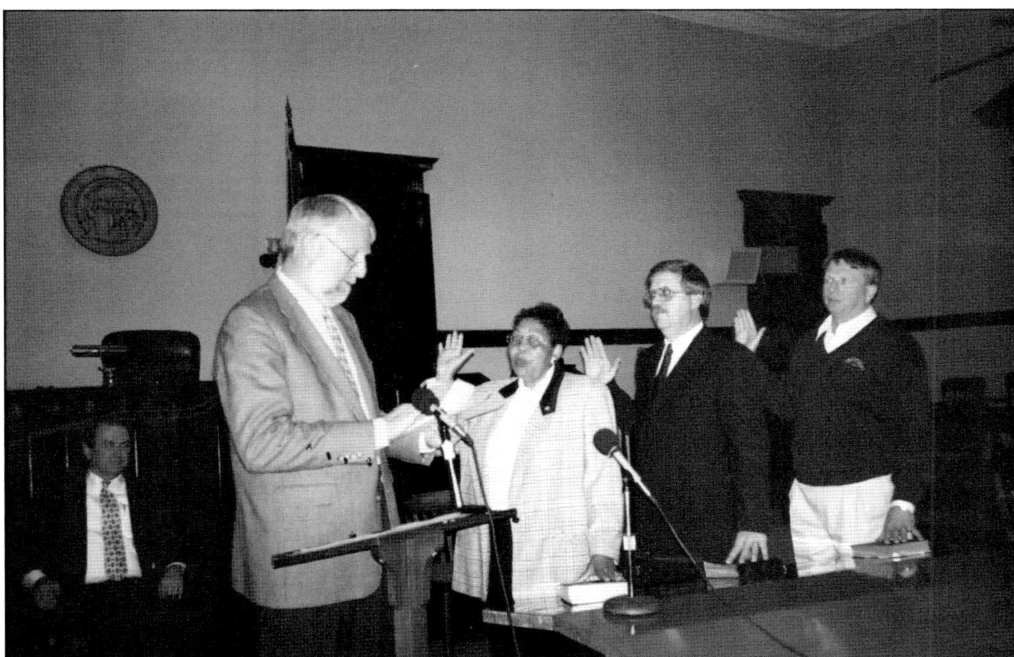

Mrs. Minnie Peek is sworn in as a member of the Morgan County Board of Education District 1 in 2000. Seated are Judge William Pryor and Judge Michael Bracewell. Members are Minnie Peek, James Paxon, and Ronnie Stapp. (Courtesy Minnie Peek.)

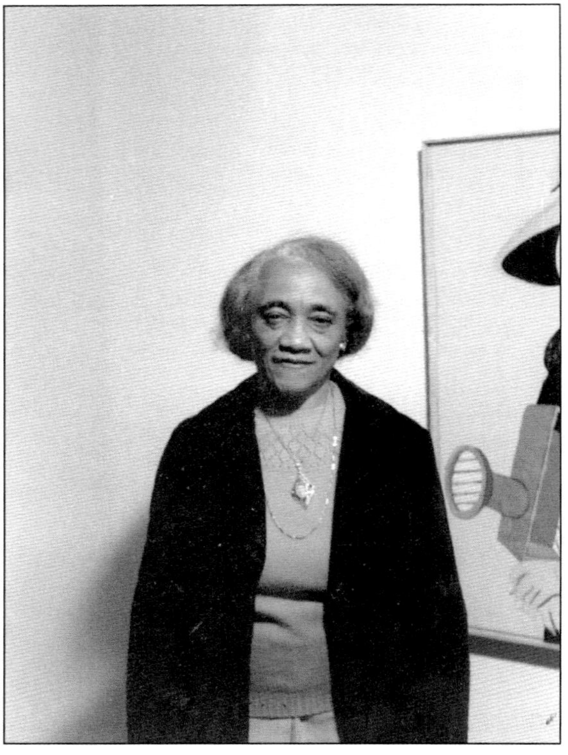

Viola Andrews, writer and mother of artist Benny Andrews, is shown at the opening reception of the exhibit "Women I Have Know Part II." This exhibit of works by Morgan County native Benny Andrews was held on March 3, 1970, at Lerner Heller Gallery in New York City. Viola became the first member of the Andrews family to have a work published when one of her articles appeared in a local newspaper. (Courtesy Benny Andrews.)

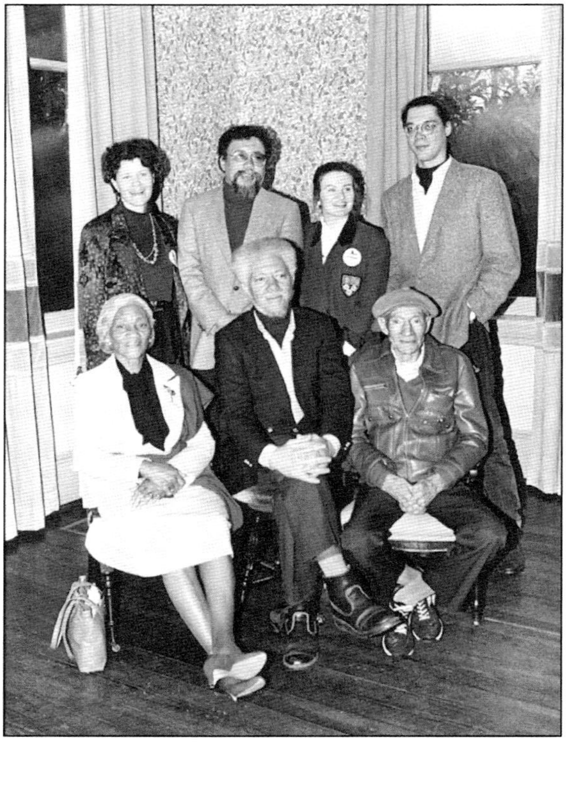

Seated from left to right are Viola, Benny, and George Andrews. Standing from left to right are Lisa Hammett, Raymond Andrews, Tamela Thomas, and Christopher Andrews. This photo was taken at the Madison-Morgan Cultural Center on February 18, 1990. Raymond Andrews won the James Baldwin Prize for fiction in 1978 for his first and best-known novel, *Appalachee Red*. He left behind three book-length manuscripts when he died in 1991. (Courtesy Benny Andrews.)

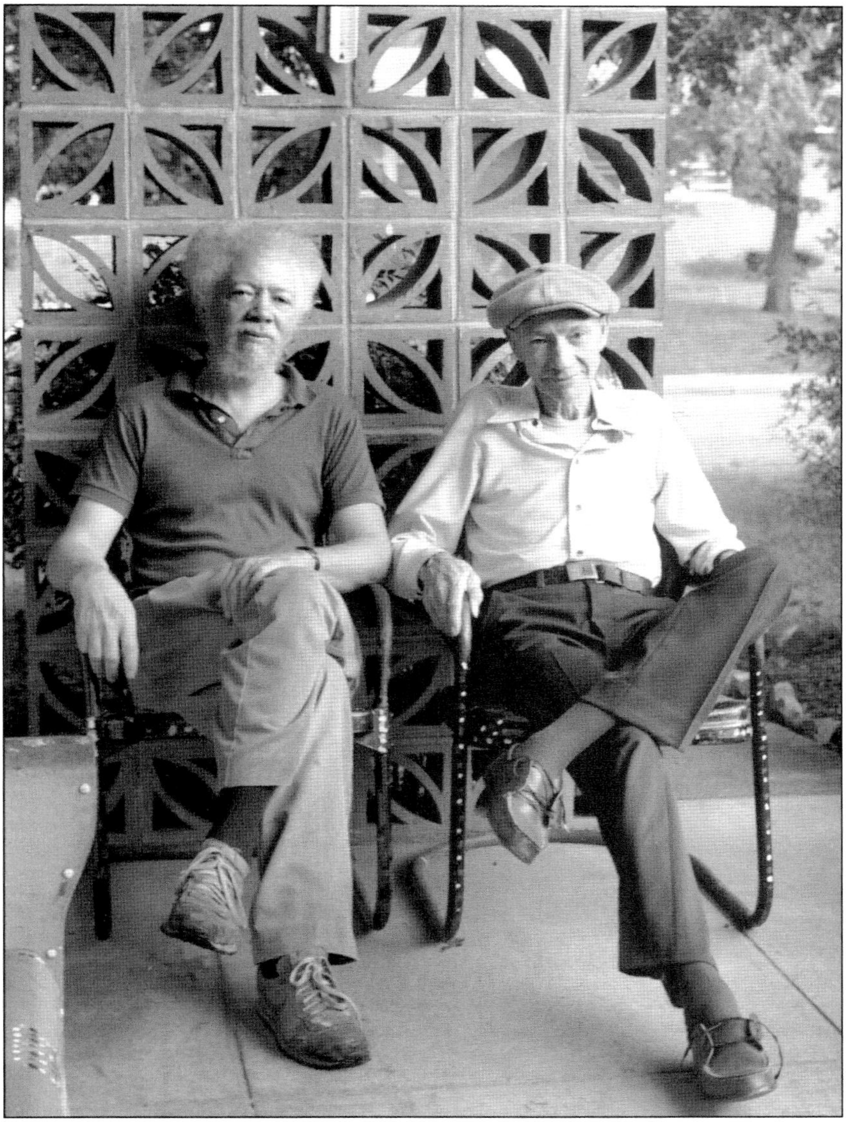

Internationally famous artist Benny Andrews and his father George Andrews, the Dot Man, collaborated on the national touring exhibition "Folk: The Art of Benny and George Andrews." This exhibit included painted objects, collages, paintings, and drawings. George, a self-taught artist, lived in the city's government housing project in Madison for 35 years. Much of George's work was inspired by elements of life in rural Morgan County and Madison. Benny, an artist, teacher, writer, and activist, has been called a master of collage. Benny's art is in the Metropolitan Museum of Art, the Museum of Modern Art, and many others. He was the first African-American director of the Visual Arts Program of the National Endowment for the Arts, was the recipient of the Abby Award for lifetime achievement in arts, and founded The Benny Andrews Foundation for the Benefit of the Arts. William Zimmer said, "Andrews is something of a latter-day Walt Whitman, the trailblazing poet who caught the nuances of American and celebrated both what was taken for granted and what was passed over, unseen by others." (Courtesy NeNe Humphrey.)

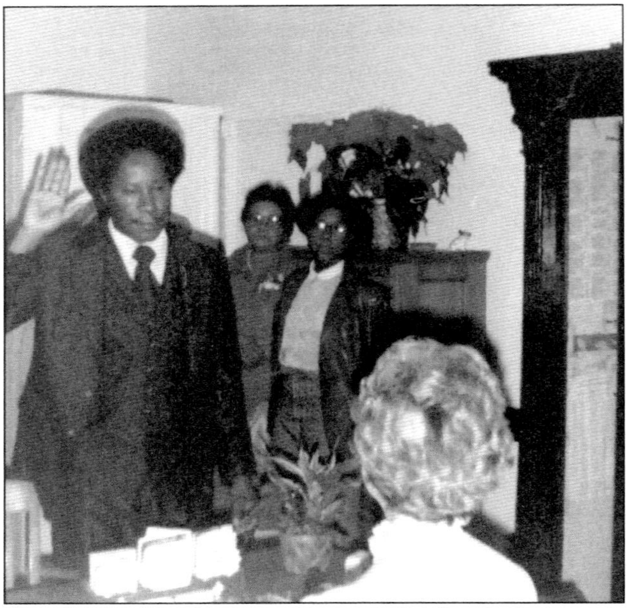

Walter Curtis Butler Jr. is sworn in as a county commissioner of Morgan County in 1983. Butler was campaign coordinator for the 10th Congressional District for Gov. George Busbee and served on the Northeast Georgia Area Planning and Development Commission, Board of Action Inc., and Community Action Committee. He is a member of numerous organizations, including Madison Masonic Lodge #209, Association of County Commissioners of Georgia, and Black Caucus of Georgia. (Courtesy Laura W. Butler.)

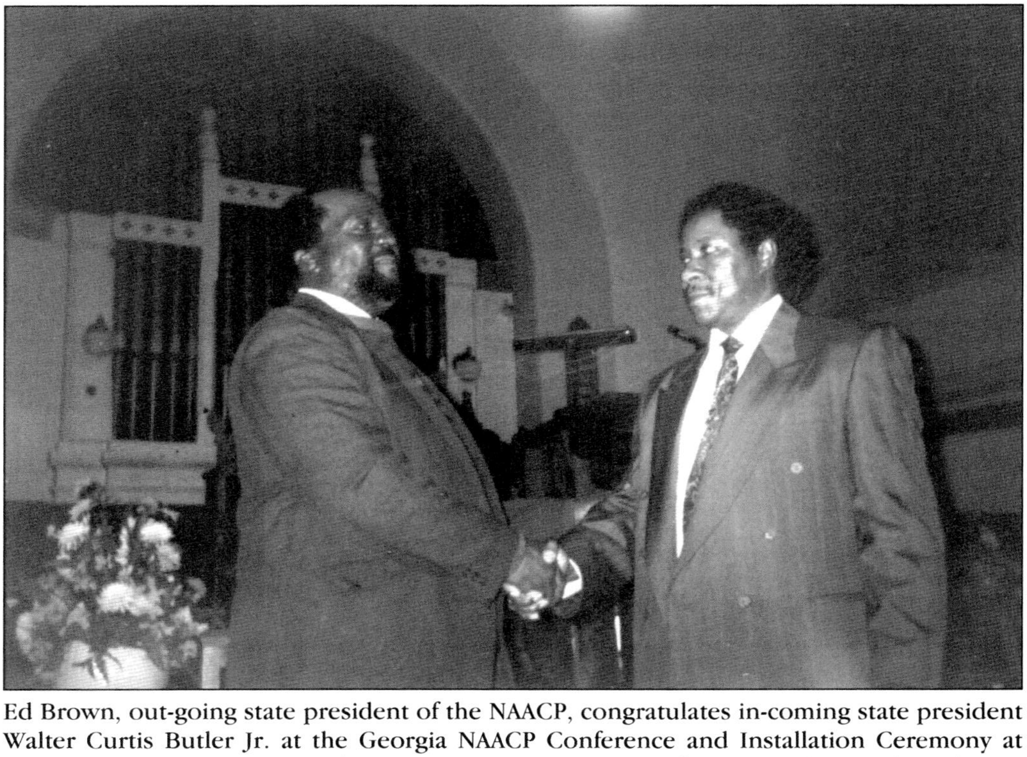

Ed Brown, out-going state president of the NAACP, congratulates in-coming state president Walter Curtis Butler Jr. at the Georgia NAACP Conference and Installation Ceremony at Stewart Chapel A.M.E. Church in Macon, Georgia, in 1994. Prior to being elected state president, Butler was a member of the state and county Democratic Party, assisted in founding the Morgan County NAACP, and served as president and vice-president of state NAACP branches. (Courtesy Laura W. Butler.)

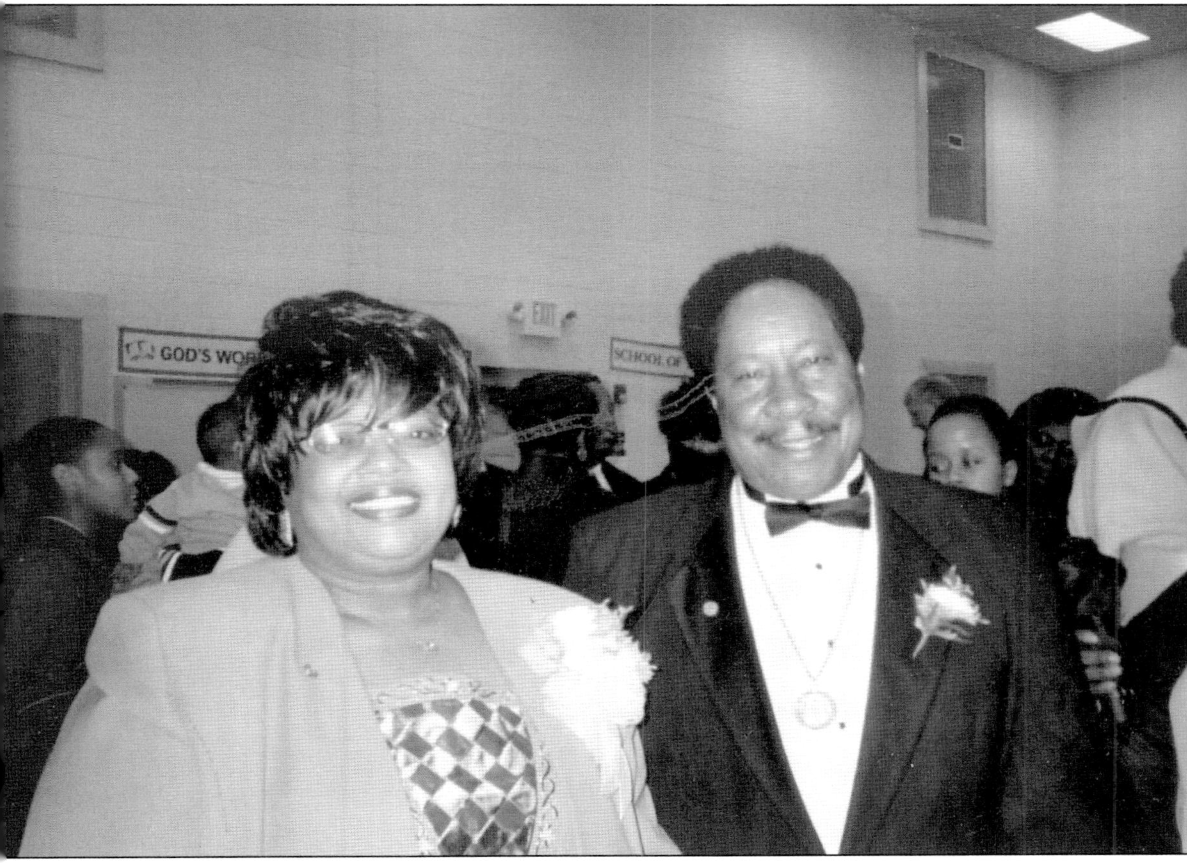

Walter Curtis Butler Jr. and Laura W. Butler are both well known in Morgan County. In addition to being supportive of her husband's political and civic activities, Laura is currently the president of the Morgan County branch of the NAACP, an active member of Calvary Baptist Church, the American Cancer Society, and Madison O.E.S. 165; a Morgan County Headstart volunteer; and owner of Ma's Butler Childcare. (Courtesy Laura W. Butler.)

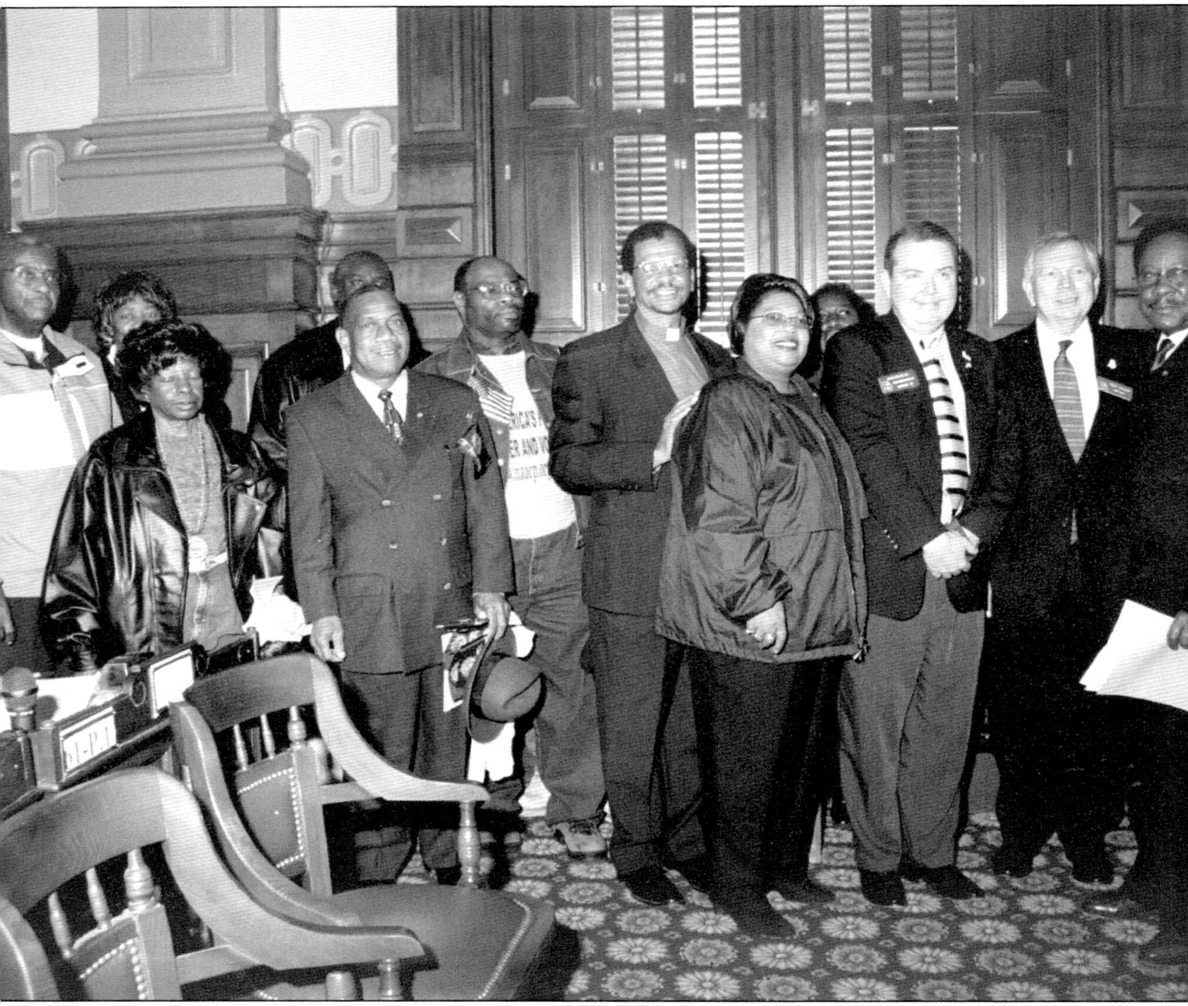

The Morgan County branch of the NAACP is shown at the Georgia capitol. They had traveled to Atlanta to discuss the issue of the Georgia flag with their state representative. Shown from left to right are (front row) Forestine Puryear, Rev. W.J. Reid, Rev. Hoke L. Smith, Laura Butler, John Douglas (state representative district 73), Terry Coleman (Speaker of the House), and Walter Curtis Butler Jr.; (back row) Joseph Biggs, Sandra Williams, Ministers W.L. Williams and Michael Ross Sr., and Cassandra Andrews. (Courtesy Laura W. Butler.)

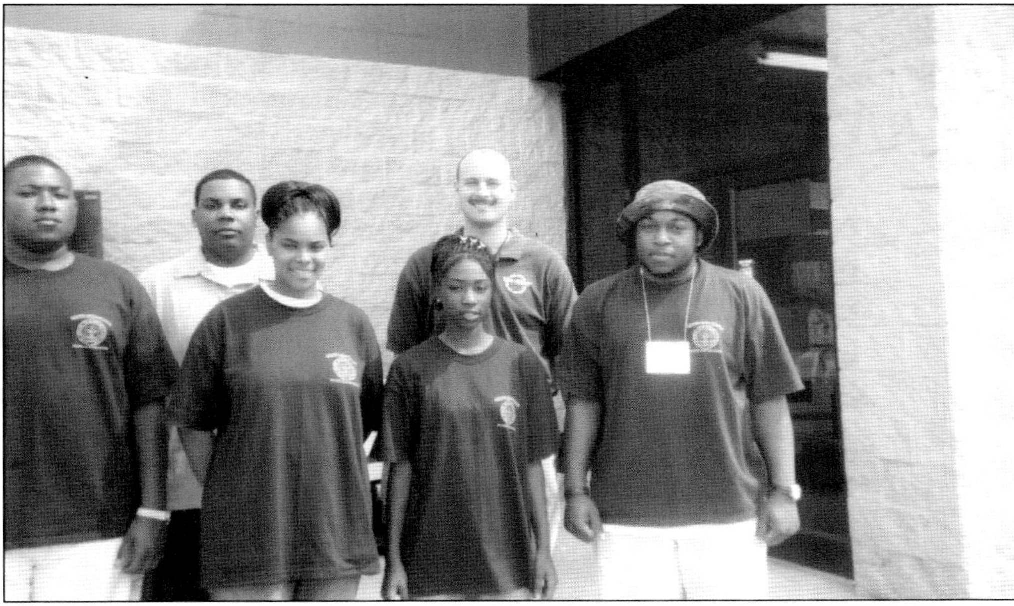

From left to right are (front row) Walter Curtis Butler III, Lashana Smalls, Kassandra McCray, and Michael Ross Jr.; (back row) Cory Colbert and the manager of Wal-Mart. Morgan County NAACP Youth Council held a membership drive for Southeast Region 5. They also held a car wash and provided customer assistance to raise funds, which were matched by Wal-Mart. (Courtesy Laura W. Butler.)

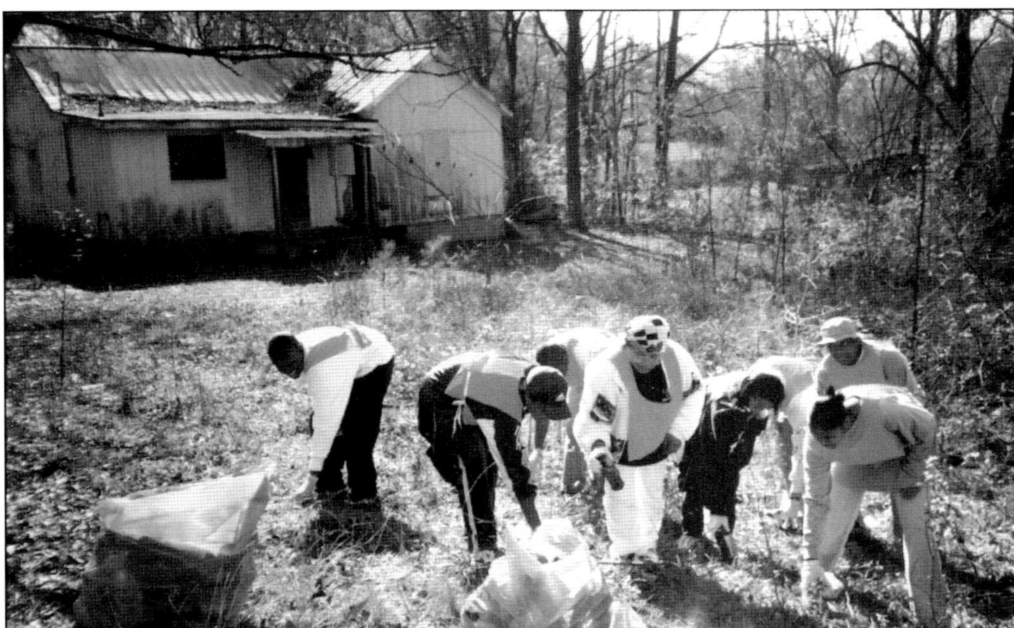

Members of the Youth Council are participating in a neighborhood clean-up project at the corner of Pearl and Eliza Morris Streets in Madison. The Youth Council was organized in 1969 and received its charter in 1970. (Courtesy Laura W. Butler.)

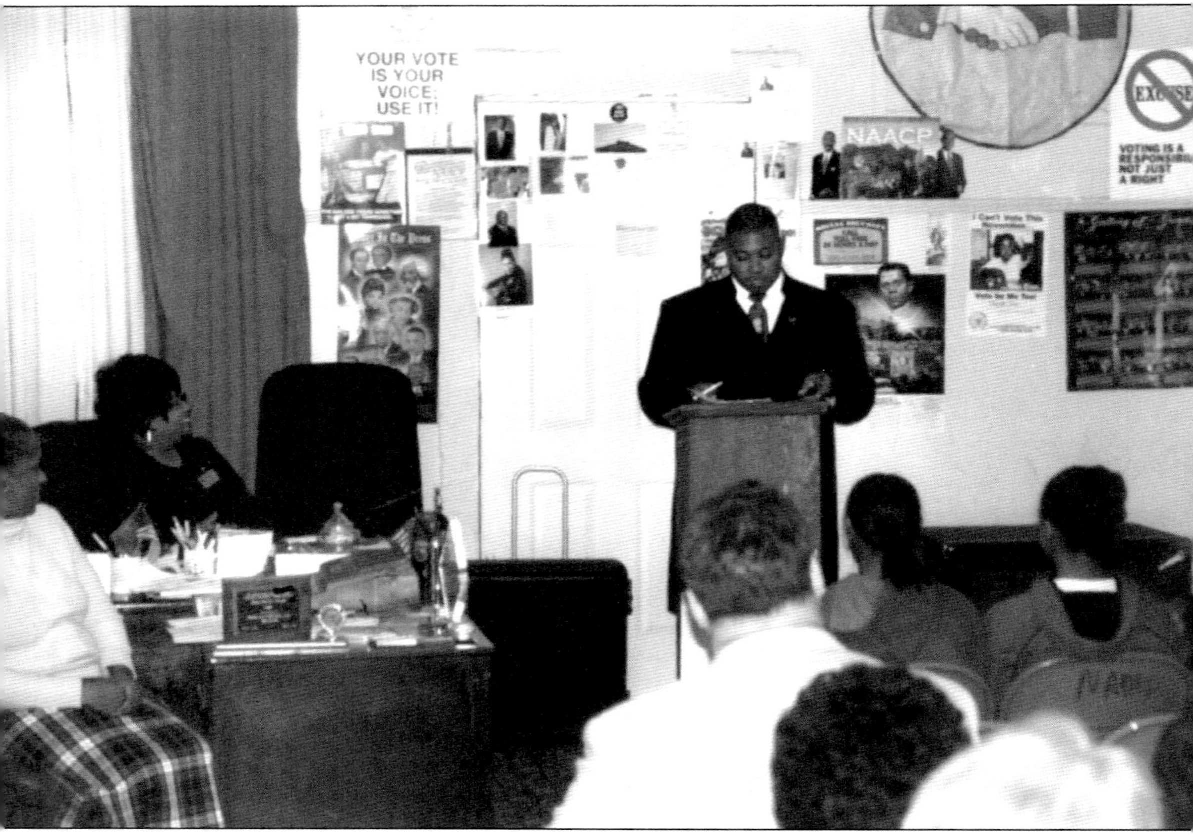

Walter Curtis Butler III was the guest speaker at the NAACP Birthday Celebration 2004. Walter is a student at Fort Valley State University where he is the NAACP president. This celebration was organized and sponsored by the Morgan County Youth Council. (Courtesy Laura W. Butler.)

Six

PRESERVING AND CELEBRATING OUR HERITAGE AND CULTURE

No man is fit to be entrusted with the control of the present, who is ignorant of the past, no people who are indifferent to their past, need hope to make their future great.
Author unknown

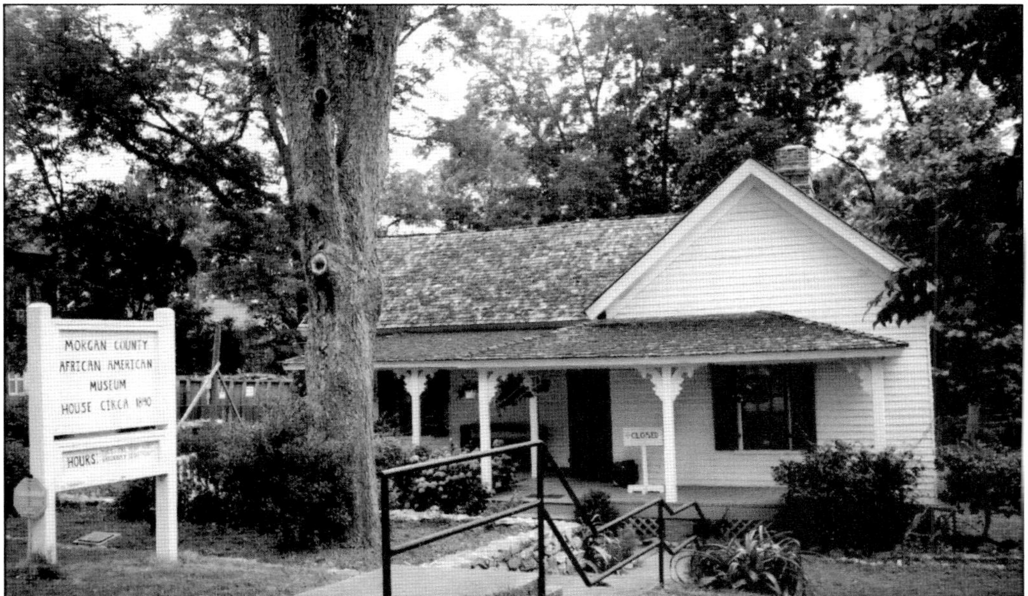

Morgan County African-American Museum opened in 1993 on Academy Street in Madison. It houses local history and artifacts from the community. Among the many supporters of the museum was Miss Carroll Hart, who purchased two paintings by St. Simons Island folk-artist Annabelle Lee for the museum through contact with Mrs. Mildred Bass. The museum has also acquired collections of folk-art and sculpture from Africa, as well as from other parts of Georgia and the United States, that interpret African-American heritage and culture. (Courtesy the author.)

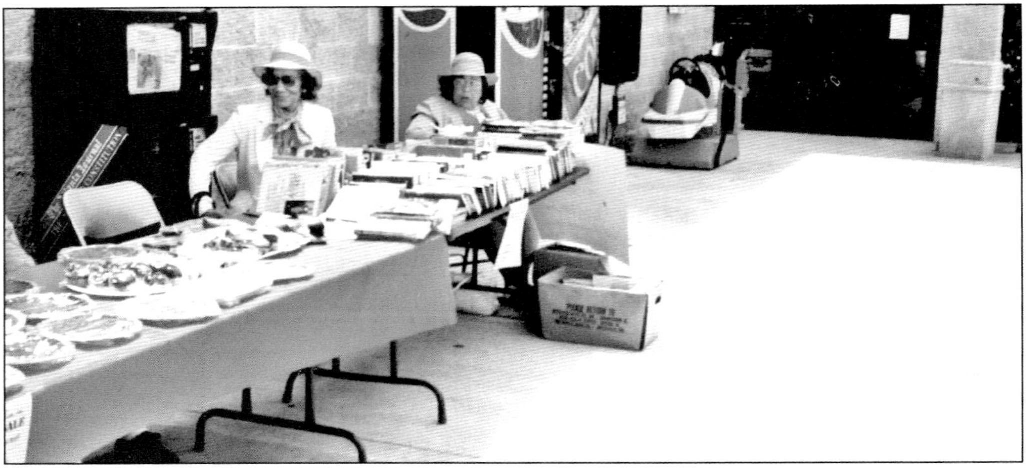

Mrs. Marie Bass Martin and her sister-in-law Mrs. Martin (Mildred) Bass Jr. are shown conducting a fund-raiser for the Morgan County Museum. Both worked to lay the groundwork for the museum. Marie and her brother, Martin, provided the land. Mildred used her exceptional communication, organizational skills, and contacts in establishing the museum. Both continue to serve on the board of directors of the museum. (Courtesy Mildred Bass.)

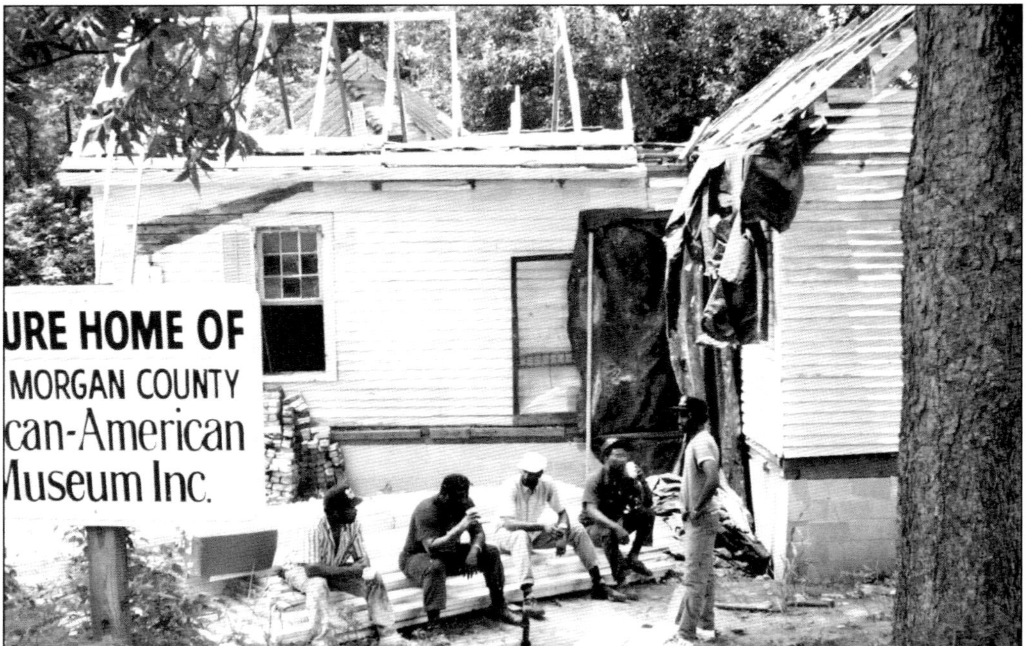

These men work at the future site of the Morgan County African-American Museum. John Wesley Moore built the house, which now is designated as the museum, *c.* 1890s. Moore was a farmhand for James A. Fanin, who deeded to Moore 41 5/8 acres of land for $5. Alfred Murray donated the house for use as the museum. The house was considered a "middle-class home" during those times and was located near Round Bowl Springs, where Madison was founded. (Courtesy Mildred Bass.)

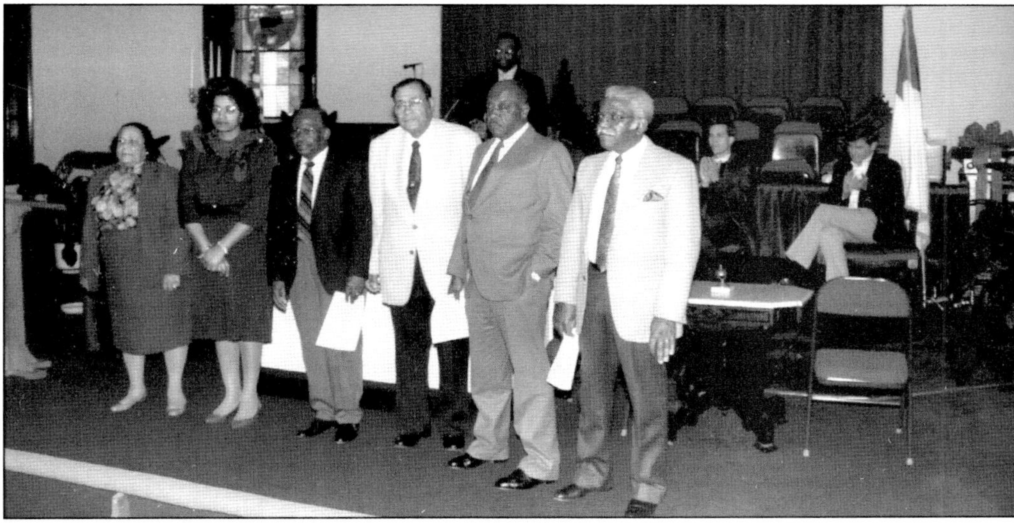

The groundbreaking and dedication of the museum was held at Calvary Baptist Church in 1993. Reverend and Mrs. Perriman hosted the first meeting of the museum officials in their home, with Martin Bass Jr., Henry Veasley, John Paul Jones, E.L. Gardner, Mamie Jackson Caldwell, and Marie Bass Martin attending. Many people in the community donated time, talents, money, and artifacts to the museum. (Courtesy Mildred Bass.)

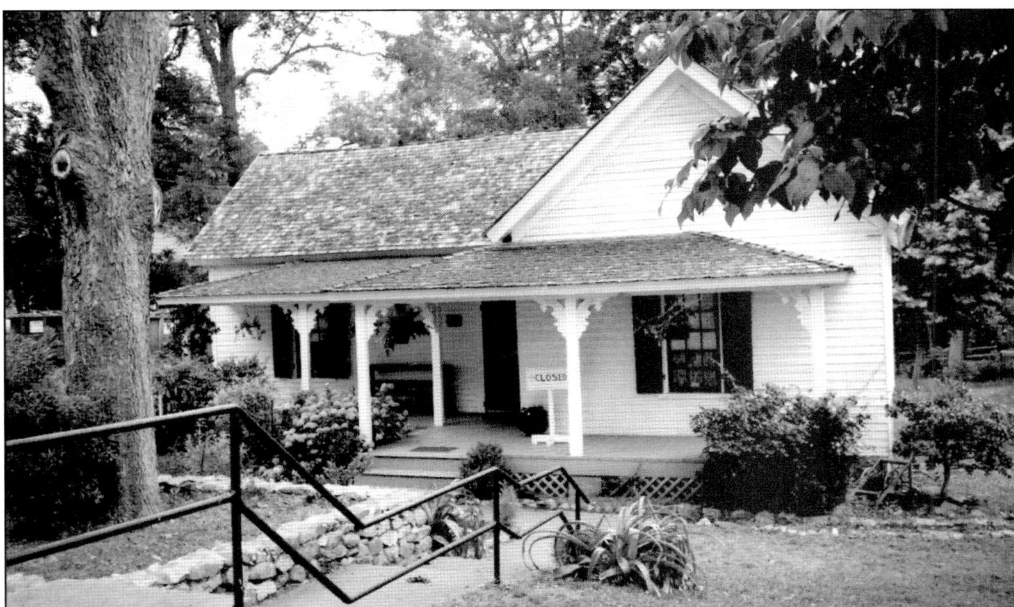

The Morgan County African-American Museum draws visitors today from near and far. Mr. and Mrs. Martin Bass Jr., Rev. and Mrs. Fred Perriman, Mamie S. Jackson, Edward Gardner, Columbus Johnson, Mrs. Marie Bass Martin, and Mr. and Mrs. Henry Veasley spearheaded early museum efforts. The museum's advisory board was Benny Andrews, Sara Harrell Banks, Rev. Brain Black, Oscar Crawford, Rev. Charles R. Hasty, and Rev. Alford Murray. (Courtesy the author.)

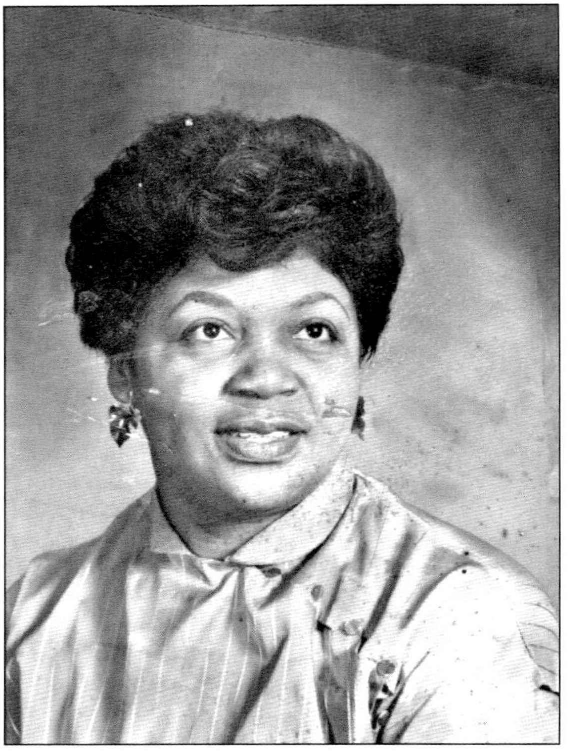

Thelma Griffin was museum director from 1997 to 2002. She graduated from Pearl High School and received a bachelor's degree in English from Savannah State College and a master's degree in English education from Atlanta University. She taught school for 30 years in Georgia, wrote a play depicting African-American life in Morgan County during the 1940s, and has now distinguished herself in the community as the first female minister at Calvary Baptist Church. (Courtesy Thelma Griffin.)

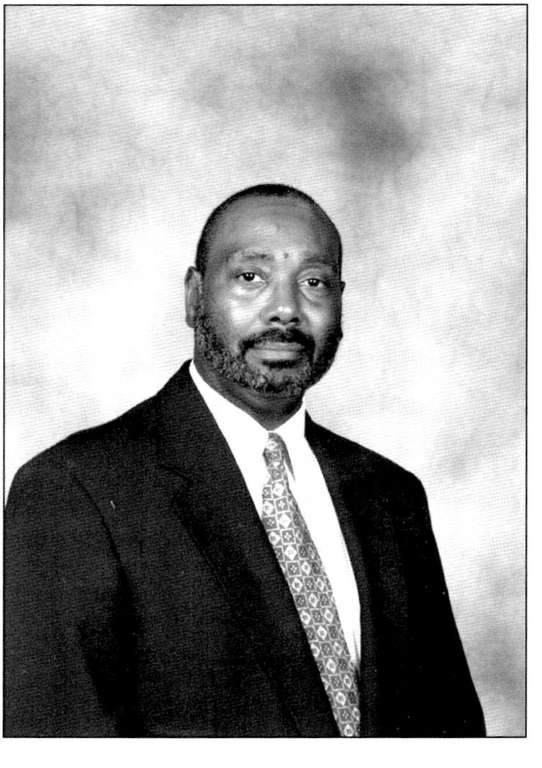

Rev. Fred Perriman, president of the Morgan County African-American Museum; is a lifetime member of the NAACP and a humanitarian. He was honored as an Outstanding Georgia Citizen by Cathy Cox, Secretary of State; has been a city council member for 23 years; and was former chairman and board member of the Morgan County Hospital Authority. He has served on numerous committees and boards. Rev. Fred Perriman and Martin Bass Jr. laid the early groundwork for the museum. (Courtesy Rev. Fred Perriman.)

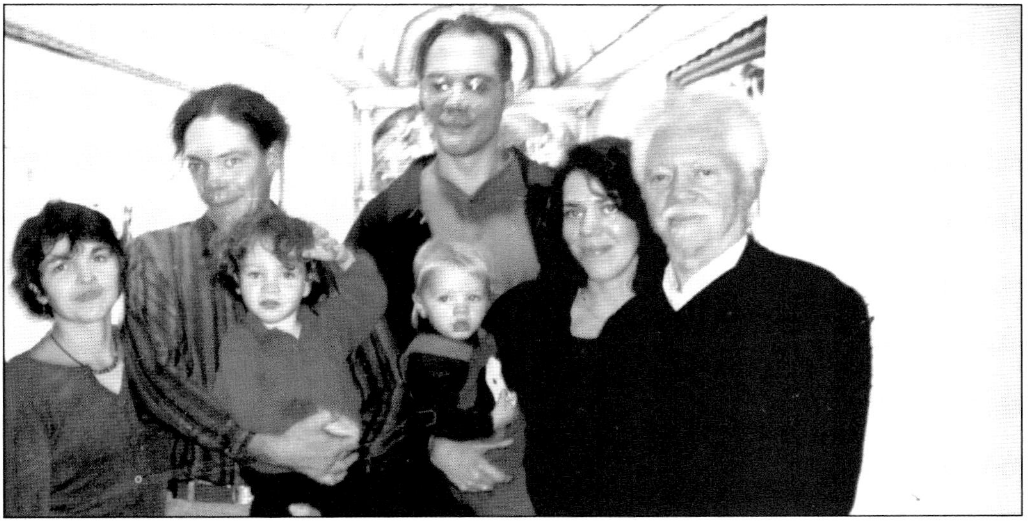

From left to right, Irene, Thomas, Julien, Christopher, Casey, Irene Julia, and Benny Andrews are at the "Critic Series" Exhibition reception in New York. Benny has exhibited his work, which often depicts life experience from growing up in rural Morgan County, in major museums around the country including the Metropolitan Museum of Art. Regarding his work, Benny has been quoted as saying "I believe I'm doing America!" Thomas and Christopher are also artists. (Courtesy Benny Andrews.)

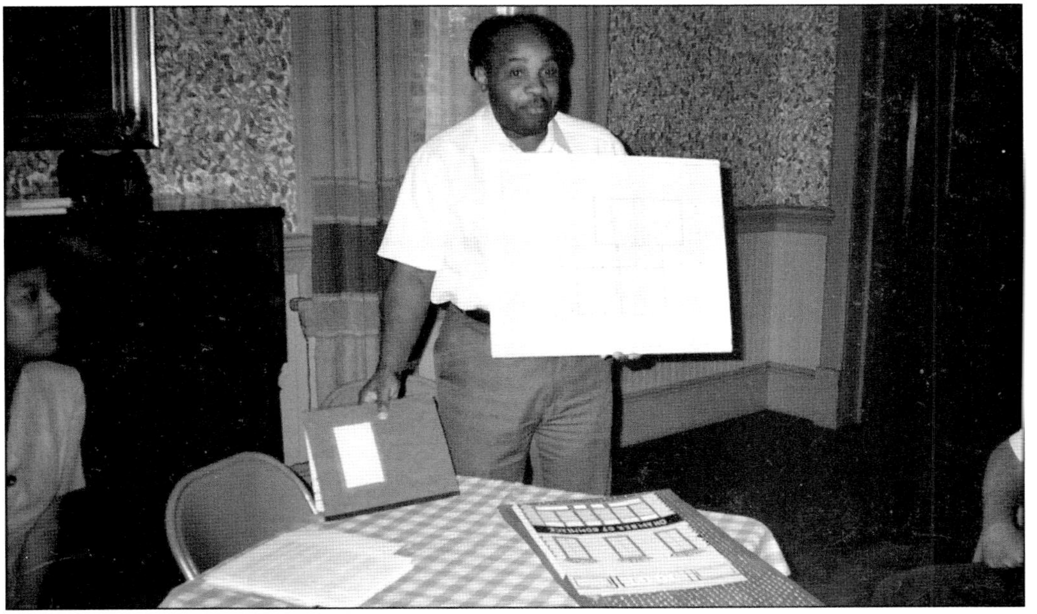

Alfred Murray shows his project while taking the heritage education class. Murray, who was principal of Morgan County Middle School from 1983 to 2002, was born in Morgan County in the Smyrna community and attended Smyrna School. He later attended Burney Street and graduated as valedictorian of Pearl High School. He graduated from Paine College in 1968 with a bachelor's degree in social studies. He has a master's degree from Atlanta University in administration and supervision. (Courtesy Minnie Peek.)

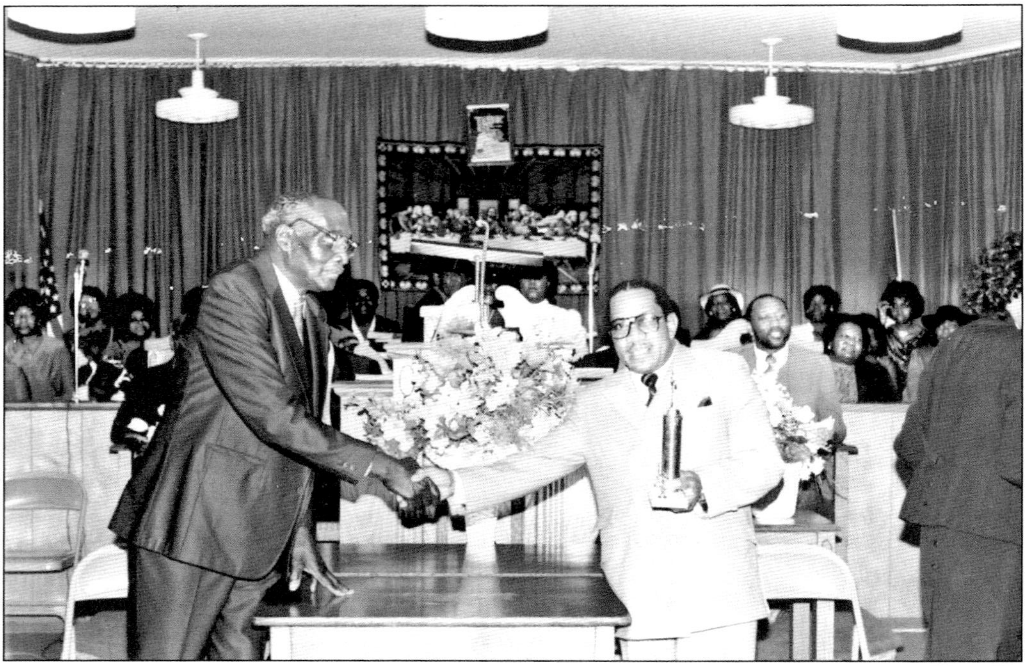

Rev. J.B. Jester and Rev. W.J. Reid are shown at the annual Religious Black History Service, *c.* 1990. Elzata Brown organized this black history celebration in the 1980s as a cooperative celebration for the community and area churches. (Courtesy Elzata Brown.)

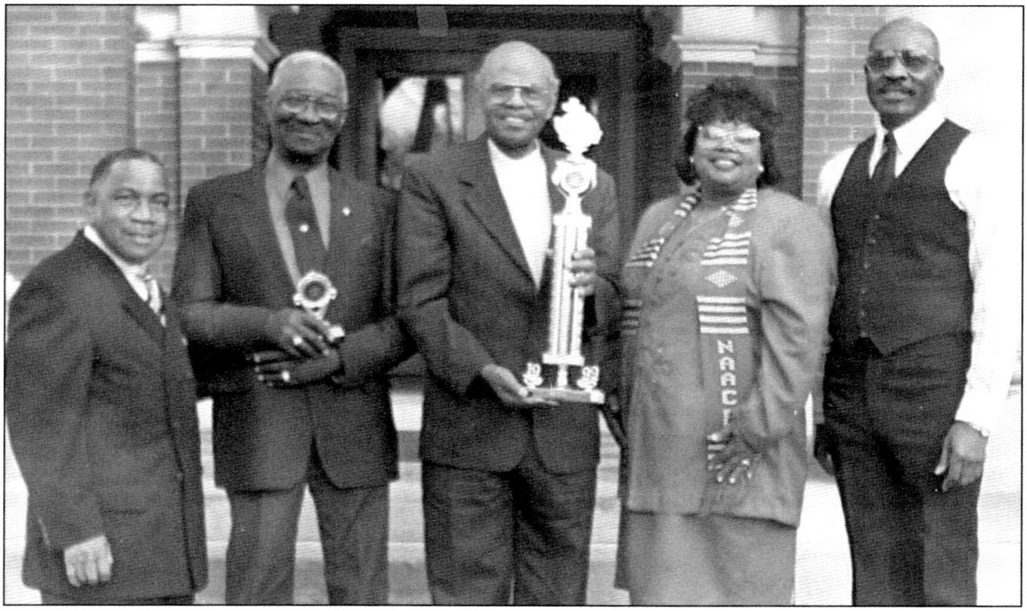

Shown here are Rev. W.J. Reid of Springfield Baptist Church; Rev. A. Baker of New Enon Baptist Church; F.D. Clark of Wallace Grove and Thankful Baptist Church; Laura W. Butler, president of the local branch of the NAACP; and James Edwards, vice-president of the local branch of the NAACP. (Courtesy Laura W. Butler.)

The Morgan County NAACP Freedom Fund Dinner was held December 11, 1977. Rev. Walter Mitchell and Hazeltine Mitchell attended the fund-raiser, where Reverend Mitchell received an award for service to education and civil rights in Madison and Morgan County. (Courtesy Dr. Rosalyn Mitchell Patterson.)

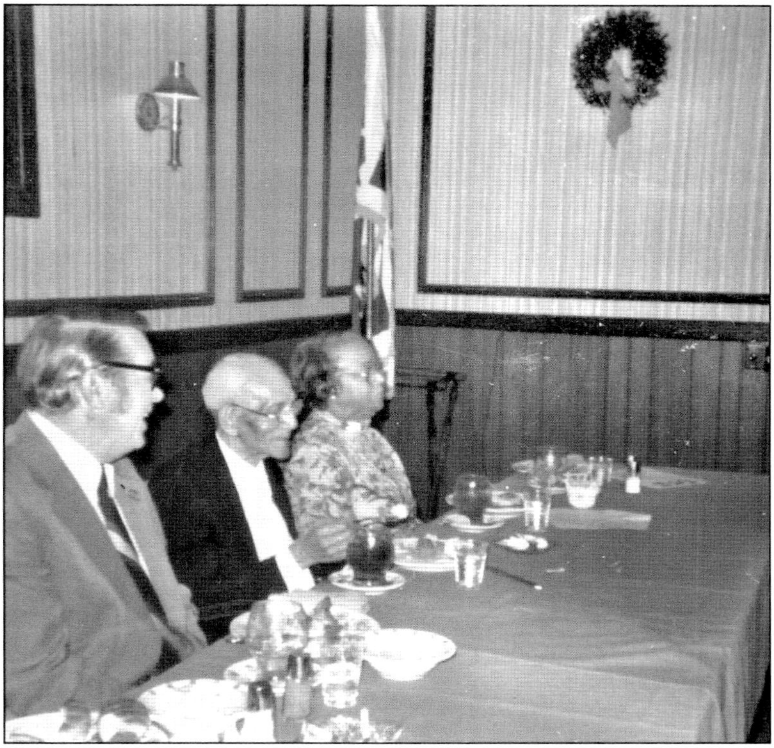

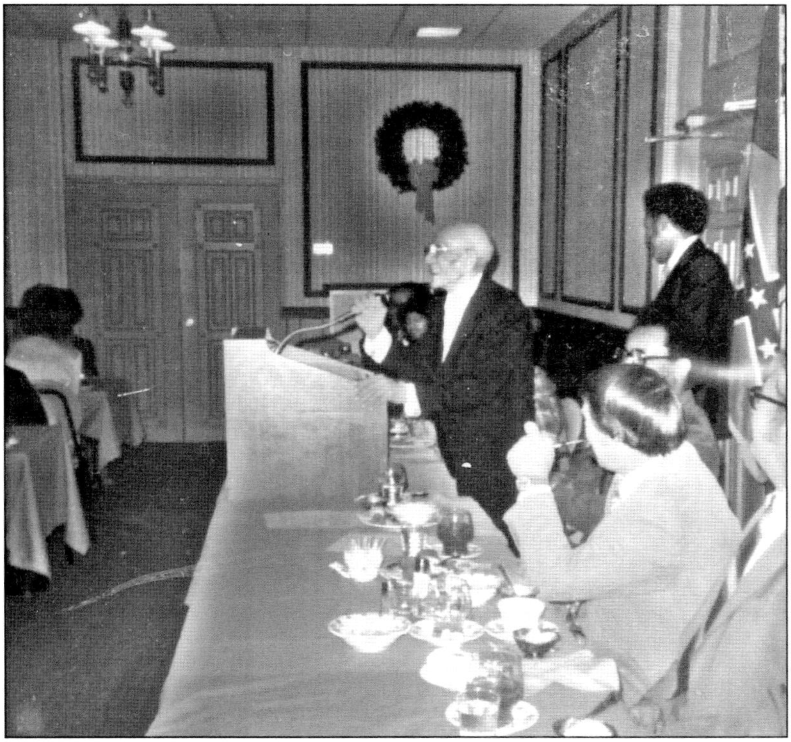

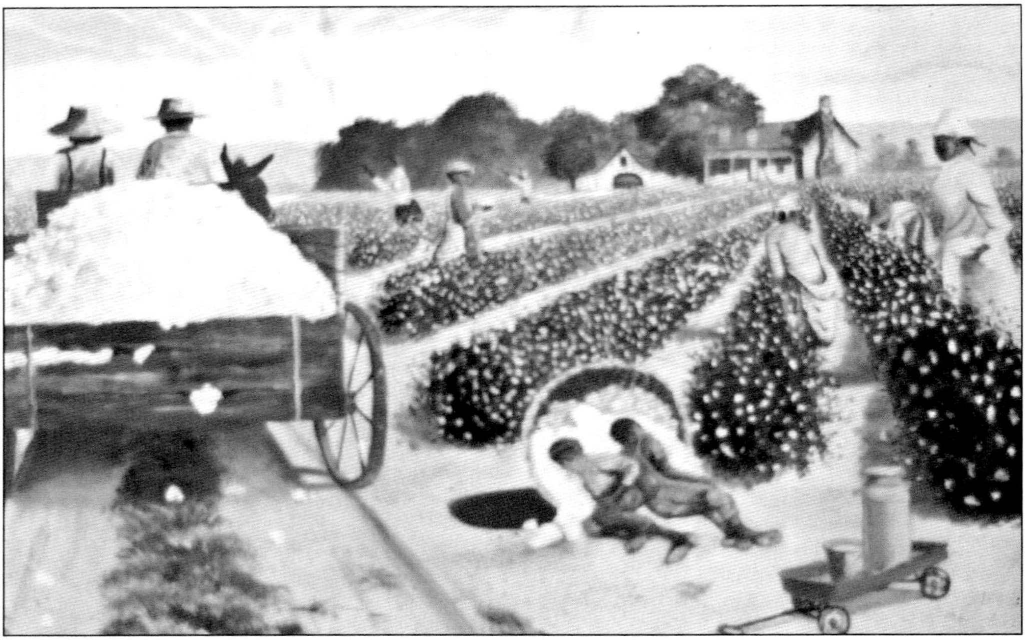

Local artist Eugene Swain paints his memories of scenes and experiences of days long since past in Morgan County. Some of Swain's works currently hang in the Morgan County African-American Museum. The painting shown here depicts a sharecropper's family in a cotton field. (Courtesy Eugene Swain.)

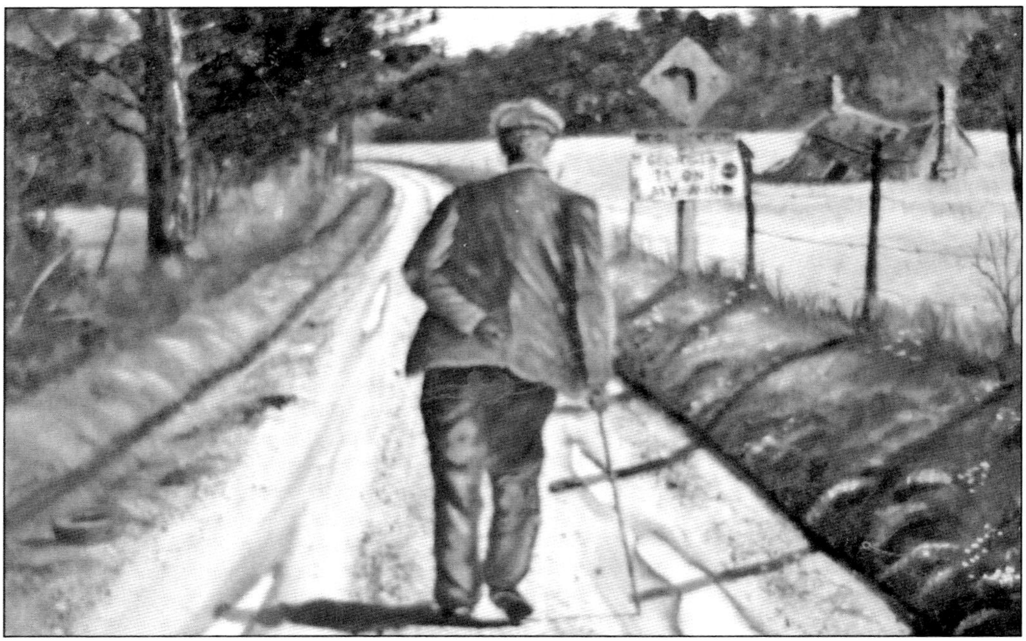

In this painting an older Morgan County resident reflects on the past while walking down a dirt road, looking at vacant pasture, fields, and deteriorating houses. (Courtesy Eugene Swain.)

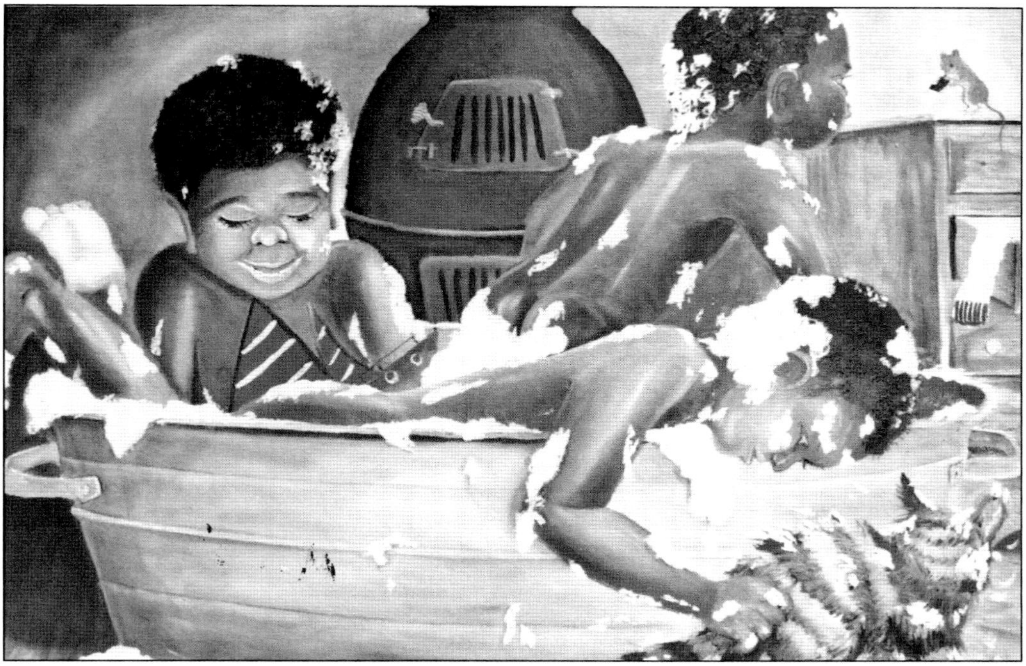

Siblings bathe in a tin tub in front of a pot-bellied, wood-burning stove in this painting. (Courtesy Eugene Swain.)

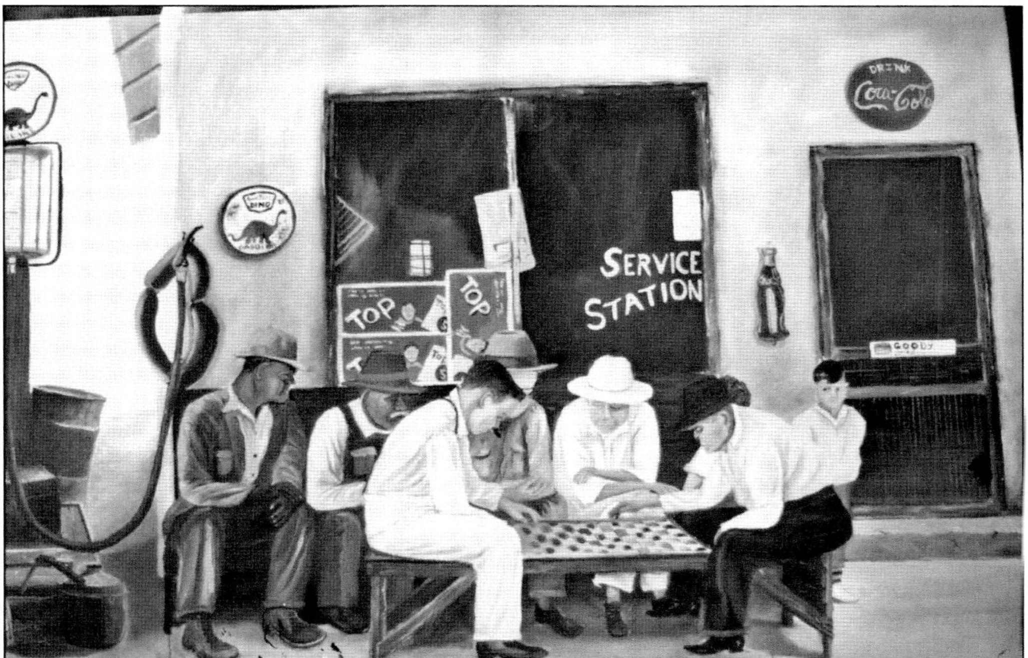

Another of Swain's paintings depicts men passing the time in front of service station by watching and playing games of checkers with neighbors. (Courtesy Eugene Swain.)

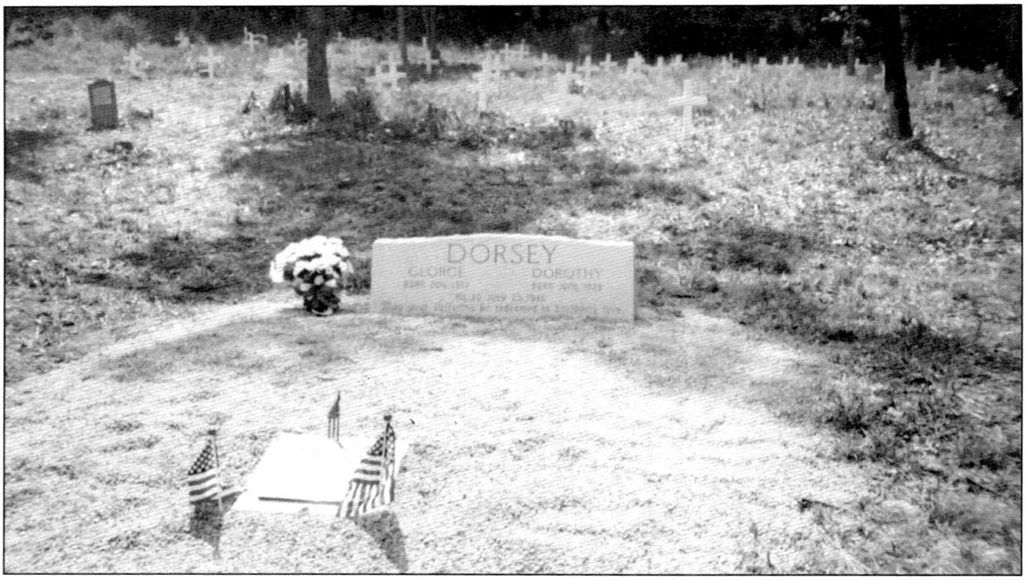

This is the gravesite of lynching victims George Dorsey and Dorothy Malcom. The Moore's Ford Memorial Committee worked 25 Saturdays to clear the Mt. Perry Baptist Church cemetery to locate the unmarked graves. A scout troop from Athens erected and painted white crosses to mark the previously unmarked graves. Neglected gravesites are a symbol of poverty and oppression, and many families leave the area or die out, causing cemeteries to become neglected. (Courtesy the author.)

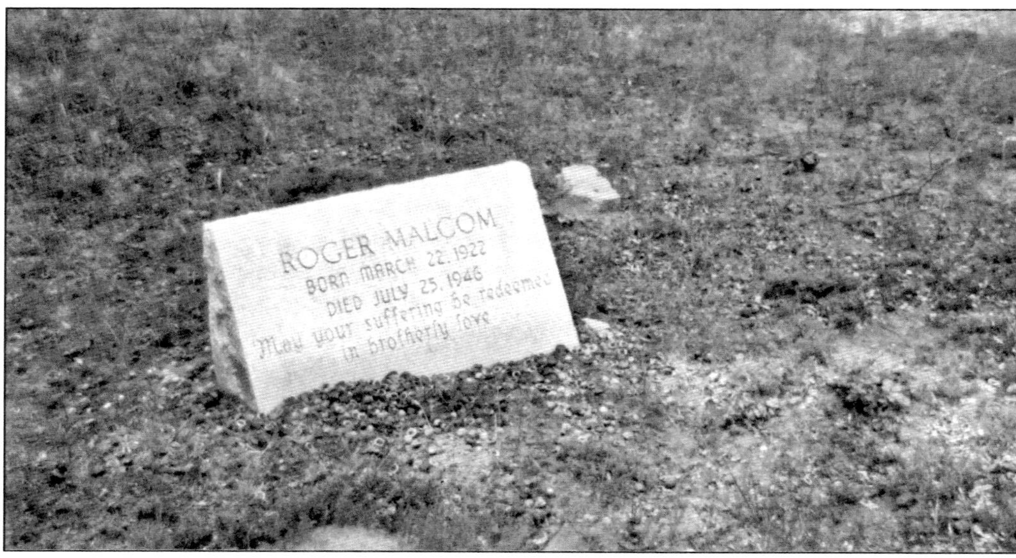

Roger Malcom's grave remained unmarked until 1998, when the Moore's Ford Memorial Committee engaged Joe Ingram to locate Malcom's burial site in the Chestnut Grove Baptist Church cemetery after being lynched in 1946. Ingram, a native of Morgan County and a founding member of the Moore's Ford Memorial Committee, recounted his childhood memories to committee members while leading the group to the grave and placing a marker on it. (Courtesy the author.)

The Robertson Cemetery is located in Bostwick on two acres of land deeded from Sarah Robertson to her former slave, William Robertson, in 1880. (Courtesy the author.)

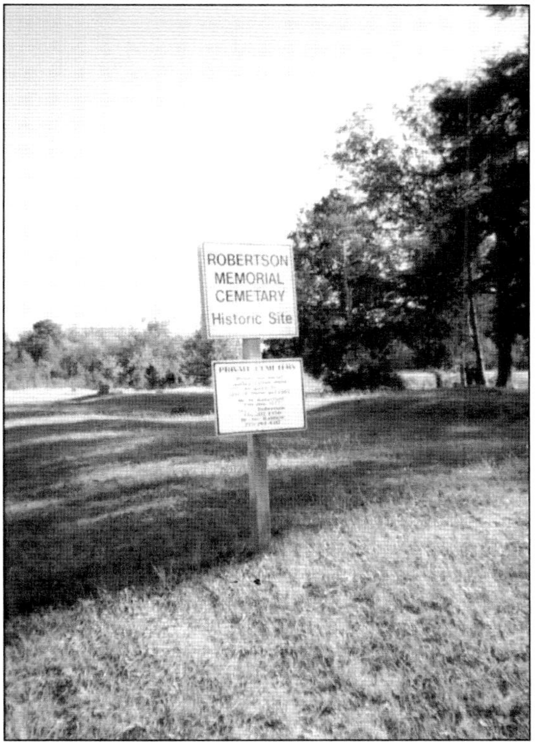

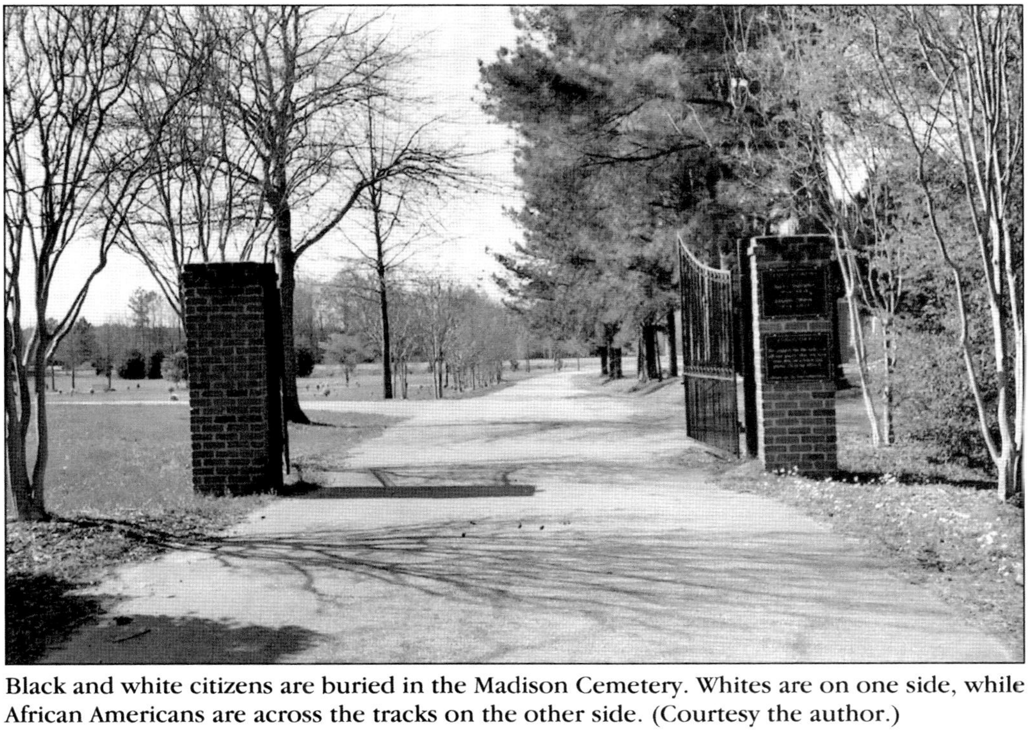

Black and white citizens are buried in the Madison Cemetery. Whites are on one side, while African Americans are across the tracks on the other side. (Courtesy the author.)

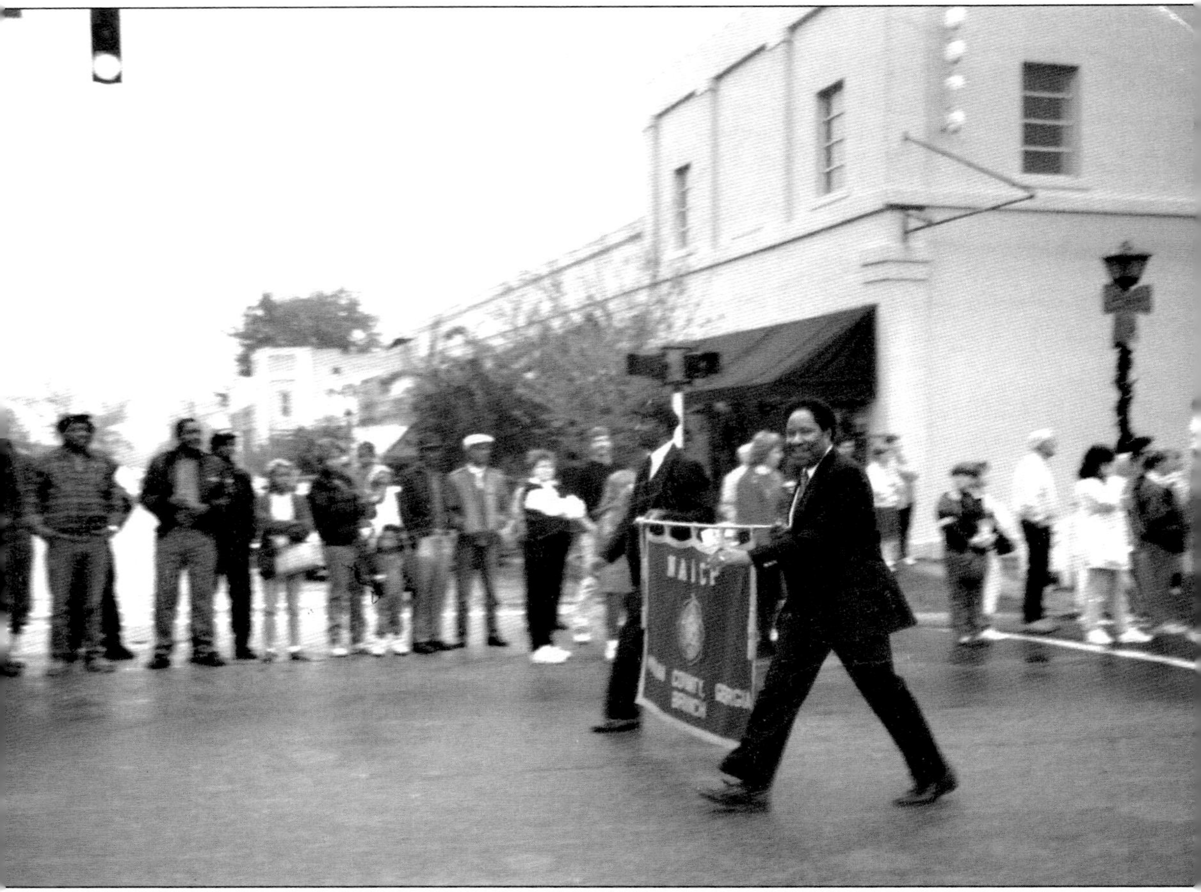

Walter Curtis Butler Jr. and James Edwards carry the NAACP banner for the first parade celebrating African-American history in Morgan County. The parade, conceived by Elzata Brown, was held on Main Street and was the only one of its kind in the area. (Courtesy Laura W. Butler.)

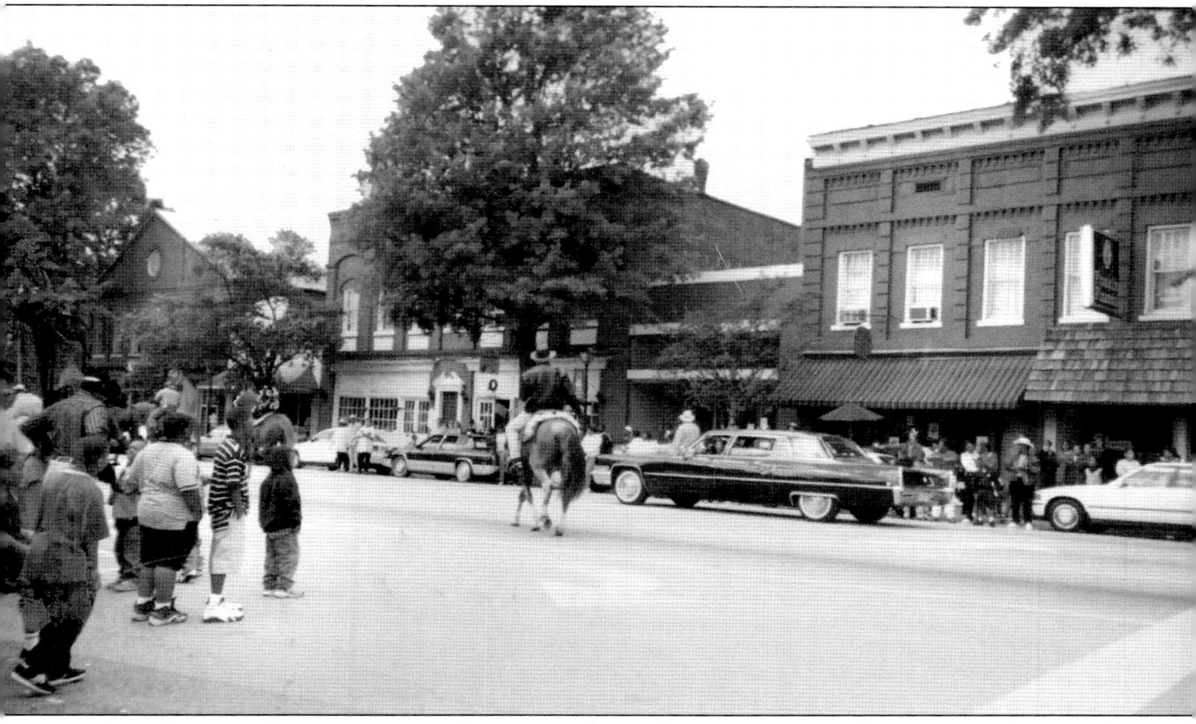

Elzata Brown rides on a vintage limousine driven by Waymon Mundy in 1998. Elzata said she got the idea for the parade while trying to think of something to bring the community together. (Courtesy Elzata Brown.)

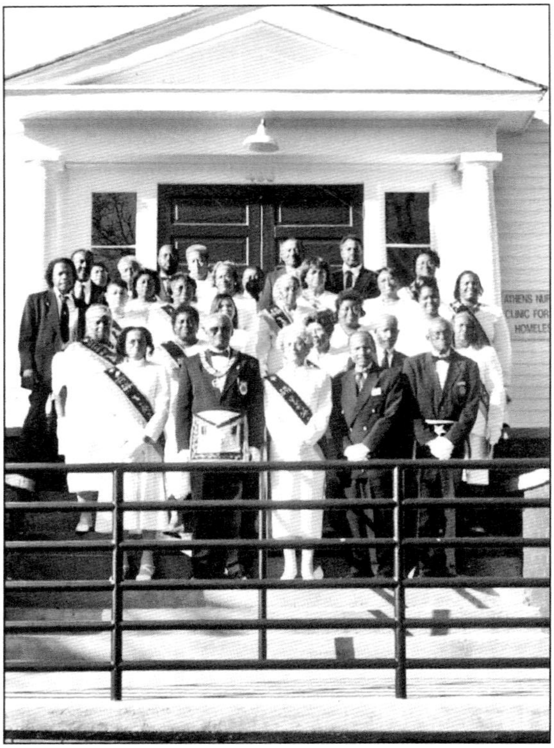

Shown here are Athens Masonic District 6 members. African-American citizens have traditionally been members of the Masonic organizations—Masons and Eastern Stars. (Courtesy Elzata Brown.)

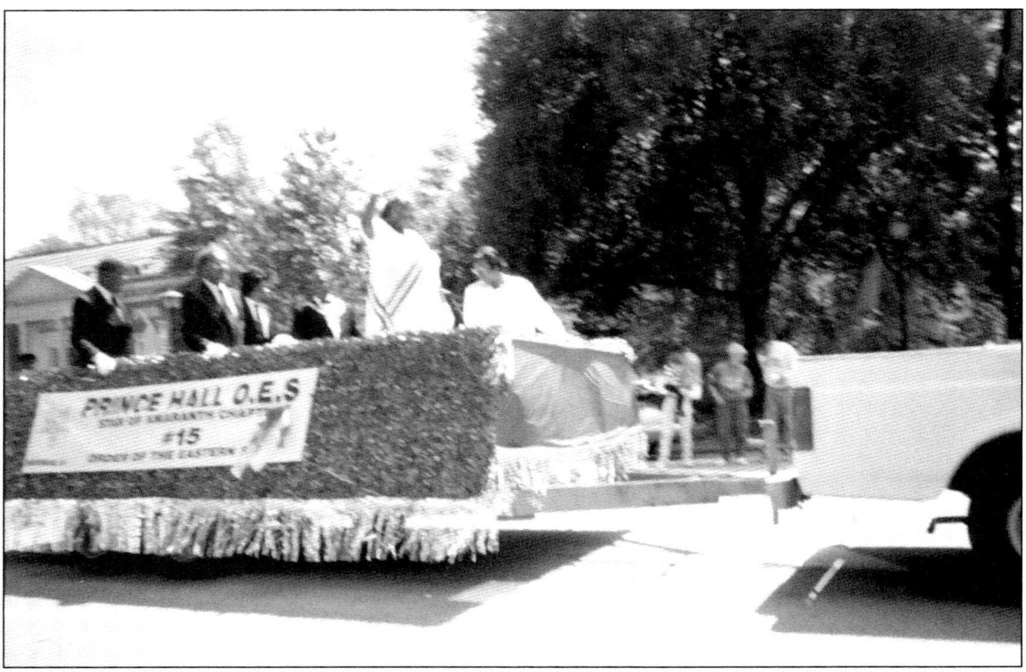

Prince Hall Order of Eastern Star, Star of Amaranth Chapter, entered this float in the parade. (Courtesy the author.)

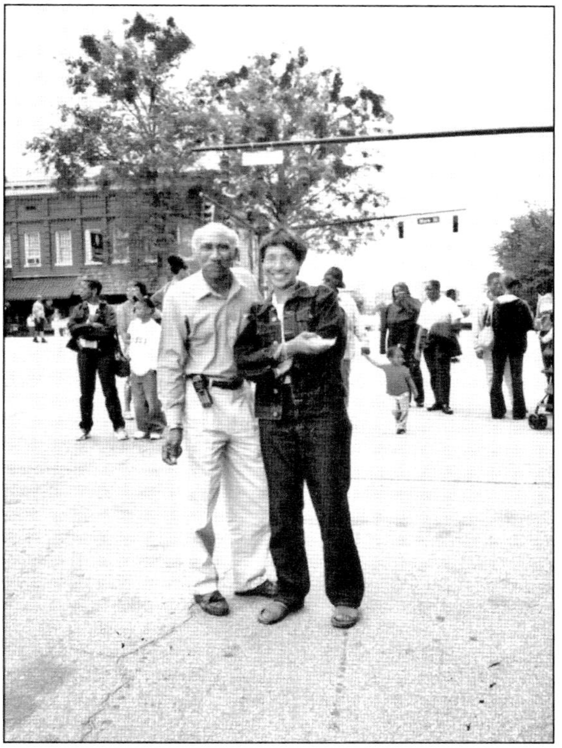

These unidentified Morgan County residents were among the spectators who enjoyed the parade in 1999. (Courtesy the author.)

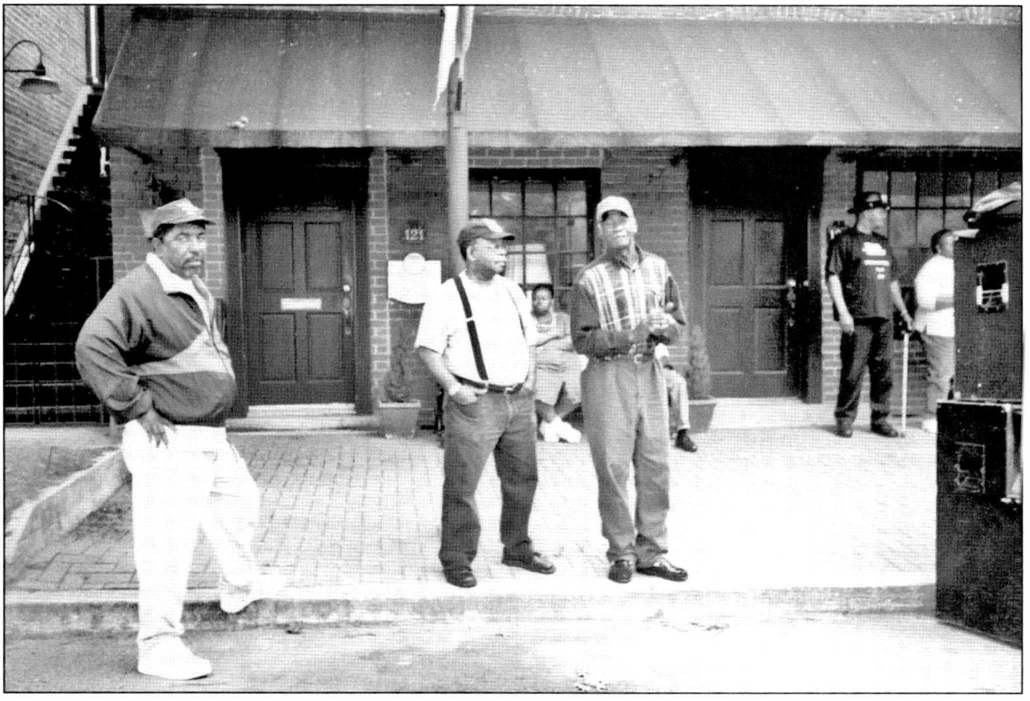

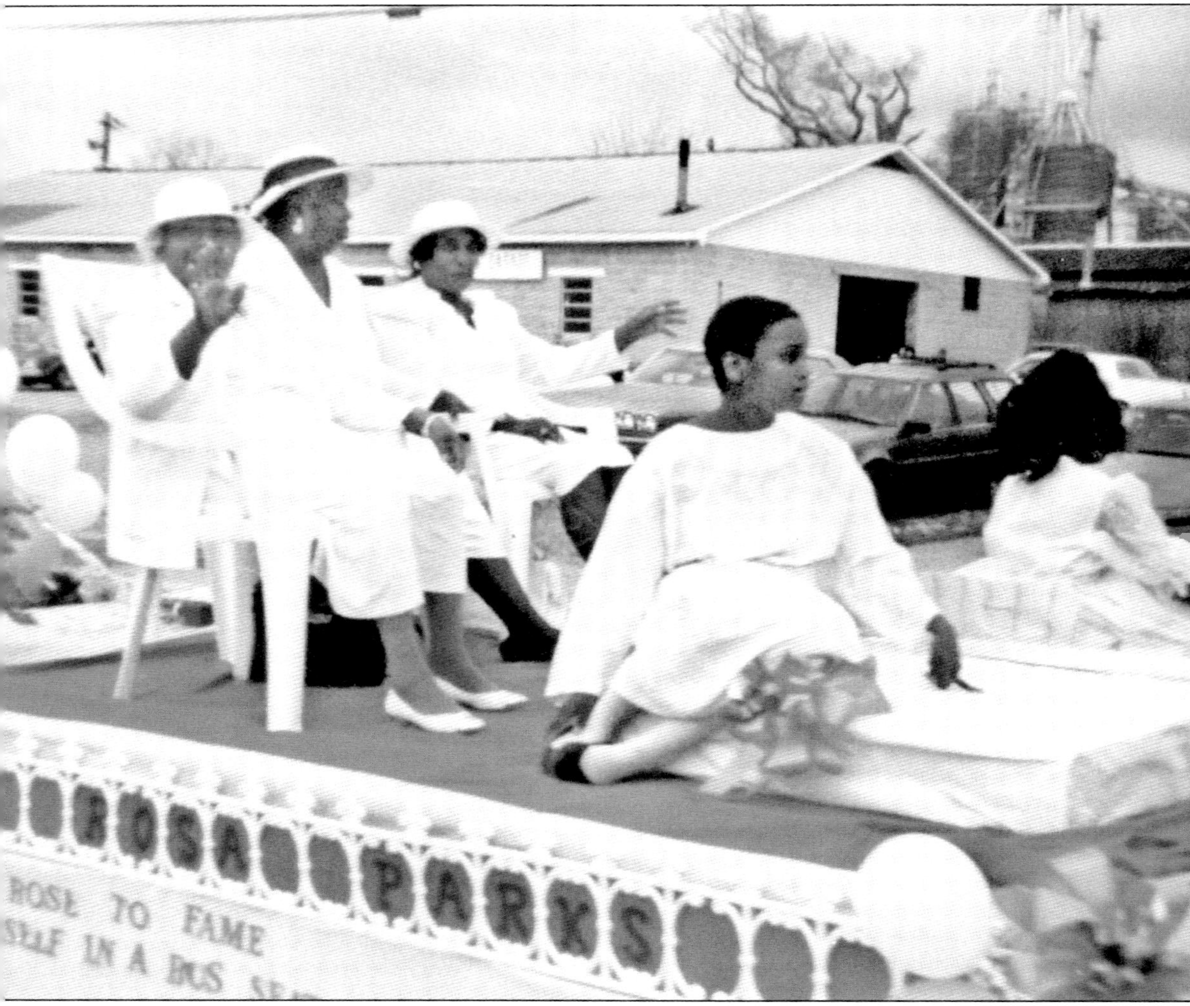

The older women—Tessie Robinson, Anna Reese, and Della Moon—represent the female workers of our culture, such as domestic workers, cooks, and housewives, while the young girls represent our future. Together, they ride on a float honoring Rosa Parks, mother of the Civil Rights movement in the Morgan County African-American Parade, *c.* 1997. (Courtesy Elzata Brown.)

This is a quote from author Henry van Dyke. It is a favorite quote of Mildred Bass, one of the pioneers of the Morgan County African-American Museum. (Courtesy Mildred Bass.)

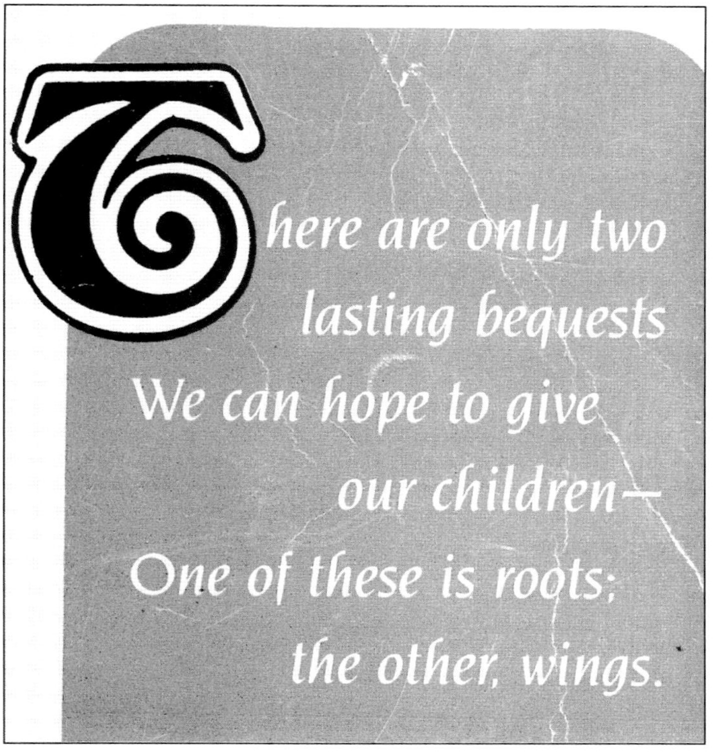

The theme chosen for this float in the African-American parade was "Reclaiming our Roots." (Courtesy Elzata Brown.)

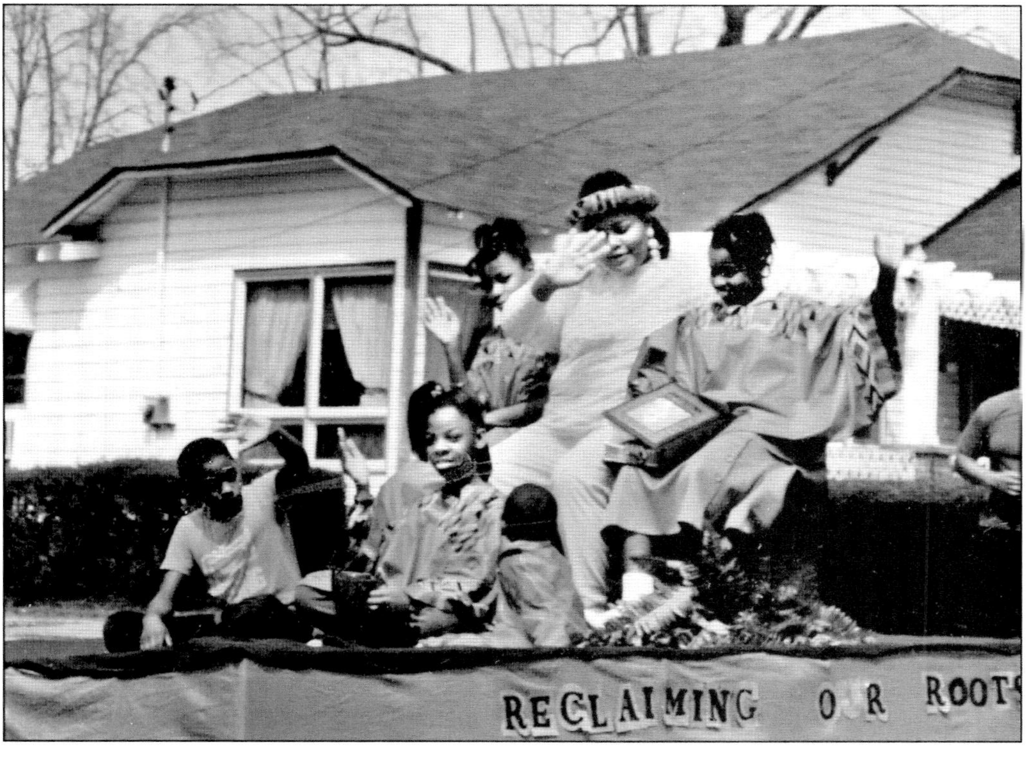

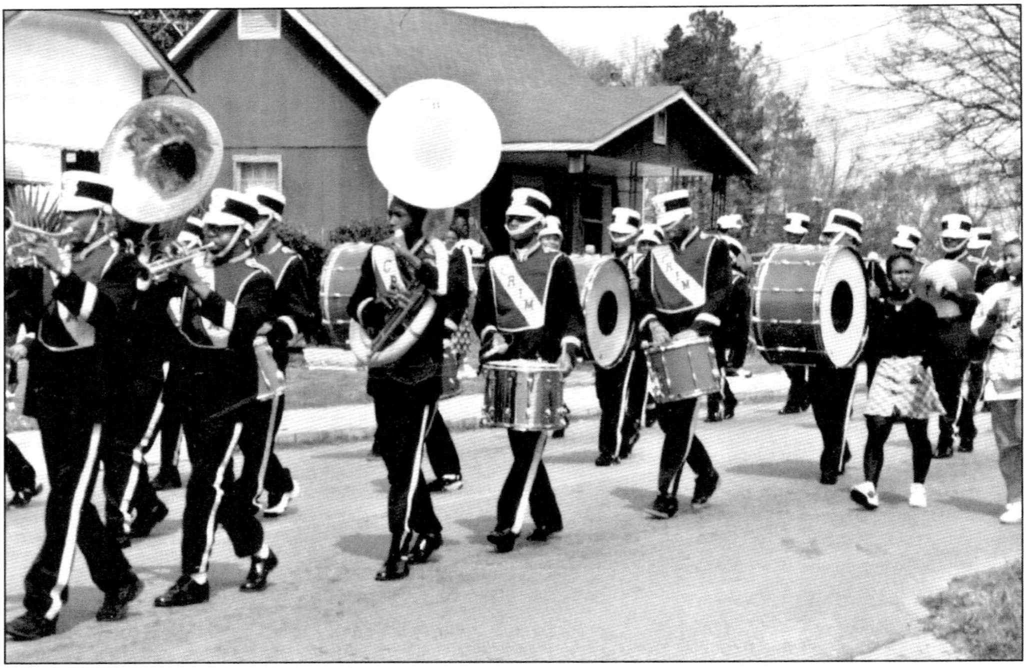

This marching band from Alonzo Crim High School in Atlanta was a parade crowd-pleaser. (Courtesy Elzata Brown.)

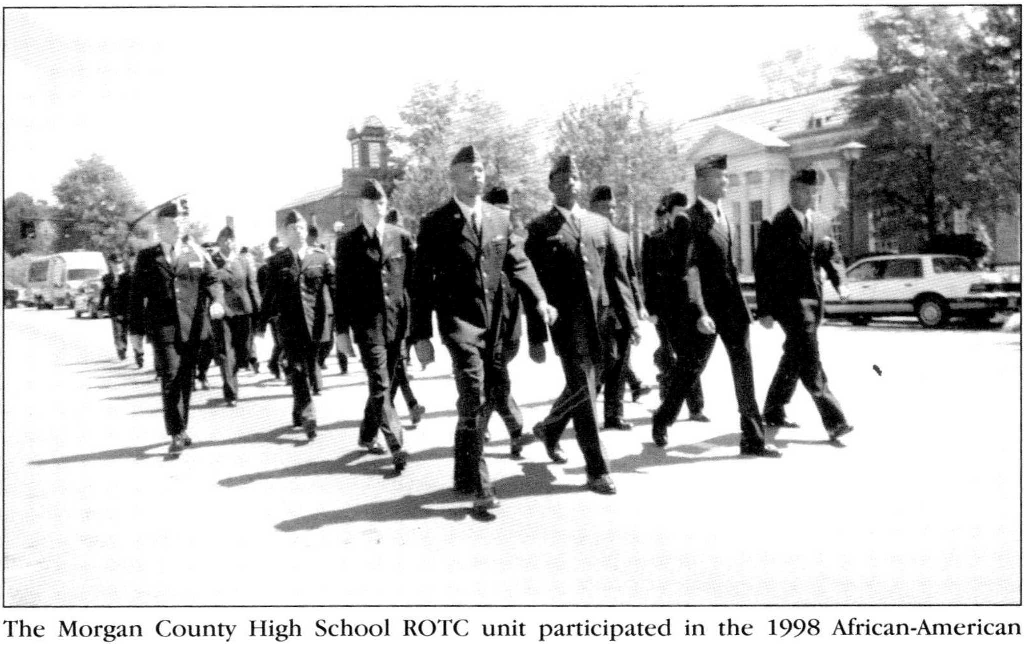

The Morgan County High School ROTC unit participated in the 1998 African-American Parade. (Courtesy the author.)

Let us march on 'til victory is won
James Weldon Johnson, "Lift Every Voice and Sing"